Eleanor Steber
An Autobiography

Eleanor Steber
An Autobiography

with Marcia Sloat

Illustrated with Photographs

WORDSWORTH
Ridgewood, New Jersey

Library of Congress Cataloging-in-Publication Data
Steber, Eleanor.
    Eleanor Steber : an autobiography / with Marcia Sloat.
    p.   cm.
    Discography: p.
    ISBN 0-9634174-0-1
    1. Steber, Eleanor. 2. Sopranos (Singers) – United States –
Biography. I. Sloat, Marcia, 1925–   . II. Title.
ML420.S816A3   1992
782.1'092 – dc20
    [B]   92-85436
                                                              CIP
                                                              MN

Published by
Wordsworth
335 East Glen Avenue
Ridgewood, NJ 07450

Manufactured in the United States of America

Produced by Millicent Fairhurst Book Production Services

1 2 3 4 5

Publication of this book is dedicated to the memory of Eleanor Steber.

For her, however, it is dedicated to her family and friends...who enjoyed her warmth, sense of humor, and *joie de vivre*...and who supported her through both triumph and despair.

For her, it is dedicated to her mentors, colleagues and admirers...who developed her talents, shared her accomplishments and cheered her impeccable musicianship and style.

For her, it is dedicated to her students...who knew her love, her kindness, understanding, and patience...and who understood her courage and determination.

For her, it is dedicated to the *old* Metropolitan Opera Company... which was her life.

And for those of us who shared the labor of this book, it is dedicated to both a great American artist and a dear friend whose life brought richness to our own.

A Preface by the Collaborator

Eleanor Steber was an astonishingly resilient person. No matter what happened, or how she felt, she always bounced back. Almost invariably she greeted each new day with cheerful anticipation.

Three years after surviving a 1987 life-threatening ulcer, she was convalescing from open-heart surgery in a Pennsylvania nursing home near her sister. Her lifelong pulmonary problems and worsening arthritis were beginning to discourage her, but she was eagerly anticipating a look at the first Voice of Firestone video. She was bucked up by the warmth of an occasional hour in the sun, the love of her family, and the cards and flowers from friends. Her days were spent in the company of her sister, Lucile, her friend, Ellen Martin, and her companion/personal representative Martha Moore Smith.

Her sudden death shortly after first light on October 3, 1990 at the age of 76 was unexpected. She was buried at a simple graveside ceremony in Greenwood Cemetery in Wheeling, West Virginia.

Steber was to have celebrated the 50th anniversary of her debut December 7, 1990. Instead, she was memorialized informally by the Metropolitan Opera and eulogized by her colleague Blanche Thebom before an audience of family, friends, students, former colleagues and fans during the hanging of her portrait in Founders Hall on January, 14, 1991. Today, her original recordings have been re-mastered into compact discs. New CDs of operas and concerts never publicly released, six memorable Voice of Firestone videos, and, finally, her autobiography—finished in the middle eighties—have all found the right moment for release.

Now that The Voice of Firestone programs are available on video, along with *Vanessa* and *The Girl of the Golden West, Les Troyens, Arcifanfano* and numerous concerts and recitals which are now on CDs, it is ironic that she is being awarded the kind of acclaim and honor she often felt she was denied in life. This radiant artist whose voice, according to the Metropolitan's Francis Robinson, "defines the American sound" is newly available for old musical friends and discovered by a few new generations.

When she asked me to help her with this book in 1976, she may have expected an easy time of it. The book originally started life as a biography because, at that time, she felt unwilling to comment on certain aspects of her life; indeed, she seemed not to have a clear idea of exactly what had happened to her. At the request of an interested publisher, I eventually reshaped it as an autobiography. Nevertheless, every word in this book was spoken or written by, read and re-read, and edited by Steber; and every word was checked and researched with one or more confirming witnesses or written sources insofar as possible.

She gave me the run of her house, and since I knew she had intermittently kept diaries all her life, I searched them out and used them, not for material but for questions. There were boxes of papers, emotional notes on envelopes, and scraps of paper stuck into books and, strangest of all, carbon copies of highly-charged letters, both sent and not sent. Steber gave it her best. When I touched a nerve or painful truth, she dealt with it on its merits. She was courageous in the search for her truth. Even the basic chronology of her life was often a mystery to her.

As we taped on and off for six months and drafts started to appear, she began to get a new perspective on her life. She was not only more forthcoming, she allowed me to probe deeper. She also reluctantly agreed that she must grapple with certain aspects of her life she had previously insisted were off limits.

There were occasions when she'd grasp some insight as to why something had happened to her in the past and burst into tears. It was painful for her and terrible for me because a writer can't comfort; a writer has to wait and listen for what may come next.

Basically she told it all. However, when we finished it the publication window had closed.

Should there have been more spicy anecdotes? Steber told me many, but refused to permit me to use anything she thought might hurt or embarrass anyone. She would not gossip, although she seemed generally to know what was going on. Nor would she judge any other artist, because she knew how it felt to stand in those shoes.

Our "Search for Eleanor Steber," she complained, was like psycho-analysis; not a new thought, of course, but the process and resulting new perspectives illuminated for her the breadth and scope of a life and career which had somehow slipped by unnoticed in the intensity of her own living. She pronounced herself satisfied.

By modern standards Steber's is far from a self-destructive story. She endured many painful and stormy passages, but kept an eternally optimistic outlook. She lived LIFE in capital letters. She persevered. And eventually she won her personal victories except for her last battle with death.

Her grace was her warmth, her open friendliness. She was generous with herself, although her rage was terrible when she felt betrayed. As she was childlike and lovable, she was sometimes downright impossible; yet she inspired lifelong faithfulness among her friends.

The production of this book has been a labor of love by all those concerned. Some, like George Cehanovsky, Bill Judd, Jimmy Quillian, Edwin Biltcliffe, Francis Robinson, Mrs. John DeWitt Peltz, and Eleanor's mother have died in the interim, but their contributions were invaluable.

Among the many others who have generously helped bring Eleanor's dream to fruition are her brother, William C. Steber, Ellen Martin, Robert Barker, Byron Belt, Richard Conrad, Edgar Vincent, Patrice Munsel, Donald McCormack, and Diana Ross. The publications of the Eleanor Steber Music Club, and the contributions by its contributing members provided an invaluable statistical resource. Very special thanks to *Opera News* and to Harvey E. Phillips for permission to reprint the "Farewell to Steber."

My personal thanks go to Dot Jenkins, Maureen Cannon, Nancy Mack, and the late Rev. John R. Rodland who sustained my spirit during the years we put this book together. I wish that both my mother and Eleanor's, Ida Nolte Steber, had lived to see it.

In May 1991 the Mozart Requiem was sung at the Transfiguration Lutheran Church in Harlem. It was directed and dedicated to Eleanor Steber by her student, Pamela Mann, because "she changed my life." Those of us who were lucky enough to know Eleanor believe she left behind a greater legacy than even she knew—unnumbered people who can say the same thing: "She changed my life." I am one of them.

I was 16 when I shared my first meal with Eleanor Steber after church on Sunday, November 16, 1942. As we finished dessert, she suddenly interrupted my enthusiastic chatter, clutched my arm and declared, "Darling, you should write a book!" It took thirty-five years of writing to get around to writing a book and I never dreamed it would be hers. She trusted me with her life. I have tried to be faithful to that trust.

MARCIA SLOAT

Overture

Some years ago my manager Bill Judd and publicist Edgar Vincent waited together at the Atlanta Airport for my arrival to sing a Metropolitan Opera Tour performance. As they chatted, black clouds mushroomed overhead, lightning crackled and big droplets of rain spat at them. Suddenly my plane broke through the overcast and, as the wheels touched down, a lightning bolt struck the runway, accompanied by an ear-shattering clap of thunder. Bill turned to Edgar, raised his eyebrows and shrugged. "Well," he said, "Steber's arrived!"

That's the way it's always been. I wasn't just born, I burst upon the world, and I have been making grand entrances ever since; and when I have to make my final exit I trust it will be a memorable one.

I celebrated the 40th anniversary of my Metropolitan Opera debut in New York's Town Hall by presenting in concert the winners of the 1980 Eleanor Steber Music Foundation Competition. Can you think of a better way to mark my career—which included literally thousands of concert and opera performances, 56 roles in almost that many operas, including 405 performances of 33 performances at the Metropolitan alone—than to pass it on to another generation?

Where do I stand today? I've encompassed more living than I can possibly write about. I am back in the world of students, teaching them, producing concerts for them, trying to prepare them in ways I was not prepared, and through my Foundation, trying to give the best young professionals I can find—those for whom just one break can make all the difference—that final boost.

As a student, artist and teacher I am forever part of the vast, yet closely-knit family of singers and teachers fathered by a handful of other singers and teachers little more than 150 years ago. And today I am part of a great new family—one that didn't truly exist in my youth—the American school of teaching.

Because we American artists have been uniquely obliged to become expert in every national style and language, our teaching is an amalgam of the best of Italy, Germany and France. American singers of the future are inheriting our expertise as an integral part of their learning experience. I believe that American singers will inevitably dominate the best in the vocal world for generations to come.

Through my singing, my teaching and my Foundation, I have scattered my pebbles into the musical waters, and I stand on the brink of the future, watching their waves spread out into endless overlapping circles. It gives me a sense of immortality to know that what I learned, what I sang, and what I have taught will extend beyond me so long as our world survives.

From the start my career simply took me over and I was merely swept through it. I threw myself with complete fervor into everything that came along—each role, each concert, each song I sang. And I thrived on it!

There were times, of course, when I ranted and raved against fate because I thought I was getting some sort of dirty deal, but when I look back on my life now, I'm amazed. What dirty deal? Nobody has ever, ever had the life that I've had!

I've never retired. I never will. I still sing an occasional concert, chiefly in connection with the master classes I give all over the country. Students again, young people—they keep my spirit young, and it's just not in me to sit back on my laurels and read my clippings or listen to my records.

There are people who seem to know more about my life than I do. I have told the story of my public life and those aspects of my private life which directly affected it, and they may draw their own conclusions.

I have touched upon subjects in this book which I have never discussed in public, and certainly don't enjoy writing about. I regret— no, stronger than that—I resent having to include such things here, but I do so because I know that if I do not my candor will be suspect.

I have heard that "Steber will never tell it the way it was; she will never tell the entire story." Absolutely correct. I don't know anyone who has ever done it or, indeed, would even be able to do it. I have found that "objective truth," that so-called "real story" is pretty hard to come by, even within my own thoughts. I have lived at such a breakneck pace that it has been an exhausting and painful task to sort it into any reasonable order at all. Detached observation and reflection are not my strong points.

There are some periods—and people—I recall only dimly, and some perhaps not at all. People who have known me may remember me or my life in quite different ways. Their memories may be correct and they may not. They have their points of view and I have mine—and this is *my* forum at the moment.

I'm sure I have forgotten almost as much of my life as I have remembered, and my memory tends to cleave to the euphoric. My hold on unpleasant memories is tenuous at best.

So my life, as I remember it, is all here. Everything falls into place as it happened, arising simply and gradually as I became aware of events.

If there is anything to this reincarnation business, I just hope I don't have to suffer for my sins through some karma before I'm allowed to do it again; because if I ever have the chance, and the choice, to sing again in another life, that is what I would like to do.

Somebody once labeled me as "the prima-tive donna"—and that's what I am: a prima donna with a small town kid inside. I've been a maverick all my life, and the establishment has often lost patience with me.

And, in spite of everything, I've done it. I've survived. And I'm still going strong! If that one fact rings clear through this book, I think that would be great!

Hotel Ansonia
New York City, 1982

Eleanor Steber
An Autobiography

River City Girl

When I was born in Wheeling, West-by-God-Virginia, river barges still anchored parallel to the shoreline of the Ohio River and off-loaded cargo directly from cobblestone ramps into horse-drawn vans parked on the narrow strip of stony beach between the river and the railroad tracks. Horses still outnumbered automobiles, but not for long. When I first burst into its life, Wheeling was a world completely unto itself, and for 19 years almost the only world I knew.

It was about 1706 when trappers and explorers canoed up the river to open the Ohio Territory. With them came Colonel Ebenezer Zane who founded a settlement he tried to name Zanesburg. (He didn't succeed, but his brother went on to found Zanesville, Ohio.) Wheeling became Wheeling in 1776. Before the Revolution it had briefly been "Fort Henry," for Henry Clay who, it was said, had the national road put into Wheeling because he had a lady friend living on Monument Place.

The Baltimore and Ohio Railroad chugged into the city in 1853, bringing lots of people and new industries. Wheeling became a manufacturing center for steel, pottery and tobacco. "Stogie," "Mail Pouch," "Wheeling Steel" and "Nail City" were familiar words to everyone.

Wheeling also became a mecca for English, Scottish, Irish, Welsh and German immigrants who brought rich musical heritages with them. They developed a strong and independent community, protected by the friendly hills surrounding them and strengthened by the diversity of trades and variety of their nationalities.

No matter where or how often I traveled the world for nearly half a century, I have remained a daughter of Wheeling with my spiritual roots sunk deeply into that unique corner of America. More pervasive than the environs themselves, however, are the stringent family bonds which have always held me fast.

Mother claims I was born laughing; probably so. I was also born with the same almost transparent fair skin I shared with my father and sister—an alabaster child, they said, and a happy one, with baby-dark eyes gradually lightening to bright blue.

I also started life with a weight problem. Nine pounds at birth, I was so fat at three months they could plunk me down on the floor to sit happily upright and steady, held securely in place by three solid inner tubes of fat around my middle.

A few miles south of the center of Wheeling at the corner of 33rd and Eoff Streets (pronounced Oaf) stood the huge brick building which housed my grandfather's prosperous general store, and above it the multi-roomed apartment in which my grandparents birthed and raised their children. It was here that I, to my everlasting delight, was born on July 17, 1914 and lived for the first three years of my life.

My most vivid early memories are of my Grandfather and Grandmother Nolte and the vast old-style emporium of which my granddad was proprietor. You should have seen my little Grandfather Nolte, for goodness sake, short and burly, as wide as he was tall. A jolly, adorable, loving man and my first real pal.

I toddled through that vast emporium, peeking into barrels of pickles, dried prunes and apricots, exploring bins of navy beans by digging out handfuls and letting them slip through my fingers. I was mesmerized by the raw red sides of hanging meats radiating bloody smells; and there was the inevitable candy case which drew me like a magnet. No matter where Granddad was, if I slid open the glass door to reach for a sweet, his voice bellowed across the store, "Eleanor, get your hand out of the candy case." Granddad was something!

He had a great booming voice and sang hymns constantly, in German of course. In church he sang them to his own tempo; his voice was so penetrating, the organist was helpless. Everyone had to sing the hymns Granddad's way because no one could hear anything else.

Most evenings I'd sit on a barrel in the store, as my mother had before me, while my grandfather set up for the next day's trade. He bellowed out his hymns as he worked and I piped up and sang along. Maybe I developed my volume then because I certainly had to sing like blazes to keep up with him.

A streetcar line passed the front of the house, and close behind Grandfather's stables were the railroad tracks. I never figured out whether we were on the right or wrong side of them, but I certainly knew they were there. Granddad's stable housed two beautiful horses, a family buggy and the delivery wagon. My love for horses began then. From the day I could walk, I regularly trotted off to the stables. I loved the smell, the sounds of the horses munching their oats, their steamy warmth and how it felt to stroke their sleek sides, always kept groomed and shining by our delivery boy. Of the many animals around us, I loved a horse called "Charlie" best. Whenever I appeared, he'd stop in the midst of chomping his oats to nuzzle me with his nose, nearly toppling me with his affections. I knew generations of cats too—always a necessity for both grocery and stable, and a succession of dogs. My constant companion when I was small was a white, overfed bulldog mongrel named "Bounce."

My grandmother's home will ever be a magic place to me, full of staircases and long corridors with doors that opened into mysterious and exciting rooms with high ceilings and tall windows with inside shutters one could pull across to create a secret alcove for dreaming.

One of my first memories is the steep and precarious stairway (22 steps) from the street to the apartment. On the landing near the top stood a great fern-filled jardiniere which fascinated me. Years later I searched for this magnificent piece, and when I found it I was crushed. It seemed so small until I realized that when I was a little girl, it was taller than I was. Today I have it in my country home, filled once more with luxuriant fern.

There was a great parlor with high windows which looked out on three sides. From there we watched the exciting torchlight Election Night parades go by on the street below, and I waved my own sparkler, breathless with the excitement of the bands and the crowds. Grandfather's special preserve was a back sitting room, but the kitchen was the real center of our life, pungent with the aromas of cookies, cakes, stews and roasts—all marvelous concoctions of German delights which inspired my lifelong penchant for hearty rich food. Grandmother cooked on a great black iron range which burned both wood and coal with gluttonous abandon. The stove was also our source of warmth and good cheer. Evenings while an old country clock ticked away the hours, I watched and imitated my Aunt Emma as she toasted her feet by propping them on the open door of the stove, while Grandmother knitted and Grandfather was forever reading his German Bible.

My grandmother was not only a great cook, she was the cleanest person who ever was. She was always washing and cleaning, washing and cleaning. Cleanliness was her religion. If I were to sculpt a figure of my grandmother, it would show her bent over the washboard where she scrubbed relentlessly until the clothes all but screamed for mercy, inevitably yielding up their dirt before her furious onslaught.

Across the street was the neighborhood nickelodeon where my grandfather took me to see the "Keystone Cops" and all the wonderful old melodramas. Granddad's sense of humor was as offbeat as his pitch sometimes, for inevitably five minutes after everyone else had stopped laughing, the joke would finally hit him and he'd bellow with laughter during some sad moment.

That little theater, the old "Southern," drew me like a magnet. I'd slip into that cool, dark cavern during the day while my friend Katie Seamon dusted and cleaned, making the air which had been hot and thick with melodrama the night before pungent with polish and disinfectant soap.

No matter. This was a real "theater" and I can't remember a time when I wasn't crazy about the theater. I'd climb up on the stage in front of the movie screen and pantomime the show I'd seen the night before or sing a song to the empty house and imagine the applause. Other times I'd sit at the pit piano and pretend I was playing for one of the heartrending romances or blood and thunder silent movies. Years later when I would walk across the backstage of the Met to my dressing room, I would breathe in the special smell of the theater and feel myself for a moment back at the little nickelodeon at Third and Eoff.

The apartment over the store was not only my birthplace, but my mother's as well. She had a unique, God-given voice (which may well have been better than mine), but she was born into an "old country" household in which women could have no career but family. Mother was born a grocer's daughter, far from poor, but somewhat short on social standing and vastly separated from the fame she unconsciously yearned for.

Consequently, when she finally had children of her own, she was determined that they must succeed where she could not. Her ambition left its mark on me and my sister. Just as I fulfilled her musical dreams, my sister lived out her social ambitions. Mother never finished high school because Granddad needed her in the office of the family store. She resented this terribly, although she used the experience to become a skilled "power behind the throne" the rest of her life.

Everybody knew she sang, and when she was 13 a local voice teacher asked Granddad if he understood the exceptional talent his daughter had. Perhaps he felt guilty for taking her out of school, for then he not only let her study singing, but he bought her an organ in addition to the Ebony piano they already possessed.

Mother was soloist and organist at the Trinity Lutheran Church when she met my father. It was just before Christmas, and she was singing, "Glory to God in the Highest" when Bill Steber walked into church with a friend. He took one look at her and asked the friend, "Who's that gal singing?"

"That's Ida Nolte. She sings."

"Well, I'm going to marry her," my father declared.

He met mother by joining the choir, and first chance he got, he took over the hand-pumping of the organ, just to get close to her.

Mother continued to study voice even after their three children were born. She sang anywhere and everywhere, and the fees she earned by singing, leading choirs and teaching piano eventually put all three of us kids through college.

The music my mother played and sang at home became the foundation of my musical education. Mother, who recounted tales of my youth relentlessly with the tireless skill of a professional storyteller, enjoyed describing how I sang the long opening "Paaaaaaaace," as in "Pace, mio Dio" sliding down the bannister. Not a bad way to learn portamento!

There is simply no way to underestimate my mother's influence in masterminding my future. When I finally succeeded, mother relished the ovations and the trappings of my fame as if they were her own. She could, and often did, steal center stage from me. She was my greatest booster, my biggest fan and constant support; yet she could praise me extravagantly in one breath and in the next cut me to pieces with a sarcastic remark or stinging taunt. My eyes often spilled over with tears of pain and chagrin, and at the height of my career, I would often feel myself an awkward, graceless child.

Even when mother was not present, I was aware of her personality on the periphery. Her influence remained profound—if not her direct influence, her imagined influence. I fought a losing battle all my life to break the silver cord that held me to her. Yet at the same time, I adored her and needed her, and I am aware how much of my strength and determination I owe to her.

My father's influence was completely different. He was a simple man, honest to a fault, and such a conservative, retiring sort of man that the whole idea of public performing alarmed him. Mother was the dominant personality in our house, always a tremendous resentment to him because he could hardly ever get a word in edgewise except when he was alone with us kids.

When I was little, Mother spent so much time away singing that it seemed to me she cared more about singing than she did about us; but in a way we got a better deal because of it, because when she was out, Daddy took care of us. He was great fun. He played games and danced with us, and quite indirectly taught us a good deal more about the internal combustion engine than we really wanted to know, because his personal idea of fun was to take the car apart and put it back together. I seemed always to be holding a light for him as he worked in some dark and greasy spot.

After I left home, although my parents traveled to Europe with me twice and often visited the Met and various cities where I was singing, I had too little opportunity to be with my father. There were always so many people around me that Daddy sometimes complained that he never had a chance to be alone with me. Because I was his first-born, I felt we had a special affection for each other. He always called me his "Miracle Kind," his "miracle child."

Mother was the one who always made a big deal about my career. If they were at the opera to hear me sing, for instance, she made sure everyone in earshot knew she was my mother and she'd always be the first one to applaud. Daddy would get all embarrassed and whisper desperately, "Ida, Ida, keep it down."

Daddy's father, Charles Stuber, was a bricklayer, and my grandmother was a darling, sweet lady who came here as a girl from Germany. She was working as a servant in Benwood when my grandfather met her and, to their astonishment, they discovered they had lived over the mountain from each other in Germany. Some years later I often programmed a Richard Strauss song, "Schlagende Herzen," about a little boy holding a handful of flowers for his girlfriend who lives over the hill. While he's dreaming of her, she's waiting on the other side, shading her eyes with her hand as she looks for him, while the gentle spring breeze plays between the two of them. Whenever I sang this song, I'd imagine such a spring wind dancing between my future grandparents long before they ever met. They had to travel 3,000 miles to find each other.

Grandfather Steber (the name was Americanized before I came along) opened a wondrous new world for me, for it was on his knees that I heard the magical legends of Wotan and Fricke, of Siegfried and the dragon. When I discovered that these stories were in Wagner's mighty operas, I was overwhelmed. It was a master mason, not a Master Singer who prepared me for the Ring of the Niebelungen.

Shortly before I turned four, my parents built their own home eight miles up the river in Warwood. I missed the Nolte establishment more than anyone knew. I went down and stayed there any time I could—it was always my second home. But gradually I grew to love the big white clapboard house with its wide front porch and the lush backyard sloping up toward the hills behind us. Our new home at 2002 Warwood Avenue had big rooms with sliding doors on the first floor, a fine long stairway to the second floor, and a large attic which quickly became my ivory tower.

My singing debut, at the age of four, was made at church. In a white ruffled dress, I was lifted to the pulpit beside the pastor where I sang the immortal aria "Buttercups and Daisies." The congregation made a great fuss over me, and I loved it. But I was considerably humbled during another Children's Day service, perhaps the following year. I was given a few lines to speak, but was so overcome with panic I totally forgot them. I burst into tears, ran down from the chancel and threw myself sobbing into the arms of the minister. What a trauma!

Speaking of traumas, my sister Lucile was born as World War I ended; my wonderful brother Bill had made his entrance the year before. Billy wasn't too strong as a baby, but Lucile and I bounced along like nobody's business. Their arrival, however, was an immediate and painful shock to my psyche. After four years of having my parents and grandparents to myself, I suddenly heard everyone exclaiming at the beauty of my new sister. Now I was told I had to be satisfied with merely my fair share of life and love, and I'm pretty sure I never quite got the hang of it. Consequently, from the time I was knee-high to a duck I tried to please everybody—absolutely everybody—because somehow, rightly or wrongly, I felt that being me was not enough. I quickly learned that performing was the way I could win approval, or get my own way.

I hated the prospect of going to school. I was miserable. Being "confined" has always tortured me, and a schoolyard filled with strange and competitive children left me isolated and frightened. But if that lost feeling about beginning at school sticks in my memory, it's probably because the remainder of the year never developed. I spent most of it in bed.

First mother got rheumatic fever. Then all of us kids came down with measles. At one point we were all bedded down together in mother's room so she could keep an eye on us. My pal Katie, from the nickelodeon, and my aunts sometimes came to take care of us, an especially lucky thing for me because I had one of my several near-brushes with death while I was recovering from the measles. In a long nightgown, I was running back and forth in front of a gas fire when my gown caught fire. I ran screaming into the hall where my young Aunt Helen was washing windows. She threw me down and wrapped me in a throw rug, burning her hands while saving me. Miraculously, I was untouched.

I had barely returned to school when I seemed to hurt my arm in a playground game. By the time I ran home, my arm was twitching terribly and the involuntary spasms quickly spread down my whole right side. It turned out I had a mild, temporarily disabling case of infectious chorea, a childhood disease chiefly affecting girls and often associated with rheumatic fever. The most terrifying part, however, was its nickname: "St. Vitus Dance." Chorea affects the central nervous system and runs a self-limiting course of six to ten weeks, but no one knew that then. My parents must have begun to despair, finally, because they succumbed to the suggestion of an aunt and took me to a faith healer. I can remember very little about it except for the marvelous player piano in the preacher's home. It didn't use the paper roll familiar to most of us, but had huge perforated metal disks that attached on the front like the giant wheel "Ezekiel saw." That got my attention, you can bet, but I remember nothing of what the faith healer said except that he spoke quietly and gently put his hands on my head. It may well be that the disease had simply run its course. I had been truly ill for only a short time, but the after-effects lingered and I was kept at home most of the winter.

Once I felt better, I enjoyed my recuperation, wandering often into the hills behind our home and spending long hours lying on the grass in a little green copse on the rocky promontory overlooking the Ohio River. It was a considerable climb for a little girl, but I loved it there. Whenever I'd sing Watts' lovely "Little Shepherd's Song" in concerts, I'd imagine myself back in that spot. I'd only have to sing the opening phrase, "Heigh-ho, what a day. . . ." and I'd feel myself back on the hill, lying on my stomach and looking down in the valley where I could see the barges and boats gliding by on the river, my own little village, the smoke rising from the canneries and the intermittent yellow-red blasts from the steel furnaces further on. I could hear the faraway sounds of streetcars and trains, the noon whistles from the factories and the caroling voice of my mother summoning me to lunch.

Her voice as she sang in church is my first profound musical memory. I was used to the sound of her singing around the house, of course, but when she sang in church it was different and exciting because everyone was listening to "her." She was the "soloist." I still remember vividly we three kids sitting together with Daddy in the congregation one night at evening service at St. Matthew's Episcopal Church. Everything was fine until mother got up to sing. Then four-year-old Lucile stood up and waved, squeaking at the top of her voice, "Hi, Mommy!" I wanted to hide under the pew.

Our Krakauer upright had fascinated me from the moment I touched its keys. As a matter of fact, my parents couldn't keep me from it. I began picking out little tunes when I was four or five, so when I was six mother decided to start me on piano lessons. No one ever had to force me to practice in those days; besides, I knew that diligence at my Czerny was one sure way to please mother.

We three kids had a great time when we were little. In later years, of course, the fact that I was three years older than Billy and four more than Lucile made a difference, but before I went to junior high school we played together a lot. Nearly every night my brother, sister and I put on "shows" for mother and daddy. Naturally I always sang, and so did Billy who has always had a lovely tenor like daddy's. Lucile usually followed our lead and then took off on her own with some inventive dance step or twirl to make us laugh with delight. She was so adorable!

The main hall of our house was divided from the parlor by large folding doors. This was our stage, and we performers entered down the stairs, or from the "wings" on either side of the doors. We danced and sang popular songs, mimicking or simply mouthing the words to phonograph records. We did a fantastic Charleston. We also created our own "show and tell," dramatizing what had happened each day at school, or after. It was important to perform in our family.

At first mother was our pianist, but when I became more proficient I took over that duty. Gradually mother turned over the role of family accompanist to me until I was finally designated to play the hymns our family sang together Christmas morning. Truthfully, I don't think I had the faintest notion about becoming a singer. My first important memory about making music was pianistic. One of my big deals was Edward MacDowell's "To a Wild Rose" and a number called "Scotch Poem," which was preceded by a recitation I recall to this day:

"On foreign Scotland's craggy shore an old grey castle stands, braving the fierce North Sea. From out the rugged casement appears a lovely face, white with woe; she sweeps the harp strings sadly and sings a mournful strain. The wind plays through her tresses and carries the song a-main."

I made the most of it. I delivered those lines with every ounce of drama I possessed, even when I practiced. I was always very dramatic, uninhibitedly theatrical, and it was probably that quality mother noticed in me as a toddler which made her wonder what the dickens she was going to do with me.

We children had another private "show business" (much of it X-rated, I am sure) which we acted out in our attic playroom, and it was also there I hid when I wanted to escape my chores or nurse my wounds. I could forget everything by losing myself in my mother's forbidden romantic novels. Sometimes when life didn't go the way I wanted, if the teasing of my brother and sister got to me—and sometimes it was unmerciful—I'd take a streetcar downtown to visit Grandmother Nolte. However, when I got seriously stuck in what mother called my "melancholy moods" she'd send me to stay with her brother Harry—my "Uncle Doc"—up at Beach Bottom where he practiced medicine. During these visits I avidly devoured all his "doctor books"; and it was there I had my first rewarded crush on the boy next door when I was 12 or 13.

My mother's sister lived just three doors from us in Warwood and I spent almost as much time in her house as in my own. Aunt Elizabeth Pell was just the opposite of my mother: tall and thin, really skinny, resembling grandmother while mother took after my roly-poly Grandfather Nolte. Aunt Elizabeth was good for me. She directed my overactive imagination by making me create and write out original fairy tales; and since she also wrote poetry, I tried that too. Reading was my lifelong refuge, but my hours alone with books were not entirely lacking in real life drama as I discovered one blustery October evening while still in my early teens.

I had remained home while the family visited the grandparents downtown. I had found a copy of Bram Stoker's classic "Dracula" and I was lost in the depths of Transylvania when suddenly I heard a strange "flumph, flumph, flumph" in the room with me. I looked up as a real live bat swooped almost under my nose and flapped around the room until it finally settled on the chandelier. Utterly petrified, I slid out of the room without scaring it into renewed flight. I trapped the bat by closing the parlor doors and then I sat down on the stairs to contemplate my problem. I considered trying to swat the thing with one of Billy's kite sticks, but was afraid I'd smash the chandelier. Then I remembered Billy's B.B. gun.

I got it from the kitchen and slowly took aim at the bat which was still hanging from the chandelier. Very slowly and carefully I squeezed the trigger—and *I got him!* Except that I had forgotten that bats hang upside down and I had only nicked his tail, so he flipped and flopped around the room until he finally landed on a window lintel. Having learned my lesson, I again took aim. With devastating accuracy I finished him off. A real Annie Oakley yet!

I was so excited when I called my grandparents' house, my father heard me clear across the room. He was so convinced something terrible had happened, he almost jumped over the table to get to the phone.

"Daddy," I shouted, "I just killed a bat!"

"Whaaat?" he shouted back.

"I killed a bat, Daddy, with Billy's B.B. gun!"

Because the Wheeling school system had a vital music program, I got my first taste of performing on a real stage in shows at Warwood High. I auditioned for the lead, of course, and was crushed when it was given to my best pal, Nancy Hill, a pretty and more popular girl than I. I was cast as an Irish maid. Broken-hearted, I raced home to mother. "Buck up, darling," she said. "If you can't be the star you're going to be the best darned Irish maid Wheeling ever saw." Whereupon she marched me to Laura Kasely Brooks, a neighbor and actress who had trained in New York. Mrs. Brooks coached me to a fare-thee-well, and my Irish maid turned out to be so aggressively Irish that I simply took over the stage whenever I was on it. I was a natural-born "ham."

Mother had already determined that whatever I did, she would see that I was prepared for it in the best way she could afford. If there were any eyebrows raised that a mere high school girl got professional coaching for school shows, I never knew it. Her decision to get the finest teacher available for all my parts set a pattern I would follow throughout my career.

I won the lead in my senior show, "The Spanish Sweetheart." For this I wore a black Spanish wig complete with fancy comb and mantilla, plus a colorful fringed shawl I swirled around me every time I moved on stage. The shawl was pure inspiration. When she was unable to find anything appropriate in the stores, Mother simply whipped the fringed shawl from our piano and threw it around me. It worked perfectly.

Mother followed me with a calculating eye as I cavorted about the stage, displaying more enthusiasm than good sense. She'd sit way in the back of the auditorium, muttering to herself, "My goodness, what *does* that girl have and *what* am I going to do with it?"

Everything I saw or heard on stage and screen became part of my education. When my old nickelodeon became the "talking pictures," I was entranced. Beginning with Al Jolson in "The Jazz Singer," I spent every Saturday afternoon for years lost in the magical darkness of a movie house—and for only a nickel. I was weaned on those unforgettable serials which immortalized Pearl White, Frank Buck, Clyde Beatty and Tom Mix.

I never missed a movie musical, including the first "Broadway Melody" and all the great movies starring Lawrence Tibbett, Lily Pons and Jeannette MacDonald—stars beyond imagining. How could anyone conceive that I would one day sing with Tibbett, be entertained by Pons, and enjoy having Jeannette as a good friend? And Grace Moore! We drove all the way to Pittsburgh to see "One Night of Love." That movie—Grace Moore herself, and the part she played—stirred something earthshaking deep inside of me, some recognition, some inner urge which fired my imagination beyond my ability to express.

Mother took me to hear every concert performer who passed through Wheeling, always watching me and trying to measure my interest, marking my intensity and complete emotional involvement with each one. She took me to hear Ampara and Jose Iturbi on their first tour. Iturbi was a dashing showman and I—about 14 or 15 at the time—reacted violently, grabbing my mother's hand and whispering urgently, "Mother, that's what I want to be." Mother smiled.

When she took me to hear soprano Grete Stückgold, I was dazzled. Half way through the program, I clutched at Mother's arm. "That's what I want to be, Mother. I want to be like her. I want to thrill people with my songs." Mother patted my hand. "First a pianist and now a singer! What next?"

Soprano Jeannette Vreeland also made a great impression on me; partly, I am sure, because she sang her concert with her leg in a cast. It was she who introduced me to "The Little Shepherd's Song." Miss Vreeland was a very beautiful woman. Although I don't think she ever sang much opera, she was a splendid oratorio and concert singer. I heard her once more as a voice student and she sang the last concert of her career, the Beethoven "Missa Solemnis" with the Boston Symphony. Once again she sang under a handicap, for this time she was pushed into Symphony Hall in a wheelchair, already incapacitated by the cancer from which she died shortly after. I have never forgotten her. Her image comes clearly to my mind even now, and I salute her artistry, her beauty and her courageous spirit.

I heard Paderewski play on his last tour through America to raise money for Poland. My piano teacher, Jessie Lipphardt, who had studied with him, introduced me. He smiled gently and patted me on the head. With what renewed enthusiasm did I attack my Chopin and my Beethoven the next day!

Groundwork

While I usually appeared a docile child, I often seethed with hidden hostility and rebellion, I am sure. My parents shared a number of prejudices quite common in their generation. Having been exposed to the suspicion directed against German-Americans during World War II, they should have been broad-minded about other national groups, I thought. But they weren't, and since I was a highly idealistic child and believed, quite literally, all the things I learned in church, like "loving your neighbor," I felt a great sense of injustice about criticisms of people who could not defend themselves. Throughout my life I often championed such people on general principles.

Still, I can't blame my parents for that or anything else. They were a product of their times, as I was of mine. I never doubted that I had very loving parents; in fact there was no end to their protectiveness toward us children, to the degree that I never really learned how to handle opposition. I simply learned how to avoid it, just the way I learned how to escape from unpleasant situations. And I've been escaping ever since.

I've always had the feeling that something beyond me has guided my life and protected me. Of course, when I was a little girl, we were always in church and the elements of religion were always around us. I must have been very impressionable, because I began to feel that there was a "presence" always along beside me.

Shortly after my visit to the faith healer, I'd had a dream or a vision that we'd come to the end of the world. All of a sudden, during the holocaust, and while everyone else is falling into the earthquake, Jesus steps out of the clouds, picks me up, and carries me off in his arms, filling me with the most wonderful warmth and comfort. I know very well that the dream was inspired by one of the colored pictures in Mother's Bible, but that doesn't make the memory less vivid to me.

Whatever it is, the Presence has stayed with me most of my life. Many times when I have been at the edge of real disaster, really on the precipice, that Presence has reached out and pulled me back. Call it psychic or mystic, or whatever you want, it has been an important force in my life.

This is one of many reasons I've always felt I've lived before, that I've known certain people before. My brother Bill and I have always had great rapport; we are very close. We are so much alike that if there is such a thing as a previous existence, Mother and Bill and I were together through centuries and centuries of time. On the other hand, Lucile and daddy were so much alike and linked in spirit, I felt they, too, had been together, and that we had all finally been drawn together into one family. All of this started working in my mind when I was a very little girl and didn't crystallize until I was a lot older. Certainly there has always been a mystical aspect to my life.

On the other hand, on my "flip side," as they say, I was always ready for fun, occasionally rowdy, and sometimes a bit naughty. Thank goodness I have always been able to counterbalance my philosophical bent with a delight in the ridiculous.

Beginning in high school I went around with a pretty wild bunch of kids. Prohibition was in full force and an atmosphere of high adventure and surreptitious activity pervaded our lives. We knew many parents had home brews and bathtub gin. I remember one night during my sophomore year being down in the basement of her home with my best friend. Her father came home to hear us whispering and giggling. He found us sitting there completely "pickled" after finishing off three or four bottles of his best home-brewed beer. I stayed the night so *my* dad never found out.

Once in a while I got caught. Daddy loved us dearly but he had a very strict standard of right and wrong. I can remember being put over a barrel more than once to receive an unforgettable strapping. Once all three of us got one of the worst—although that time I was innocent of the now-forgotten offense; but it all evened out because the one time I probably deserved a first-class beating, I got none.

The kids from school all had crushes on each other sooner or later, and I did a great deal of agonizing about it. My theme song during those years must have been "All Alone by the Telephone" because I certainly spent a lot of time hovering around it and watching it. It was during those days when I was a young kid and feeling frustrated or unwanted that I discovered that if I took a drink or two with the gang, it made me feel good. Then I felt witty and could tell jokes and make them laugh. I felt it enlarged me a little, I guess. It certainly made me feel more confident and at ease.

I was 17 when I fell desperately in love for the first time and of course I couldn't tell my parents. It all shook me up pretty well at the time, because goodness knows, I have always suffered dreadful guilt when I've done or felt things contrary to my Puritan upbringing. I mean I've always been a willful person, even in high school, but I've also done my own worst punishing of my own self.

Still, with all my escapades with my gang, I felt set apart and tried desperately to fit in. Maybe I tried too hard, because one day as we were driving to a dance and I was chattering along, my date suddenly declared, "You know something, Steber, you're a grandstander!" That bothered me so much I never forgot it, probably because I knew it was probably true.

But, all in all, I don't think we were any different from other teenagers of our day, and maybe not so different from the kids today. Actually, I think we were much more romantic. Today everything has become so graphic that the wonderful mystery of it all has disappeared.

No one knew what I should do after high school. Even if there had been enough money to send me to college, no one knew where or for what. Even I wasn't yet clear whether I wanted to act, play the piano or sing—or all three—I just knew the stage was my destination. So I stayed in Wheeling where I got my first paid singing job in the quartet of the Second Presbyterian Church, taught piano to beginners and studied at Idabel Waggoner's School of Dramatic Art. I paid for my lessons by playing background music for the recitations of other students.

I adored drama school. I got to sink my teeth into such histrionic morsels as Edgar Allen Poe's "The Raven" and "The Return of Enoch Arden." I threw myself into this new world with such enthusiasm that my parents complained that I spent more time at the school than I did at home, and that I was running with a crowd too old and too "fast" for me. But I knew better. I was in my element now, not only loving every minute both on and off stage, but increasingly stirred to explore the world beyond Wheeling.

How could I realize when I played the Mother Superior in our graduation production of "The Nursery Maid of Heaven" that some 30 years later life would come full circle and I would play almost the same role again when I did the Mother Abbess in Richard Rodgers' "The Sound of Music." Mother discovered an old picture of me as that first Mother Superior and brought it with her when she came to see me play the Abbess at New York's City Center in 1968.

While I studied acting, there was a pitched battle going on at home about my future. The struggle was strictly between my parents and other relatives, because I certainly wasn't consulted. Mother was determined to get me out of Wheeling, but she didn't know how she could manage it because my father dug in his heels and rejected every idea mother put forth—and Grandfather Steber backed him up—not to thwart me, but because daddy loved me. He just wanted me to stay home, get married and have a lot of kids. He wanted all of us to stay near him.

To make matters worse, the "theater" was an anathema to him. He loved to watch us perform at home, but to make a living at it, no! The "stage" held terrible connotations for him. He firmly believed that everyone on it was immoral (which may well be from his point of view), but mother stood firm. "Bill," I heard her say, "that girl's going away to study if I have to scrub floors!"

Daddy helped work it all out in spite of himself, for he drove us on half a dozen trips during which Mother checked out various music schools. Philadelphia's Sesquicentennial was her excuse to look over Curtis Institute, and she manipulated investigations of the Cincinnati and Cleveland Conservatories as well. We even visited Juilliard, although it was never in the running because, to my father, New York was the twentieth century Sodom and Gomorrah. To this day I believe Mother chose the New England Conservatory because it was farthest from home, and she knew that if I studied in Boston, she'd eventually get to visit the city herself.

That decided, Mother's problem was money. Daddy couldn't have come up with it even if he wanted to because he probably never made more than $7,000 a year in his life and that didn't happen until much later. Eventually Mother finagled it by using everything she had saved from her singing and teaching. Then she coaxed some from Grandmother Nolte and yet more from my "Uncle Doc." She eventually raised $1,250, just enough for one semester. So Boston it was, and on a warm September day in 1933 our little party huddled together, hugging our farewells on the train platform in Wheeling. I was dressed fit to kill. Mother had created a glamorous new wardrobe for me which was probably far more appropriate for a bride's trousseau, I am sure, than for a college freshman.

As the train started to pull away, I looked down from my window to see my mother weeping and my father glum and pale. Tears trickled down my sister's cheeks and even my brother Bill looked uncharacteristically downcast.

Perhaps it was devastating for them to watch their first-born leave home, but I was on top of the world. I was on the road to freedom and so excited I could hardly contain myself. I was bursting with confidence and hope, not even bothering to imagine what my new life would be like. I intended to love it. As the train gathered speed, I sat lightly in my seat, eyes glued to the window recording the changing scenes, eagerly waiting to embrace my new life with open arms.

Boston

I arrived at Back Bay, Boston with a warm feeling of homecoming and a surprising assurance that I had found the place I was destined to be. I grappled successfully with all my bags and found my way to Frost Hall, my dormitory. I was so overwhelmed with excitement I can't even remember entering the Conservatory, but meeting Charles Dennée, head of the piano department, stuck in my mind because I had entered the Conservatory as a piano major.

This was entirely logical to my parents because as I was preparing to leave for school the Depression was at its worst. Mother minced no words. "Eleanor," she said, "if I can't find a way for you to stay a full year, even one semester will mean you can return to Wheeling and ask $1.00 for teaching a piano lesson instead of 50 cents." Thus, the practical importance of piano study was impressed upon me from the start, although singing, which was my minor subject, was already as much a part of my life as breathing, so much so that although Mr. Dennée always was very encouraging, I simply didn't practice as I would have if I'd truly set my heart on becoming a concert pianist. Not so with voice. Although I never agonized about whether or not I would be a "singer," there was *never* a possibility of my *not* singing. I couldn't help singing. It simply wasn't immediately clear that it was to be my whole life.

Mother somehow contrived for me to finish that first year, and by that time my voice teacher, William L. Whitney *was* sure. He told me to change my major, which enraged Mr. Dennée who was furious at Mr. Whitney for taking me away from him. The idea of those two darling old men fighting over me was something! But Mr. Whitney prevailed, and rightly so, for he already knew I had neither the patience nor the temperament to become a great pianist. Anyway, by then I was dedicated to singing and to Mr. Whitney, who helped me win a full scholarship which kept me going for the next five years.

Mr. Whitney was 72 years old when I met him. So profoundly did his personality impress itself upon me that he is as vivid to me today as he was then. A gentleman of a very "old school," he was always impeccable in striped trousers and cutaway coat, his white goatee and moustache precisely trimmed and a scruff of white hair fringing his pink pate. He carried a touch of the Victorian age well into the 20th century.

William L. (as we called him privately) began as a pianist who "incidentally" studied voice. He, too, left piano to study voice, undoubtedly influenced by his singer-father, Myron Whitney. Toward me he was gentle, kind and considerate and above all, wonderfully intuitive. He always seemed to know whether I was on top of the world or under it and what to do about it. I never thought of him as "old," but I was awed by him. He warned me from the start that I would have to work harder than I could conceive possible and I vowed I would. I wanted only to please him.

His white gloves were his trademark. He wore them everywhere — ordinary workmen's gloves in the studio and, for public occasions, sleek, skin-tight silk gloves that hugged his extraordinarily large hands and long fingers. We were fascinated and puzzled to know how he could play even the most florid passages so cleanly in gloves. No one dared ask him why he wore them, but one night an old pair which had taken a pretty heavy pounding during the day wore through during a group class and we saw blood seep through them, smearing the keys. The gloves were protection for his tender, allergic skin. He was also allergic to flowers which I discovered the day I brought some lilacs to please him and he exploded with terrible sneezing and frantically waved me out of the room. I was heartsick.

His "office" was a shopping bag in which he kept everything from tissues to candy, his appointment and address books, his *Argosy* pulp magazine and paperback mysteries; medicines for headache and hay fever, extra white gloves and a jumble of keys. I can still see him bending over it searching its contents with a playful shrug and a quick cock of his head. Whenever I had to wait for my lesson in the corridor, he'd dart out of his studio to hand me an adventure or mystery magazine saying, "Here! Improve your mind while you're waiting." So I'd read until I heard the great discordant crash on the piano inside which signaled the end of my predecessor's lesson.

The bel canto I learned with Mr. Whitney came to me in the pure form in which he had first learned it with Luigi Vannuccini in Florence in the late 1800s. He had remained with Vannuccini and taken over his school when Vannuccini died, returning to head the voice department of the New England Conservatory in 1915 before World War I. Slowly and methodically he subdued my enthusiastic but undisciplined vocal delivery. He taught me to "mount the breath," which means bringing support up under a phrase and keeping it there so that the sound is riding *on* the breath. It is the breath, vibrating as it passes through the vocal chords and resonating against the mask (the face and its resonant cavities), which produces the quality of the tone. With hundreds of exercises, many of them of his own creation and others by Panofka and Vaccai, he eased my voice down to the essential core of my middle range, then gradually extended it in either direction, letting it grow naturally in strength and quality.

My Maestro's approach was completely classical. Recently a professional colleague insisted that Mozart should not be attempted until one had already learned to sing. On the contrary, Mr. Whitney schooled me *first* on Mozart — and then Haydn, Handel, Rossini, Bellini. He taught me, of course, to float a tone and to perfect the fine art of "messa di voce" (a tone beginning pianissimo, gradually swelling to forte and just as gradually decreasing to the ultimate pianissimo). He drilled me in coloratura, cadenzas, appoggiatura and embellishments until they were my second nature. He taught me to use my voice like an instrument.

I had to learn that it takes a good three years of study for a voice to "find itself." Sometimes I felt I was only marking time. I had too much energy and eagerness for comfort. All the time I yearned to dig into something meaty — something more dramatic than my tranquil diet of Mozart and company. So one day I timidly asked if I might bring something of my own to work on. When he said yes, I fairly bounced out of the room. Next lesson I set a copy of "Pace, mio Dio" on the piano. He peered at the music, withered me with a glance and, with a flip of his wrist, scaled my sheet music across the room. Then he said quietly, "Now we will sing 'Batti, batti, O bel Masetto'."

Despite all the drilling in technique, however, I was never really analytical about the mechanics of singing until I began to teach others. It just wasn't my nature to question or analyze. Yet it was this technique, absorbed almost by osmosis, which gave me the freedom and ability to sing in so many styles.

Everybody wants to go for the "big" voice today. Mr. Whitney taught me that you cannot make even a "big" voice bigger. You must first find the core of the voice and make *that* beautiful. He taught me that the timbre of a voice remains constant; that I, for instance, was a lyric soprano because my timbre was lyric, but that I could learn to *color* my voice to encompass almost any role.

Some years later, when I first arrived at the Metropolitan, there were a few who said my voice would never be heard. With the technique Mr. Whitney gave me, it is not necessary to hear "bigness" of sound at the source. When a tone is well focused against the mask and resonators, this starts everything going ahead of it so that it will project and grow into the qualities and acoustics of the hall. Tenor Paul Althouse said, for example, that when he sang with Kirsten Flagstad, her voice did not seem big at all when he was close to her. It had a lovely lyric quality, but its sound grew in size and brilliance as it flowed into the opera house.

The process of learning to sing is seldom obvious, logical or demonstrable either to the beginning student or untutored listener, so that with the best intentions in the world, friends and family sometimes cast doubts in a student's mind. Toward the end of my first year at NEC (probably the point where Mr. Whitney had succeeded in reducing my voice to its core), some of my friends tried to pressure me to leave Mr. Whitney. I was beset by such urgings and advice and it troubled me terribly until I made up my mind to stop listening to anybody but Mr. Whitney. I simply had faith that what Mr. Whitney was teaching me was absolutely correct and that I could not possibly leave him until he sent me away. I accepted and obeyed, absolutely, everything he told me for the next six years. Total trust in my teacher was a fundamental instinct in me. Mr. Whitney's greatest praise was never more than a casual, "Pretty good, Steber." His uncompromising standards for me never wavered.

I visited him in Boston many times after I joined the Met. In 1949, when he was in his late 80s, I found his mind sharper, if possible, and his wit keener, his convictions even firmer than I remembered. I called him on the phone when I arrived in Boston that year and at once he demanded, "Can you still sing, Steber?"

"Maestro," I protested, "I've just sung my 16th major role at the Metropolitan Opera and everybody wants me for concerts, radio shows and recordings!"

"Yes, I know," he replied softly, "but can you still sing?"

He made me vocalize for him on the telephone to prove it.

During my entire life I can remember being terrified on stage exactly three times. The first was my initial appearance in an afternoon student recital in the Conservatory's Jordan Hall. I sought courage by dressing to the ears in one of the voluptuous gowns mother had sent with me, but when I walked out to sing "Il Bacio" and "Freulingsglaube," I shook in near panic and I knew people could see my knees shaking under my skirt because I had not even worn a slip. But I took a deep breath, pulled myself up and sang with all the bravado I could muster.

Mr. Whitney didn't play for me that day because he wanted to see how I conducted myself on stage. His young wife Leta was watching with him. Later she told me she had whispered to him that she thought I was overly theatrical and my voice was somewhat shrill, and said that she really didn't understand what he saw in me. He whispered back, "Don't worry. You'll see. Steber's got it."

If I threw myself into my singing, I certainly didn't apply myself with the same dedication to the rest of the curriculum. Like so many of my students today who balk at courses which seem to have nothing directly to do with singing, I slithered through the academics. Even in retrospect it scares me because I still have nightmares that I never got my degree.

Why did I have to waste my time on Composition and Analysis? I wasn't going to be a conductor or composer. I already knew chord structures from playing piano. It was enough that I understood them and their progressions. What saved me was a retentive mind and the concentration to absorb everything I heard and read, because, quite honestly, I didn't devote all that much time to my homework.

Later, however, I began to get new vistas of harmonics and rhythms. I became fascinated to see how my songs were constructed. I can remember sitting at the piano one day learning Debussy's "Mandolin" and discovering the contrasting rhythmic patterns and variations. After that, with tremendous excitement, I began to explore all the new music I could find. I don't think my mind was ever still.

I cannot over-emphasize the importance for any child to have good early instrumental instruction, particularly piano or violin, long before the voice potential becomes evident. The voice is an instrument, too, of course, but the voice is "us" and it matures so comparatively late that it's essential to start building the musical foundation long before.

If I have been known as a good musician, an accurate reader and quick study, it was 90% my solid technical background; the rest was desire and the talent God gave me. With a solid background, a singer can handle anything that comes along; without it, any career, no matter how beautiful the voice, has built-in limits.

One of my classes was Vocal Pedagogy which qualified me to teach beginning techniques to new students. I had a natural aptitude for teaching from the start, and knew it was my eventual destiny. I also played accompaniments for the Hans Weiner Dance School, in return for which I was allowed to take classes. I also became soloist with a violin, cello and piano trio which played short concerts of light classical music for high schools within driving distance of Boston. We called ourselves "The Barnstormers." Outside of class I settled in with a congenial group of older students and young professionals who kept me on my toes. To me they were the heart of it all—experienced, sophisticated people who *did things*.

My theatrical baptism of fire came when Arthur Fiedler called on NEC students for a production of Reginald DeKoven's "Robin Hood." My friend Thelma Jo Fisher and I auditioned together. She was cast as a milkmaid and I, believe it or not, became one of Robin Hood's Merry Men, proving how slim and boy-like my figure was in those days. The Friar Tuck, a horse-loving Irishman named Henry Kelly, caught up with me backstage one day and told me that I reminded him of a young colt. Oh, the dreams of yesteryear!

The backbone of my performing experience, however, and the job which contributed most importantly to my future, was the music program developed by the Works Progress Administration (WPA), part of President Franklin Roosevelt's National Recovery Act. The WPA provided work for thousands of unemployed professional musicians, kept music in the theaters, and introduced live music to audiences who couldn't ordinarily afford tickets. I was hired as a non-relief performer, receiving a grandiose $19 per week. For this I rehearsed for three hours every morning in the chorus and was expected to handle the soprano solos in everything we performed.

I had been weaned on oratorio, and with Alec Simson and the WPA Choral Symphony I sang some two dozen of them. I rehearsed and performed constantly not only the familiar "Messiah" and the various Requiems, but the Beethoven Ninth and Missa Solemnis, "The Beatitudes" by Cesar Franck, Mendelssohn's "Elijah," "St. Paul" and "The Hymn of Praise" and the great Bach cantatas and Mozart masses—a priceless experience.

If there was anything missing from my conservatory experience, it was an opera school, or even a course in dramatics. This omission has been rectified in conservatories everywhere, and for me, it wasn't as crucial as it might have been. After all, I had not only studied drama for a year in Wheeling, it permeated my whole nature. I wasn't aware of it then, but I was a born performer; what I needed was a stage!

Love Along the Fenway

I needed a church job to supplement my limited finances. Unable to find a solo position at first, I sang in the choir of the little Union Congregational Church on Westland Avenue for $5 a service. There I became acquainted with Gladys Miller, contralto soloist and a teacher at the Conservatory. As we strolled away from rehearsal one night, Miss Miller murmured in confidential tones, "Eleanor, there's a young fellow in the tenor section who thinks you're the most wonderful thing on two feet."

Now who could resist that? Certainly not me. Nothing has ever dampened my interest in handsome young men. So, the following Sunday I took a look at this Edwin Bilby fellow and decided I'd like to know him better. He began to walk me home from church and now and then we'd stop in at the Old France Restaurant or stroll along the Fenway and talk for hours about music and books.

Edwin was older than I and had already graduated from Harvard with a degree in Liberal Arts. Now he was trying to make his way as a singer. He seemed a wonderfully enthusiastic young man, very slim, with wavy brown hair and beautiful blue eyes and had the look of a poet about him. It was an idyllic time for two youngsters like Ed and me, with our highly romantic imaginations. As we walked or sat together over a meal, Ed read all the major poets to me—Keats, Shelley, Wordsworth. He knew a great deal more about opera then than I did, and we often spent Saturday afternoons listening to the opera broadcasts on a friend's radio.

We began going together in February of 1934, and by spring I no longer wanted to go home for the summer. I wanted to stay and take a summer housekeeping job in Maine with Ed, but my mother would have none of it, and not just about the job. She took a very dim view of my whole association with Edwin for, in spite of his Harvard degree, he was having a tough time making a go of it. A Harvard degree didn't count for much in the mid-1930s, and a future with Ed Bilby was not at all what mother had in mind for me. She made life very uncomfortable for him when she visited Boston that first spring. I always felt sorry for anyone on the receiving end of mother's piercing "gimlet-eye," but Ed just smiled in his pleasant way and pretended not to notice.

By the fall of that year I secured a solo job at the Eliott Church in Newton, and by Christmas Ed and I were formally dedicated and engaged. We were constantly together and my life was hectic indeed, for it was simply not in my nature to say "no" to a party with our gang or a date with Ed. (Ed, in fact, helped me with some of my academic papers.) I was caught one night trying to sneak into a dorm window after curfew, and the powers-that-be immediately reported my misdemeanor to Mr. Whitney: "That girl is nothing but a southern butterfly, staying out all night and who knows what-all!" Whereupon dear William L. replied that as far as he was concerned, "Steber works hard, so let her play."

During my third year I met Hans Hoffman, conductor of the WPA Opera Project, who asked me to sing Senta in "The Flying Dutchman." I ran immediately to Mr. Whitney to ask if I could do it. He said he thought I could if we were very careful. He coached me every step of the way and I finally made my opera debut in 1936 singing Senta in English—age 21. A year later I sang the Mother in Louis Gruenberg's "Jack and the Beanstalk" with young Eugene Conley singing with me. Years later Gene and I sang together at the Met and recorded the official Met "Faust." It really has been most mysterious how so many people I met or heard in Boston—and even back in Wheeling—eventually became part of my career life.

Things really began to look up professionally after I got my vocal diploma. I was working on my Bachelor of Music degree when I won a regular job as featured singer on the I.J. Fox Fur Trappers Radio Show. The program's theme was the "Indian Love Call" ("When I'm calling 'U' double 0, double 0") and offered light classics and popular songs. The program often featured such guests as tenors Morton Downey and Frank Parker, from whom I learned a lot about mike technique."

My sponsors offered me an attractive fringe benefit. I was told that I could stop down at their main emporium and pick out "a little something" for myself. Well, they hustled me past the silver fox, the sable, mink, Persian lamb, the beaver—even past the rabbit. I landed in a room filled with fur-trimmed cloth coats and suits. I finally found a beautiful three-piece suit with a jacket of fur with stripy brown, black, white and burnt orange markings which they called "barondukie." I was quite charmed with it until I discovered a few weeks later that "baron-dukie" was part or all chipmunk. I wore it, but I still can't look a chipmunk in the eye.

My first experience with "live" opera came at the end of my first year in Boston when the "old" Chicago Opera Company presented "Andrea Chenier" with Mario Chamlee. The following season the Metropolitan included Boston on its tour, and I nearly jumped out of my skin when a call for "supers" to appear in "Die Meistersinger" was posted on the student notice board. I raced to the opera house to apply and was interviewed by Etienne Barone (who was still in charge of supers for the Met when I got there myself). My very long brown hair (usually braided, twisted in a bun or wrapped in a corona around my head) must have given me a sufficiently German mädschen look, for he immediately instructed me to return that night to be a garland-bearer in the third act. I was thrilled silly and told my good news to everyone I met. I should have known better. When I arrived backstage that night and tried to get in, I discovered that someone who was not even a music student had used my name and swiped my job. It was a crushing disappointment and a hard lesson, but it has never been easy for me to keep my mouth shut.

All was not lost, however. Barone took pity and sent me to the wardrobe mistress, tiny, plump Jenny Cervini, who found me a costume. Thanks to them, I enjoyed my first opera on stage and walked the boards with real opera stars. Viennese soprano Irene Jessner was singing Eva that night (she would sing many performances of the Marschallin in "Der Rosenkavalier" with me during the 1940s) and tenor Paul Althouse (so important to me a few short years into the future) was Walther. The great Friedrich Schorr was Hans Sachs.

I was dazzled by their very nearness as I watched them on and off the stage. That memory came back to me often in later years at the Met when young people came into my dressing room with stars in their eyes, stammering in their nervousness. I understood them so well because that was the way I felt that night when I tried to approach those three awesome opera personages. I was fascinated watching Irene Jessner swishing in and out of her dressing room, each time munching some different appetizing morsel. "Did opera singers eat all the time?" I wondered. Some of us do! Some of us do!

I was graduated from the Conservatory in the spring of 1938, and as a final gesture of recognition, I was invited to sing at Commencement with the Conservatory Orchestra. More importantly, I finally got my chance—at last—to sing my adored "Pace, mio Dio" as guest artist with Arthur Fiedler and the Boston "Pops" Orchestra.

Although my days in Boston were already numbered, I was unaware of it and continued studying with Mr. Whitney while I planned a September wedding. Until then I had had my own little apartment on St. Stephen's Street, which I loved; but it was barely big enough for me and certainly impossible for two of us, so I was apartment-hunting, too.

Finally, on the afternoon of September 25, after I had completed my regular musical chores at the Eliott Church, Ed and I were married there. The event had all the elements of a theatrical cliff-hanger. Hitler had invaded Czechoslovakia, and two days before the wedding the big hurricane of 1938 hit New England hard. The trees along our beloved Fenway were laid low, scattered like toothpicks. My family, which wasn't keen on our marriage anyway, was forced to detour across western Connecticut and Massachusetts, nearly driving off a cliff, to get there at all.

We settled into our new little apartment, and like so many couples of our time, lived a hand-to-mouth existence. Most of the time we were so blissfully happy we didn't care. I had my church job and occasional concerts, and sometimes mother sent along a little something extra. We even managed a small second-hand car. We tried getting work as a concert duo and dreamed of singing opera together one day. Then a job came through from a group who wanted me, but not Ed. Almost simultaneously he lost his church job. It shattered him when his bright hope of our singing together burst like a bubble. Ed seemed to give up on himself; and he began to pour all his energy and ambition into my career. He became intensely enthusiastic about his dreams for me, which were often impractical, and subsequently often brought more disappointments for him.

Through the years that followed, he became so eager for me to succeed and urged me forward with such ardor that I was never quite sure what to believe or what to do. The patterns set during these few months in Boston persisted throughout our marriage with results which were, I know now, inevitable.

While still in the Conservatory, I had won the regional competition of the Federation of Women's Clubs and was scheduled to go to Baltimore to compete in the national finals. This was terribly important to me because the previous year I had failed even to "place" in the Naumberg competition, which awarded a Town Hall Recital to each winner. In 1938 this was equivalent to about $1,000, and if recital notices were good, the chances of securing top management were excellent. I had to get to Baltimore, but I was broke. In desperation I borrowed money from one of those storefront loan companies. I thought of it as my "loan shark."

So I got to Baltimore, but I lost the competition by one point to mezzo-soprano Martha Lipton, a future Metropolitan colleague. Among the judges in Baltimore were conductors Eugene Ormandy and Fritz Reiner and Robert Spalding of Juilliard.

My disappointment in placing second turned to fury when I heard that although the judges had found no violinist worthy of first place, they had split the prize money between the two second place violinists. I would never dispute the judges' decision about my performance, but I was desperate about the money and bitter that there wasn't even a token for second place. (This is a major reason I made sure that all finalists in my future Eleanor Steber Music Foundation Competition always went home with something!)

It was in Baltimore, however, that I met Orville Moore, a young baritone contestant from Denver who was full of the excitement of singing and wonderfully knowledgeable about new music. He heard my performance, comforted me in my loss and urged me to stop over in New York on my way back.

There I discovered that I had again not placed in the Naumberg competition. I couldn't believe it. As my train headed for Boston I got madder and madder; by the time I arrived, I was furious! I poured out my frustrations to Mr. Whitney, who listened patiently to the whole story. Then he said, "Steber, it's time for you to leave Boston – now – as soon as you can. I have taught you all I can. You don't need any more vocal training; what you need now is a first-class coach."

I think Mr. Whitney, then nearly 78, had been through so much with his students that he was beyond anger, but his vision was absolutely clear. I didn't question his decision. I had obeyed him for six years and I obeyed him now. I packed up as quickly as I could and headed for New York.

Siren City

Since Edwin had to stay in Boston at his job, pending the success of my ventures in New York, Orville helped me search for a place to live. I had been told that a good address was essential, so when I found a room I could afford on the fourth floor of a brownstone walk-up at 18 East 10th Street, I took it. The address had to be good – didn't the great *New York Times* music critic Olin Downes have a town house just across the street?

Talk about starting life as a Bohemian Mimi! I lived in a garret, literally, so tiny that when Edwin came to visit, I kept a folding cot in the closet for him. I did all my cooking in a coffee pot on a hot plate, and both my air and light came from a skylight which I kept open constantly – except when it rained. But the address *was* good.

With Orville as my guide, I made the rounds of the agencies for church soloists. Almost at once I landed a great job for the summer in a quartet in Elberon, New Jersey, near the shore, where Norman Vincent Peale was preaching. I had to be on the road by 6 A.M. each Sunday to keep this job.

I scouted the Naumberg finals at Town Hall where the winner turned out to be an attractive young soprano recently graduated from Juilliard. Her name was Gertrude Gibson. Her presence in New York was to haunt me during the next 12 months.

As soon as I got the Naumberg blues out of my system, I shopped around for a good vocal coach. Mr. Whitney had suggested Frank St. Leger, but he was now working at the Met and, I assumed, unavailable to me. I also sang for some managers, including a couple of impresario types, Zanatello and Guy, who declared they could make me the leading Tosca at the Met within two years! Thank goodness I had the sense to realize that nobody could make me a Tosca in two years—Violetta, I thought, *maybe*, but not Tosca. As I escaped from their office, Orville spoke up. "Eleanor, I really think you ought to sing for my teacher, Paul Althouse." I agreed at once.

Paul Althouse, who lived in one of New York's marvelous music-filled apartment houses on West 72nd Street near Riverside Drive, was nearing the end of a splendid career as one of the few American tenors to excel in singing Wagnerian opera at the Metropolitan. Some years later, he told me that the first time I sang for him, goose bumps ran up and down his arms. When I finished, he said, "Eleanor, I can't teach you a thing as far as your technique's concerned, because it's already superb, but your voice should be opened up. He was right, of course, and that's exactly what he did. He became my mentor, my "ears" and my faithful friend who helped me as long as he lived. He was a dear man and a peerless coach.

As Ed wound up his affairs in Boston and joined me on East 10th Street, my parents descended upon us, combining an inspection visit with a trip to the 1939 World's Fair in Flushing Meadow. When they took one look at my tiny "digs" at the "good address," they mobilized instantly. Before we knew what was happening, we had been moved to more spacious quarters on the floor below. This time there were actually a few windows from which we could look out over a tiny backyard garden. We also inherited a pair of studio couches and two closets, one of which we converted into a kitchenette. Why we didn't burn the place down, I'll never know.

Edwin had sold our little Boston car to get the money to move to New York. Then, when the only suitable job he could find was with a church publishing house in New Jersey, we again needed a car—so back to a second-hand car we went. Our routine was simple. We rose at 6 o'clock and had breakfast together at Stewart's Cafeteria at the corner of 9th Street. Then Ed headed for New Jersey while I hiked up to 13th Street to what we laughingly called "Manhattan School of Music downtown," actually a bare loft on the top floor of an old warehouse with a single battered old upright piano, but I could vocalize and study my music there for 25 cents an hour.

Whenever I could, I worked on repertoire with Jimmy Quillian, a delightful coach-accompanist I had met through Orville during my post-Baltimore stopover in New York. A graduate of the Eastman School of Music, Jimmy was also an honest-to-goodness "su'thun gentleman" with a pixy sense of humor. Competition for jobs in New York was fierce (although it's much worse today) and I auditioned for anyone who would listen to me. Since it was routine in those days for every young singer to apply to the Metropolitan Opera Auditions of the Air, I also did that.

Ed and I explored New York. We were thrilled by the gorgeous stage extravaganzas at Radio City (Jan Peerce, Leonard Warren and Robert Weede got their starts in them) and I whispered to him, "Someday I'd like to sing here." Or, maybe on a Sunday we'd attend the Evensong oratorios at St. Bartholomew's on Park Avenue and I'd wonder to myself if maybe I could get a job there. Actually, I had already found a very fine church job. Immediately after my stint in Elberon I became soprano soloist in the quartet at the Methodist-Episcopal Church of St. Paul and St. Andrew at 86th Street and West End Avenue. It was an excellent position and a happy one. I sang there as long as I could, well into my third year at the Met, until my concert and opera schedules made it impossible. However, my association with that fine old church never completely severed and I returned to it often over the years. I made several recordings there as well. I was always happy singing in church.

The job kept me from starvation, but you can't live on church pay, but for the moment, it was all I could add to Ed's income. There were many days I nearly lost hope, and sometimes in church I caught myself crying, "Dear God, where are we going? What's going to happen to us?"

Only Paul Althouse seemed completely assured about my future—so sure that he was willing to wait for his fees, which were some time in coming. But when I was finally on my way, I made sure he got every nickel of it. Paul looked like a Wagnerian tenor: hefty, somewhat short, with a receding hairline and kindly face; he was a warm, honest man who never made any demands upon me, never tried to capitalize on my ultimate success and always made certain people understood I was Mr. Whitney's pupil and he was simply my New York vocal coach. His remarkably generous attitude helped maintain my faith in people, which wavered more than I care to admit. This is a tough business.

I was summoned in early fall to sing for Wilfred Pelletier, musical director of the Metropolitan Opera Auditions. He listened to me in a small studio at NBC. I still have a vivid mental picture of standing before the big floor microphone watching the expressionless faces in the control room and waiting for some sort of reaction. I was placed to sing on the first broadcast of the 1939–40 Auditions together with a fellow named Bill Greenstreet. I sang "Ah fors e' lui" from "Traviata" and Friml's "Donkey Serenade" in duet with Bill.

I certainly never gave a thought to winning. After the fiascos of the Federation and Naumberg competitions, I wouldn't let myself consider it. I felt that the radio auditions were giving me a chance to be heard by some important people and a big step toward getting ahead. More importantly, I was being *paid!* I was dumbfounded when I heard myself announced as winner of the first half of the Auditions. If nothing else, it meant another nationwide broadcast and another much-needed check.

This time Maestro Pelletier instructed me to learn a specific aria. I was sent down to the Metropolitan Opera House where I climbed the creaky old stairs on "the men's side" to a dusty little dressing room where Maestro Fausto Cleva coached me in the brilliant bel canto aria, "Ernani involami."

As the Auditions came down to the wire, the second-half winner turned out to be—guess who?—Gertrude Gibson, the Juilliard graduate who had won the Naumberg prize. I wasn't encouraged.

I sang my semi-final Audition of the Air on March 9, 1940, and went directly from NBC to sing "The Seven Last Words of Christ" in a small New Jersey church for a $10 fee and carfare. Gibson would sing the following week and the winners would be announced the Sunday after that. Ed and I spent "Gibson's Sunday" with friends, playing Mah Jongg, listening to the broadcast and conjecturing about my chances, if any. I was in limbo.

Back home again late that evening, Ed and I were still debating my chances when our landlady called up the stairs to say I was wanted on the telephone. I ran down three flights of steps and picked up the receiver. It was Maestro Pelletier.

"Eleanor," he asked, "do you know the duet from 'Madama Butterfly'?"

"No, Maestro."

"Do you think you can learn it?"

"Oh, yes, Maestro, I can learn it."

"Do you know the quartet from 'La Bohème'?"

"No, Maestro, but I can learn it."

"Do you suppose you could learn them both fast enough to sing them in Cleveland next week?"

Cleveland was the corporate home of the Sherwin-Williams Paint Company which sponsored the Metropolitan Opera Auditions and the location of the giant auditorium used for the gala pre-opera concert at which the winners and finalists of the Auditions were presented.

Pelletier persisted, "Do you think you would be able to go out to Cleveland to sing next week?"

"Oh, yes, Maestro."

"Eleanor, do you know what I am saying? You have won the Metropolitan Opera Auditions of the Air."

Silence.

"Eleanor, are you there?"

"Yes, Maestro."

"You have won."

"Oh, yes, Maestro."

Slowly I hiked back up the "leaning stairs" of 18 East 10th Street, carefully feeling each step. Finally I reached the third floor. I opened the door.

Ed looked up expectantly, "Well, who called?"

"Presentation of the Rose"

In this most sacred hour, my God,
When Thy great blessings lift me high above my worth,
I thank Thee.
Oh, grant that the sin of vainglory be ever far from my soul...
Let me not be puffed up with pride unduly
by the honors of my new station.
Ye Saints in Heaven, I know that pride is a most deadly sin;
But this day, all my prayers are in vain —
I cannot be duly meek — For it is all so fair! So fair!

—Sophie, *Rosenkavalier, Act II*

If ever anyone was as dazzled in real life as young Sophie in "Der Rosenkavalier," it was me on that unbelievable Sunday afternoon when the Metropolitan's General Manager Edward Johnson asked a nationwide radio audience, "Do you remember this voice?" and gave me the cue to sing the opening bars of "Ernani involami."

People who heard the Metropolitan Auditions broadcasts can't understand why I ever doubted the outcome. Even Kirsten Flagstad, then riding the crest of her fame in the U.S., confidently told her accompanist, Edwin McArthur, that "no one but Steber could win," and some time later when I was taken to visit the legendary Emma Eames, she declared to me, "I knew the moment I heard you that you would win. I recognized the technique and I knew no one could touch you."

Back in 1940, winning the Metropolitan Opera Auditions really *meant something*! Metropolitan Opera Manager Edward Johnson, who had originated the Auditions of the Air, awarded each winner a contract with the opera company as well as a cash prize, and both the Metropolitan and Sherwin-Williams honored the winners in magnificent style. What I didn't know is that while my co-winner, baritone Arthur Kent, and I were being feted at NBC, along with former winners and the entire Metropolitan hierarchy, my home town went wild. For days my parents' phone rang off the hook, and my friends began to plan a gigantic home-coming for me.

My triumphant return home on "Eleanor Steber Day" in early May was a storybook affair and has been recorded by photos of me and my entourage of family and friends waving to a crowd of fans from a train observation car marked with a big circular "Eleanor Steber Special" sign. Actually, I'd already been home for a day or two, long enough to get the beautiful silver fox stole which Mother insisted I needed to give me that "real prima donna" look. Mother also hatched up the "Eleanor Steber Special" by arranging with the B&O Railroad to back a rear car out into the train yard so we could take the "homecoming" pictures. Machinations already!

The parade through town, however, was the real thing. "Eleanor Steber Day" signs and billboards had sprouted on storefronts everywhere along the way, and all of Wheeling seem to jam the sidewalks. The Warwick High School Band led the way followed by 90 cars filled with my family, friends and everyone from the Governor to the Mayor to the Sheriff. That night I sang the first of my 16 annual "Homecoming Concerts." So great was the demand for tickets that I had to repeat the program the following night at a different theater. My people—almost everybody in Wheeling—sent me back to New York with an unforget-table memory and a gift of $2,000. So, together with the prize from the Auditions of the Air, I had a financial stake of $3,000 plus my good church job to hold me until I could start realizing the income from my future concert and opera career.

We had already moved from the East 10th Street walk-up to a delightful little apartment at 55 West 11th Street. I used some of my precious new largesse to secure a spinet piano so I could work at home instead of renting the dusty loft studio. Not long after this I hired my faithful and patient Rena Fludd to take care of our housekeeping and meals so I could concentrate on my work. I found it not the least bit strange to shift suddenly from a single room walk-up to an apartment with a housekeeper. I slipped into this new lifestyle easily and gratefully. Oh, I could be a good housekeeper when I had to (I have a keen eye and nose for the musty, the stale, the sour and the unpolished), but it was seldom a matter of choice.

A dear little old lady I knew in Boston had once caught me most uncharacteristically washing windows in my little St. Stephen Street apartment. She chided me gently, "My dear, you oughtn't to do that kind of hard labor. You're an artist and you should reserve yourself for your music." My idea precisely!

During what remained of the spring and throughout the entire summer, I had mammoth tasks to master. Not only did I have to learn and polish recital programs for my first concert tour in the fall, I had to study and memorize more than half a dozen roles assigned to me by the Metropolitan. At the same time, I made recordings of opera excerpts with other rising artists at the Met like Armand Tokatyan and Leonard Warren. In quick order we recorded highlights from "Butterfly," "Bohème," "Traviata," "Pagliacci" and "Faust." None of us was named on the records, but the operatic cognoscenti quickly identified us all. I think I got something like $500 for that whole set of records, which are collectors' items today.

Among the first roles I was told to learn were those of Oscar, the Page, in "The Masked Ball" and Sophie in "Der Rosenkavalier." During that hard but exciting summer before my debut, I coached the role of Sophie under the masterful guidance of the gentle and sensitive Felix Wolfes, finding it surprisingly hard to learn. I could have picked up operas by Bellini, Rossini or anything else from the classical or bel canto repertoire quite easily, but I had had little exposure to Richard Strauss at that time and it took me nearly that whole summer to learn Sophie. Once I finally learned the role I had the Strauss idiom, and Strauss came easily to me after that.

With the arrival of autumn I left on my first concert tour with masses of new music whirling around in my head. It was a strenuous tour, extending from the eastern seaboard across the southern states into Texas. It was my first experience at being "courted" by audiences and lavishly entertained by sponsors, those devoted and influential ladies who were the driving force behind the then-booming American concert organizations.

Because I had spent so much time on my Sophie and my other roles, the records and the recital programs, I hadn't finished learning Oscar in "Ballo in Maschera" which was scheduled to open the opera season. I worked on it with Jimmy during moments stolen during the tour.

I returned to New York dead tired. Because it was my first tour, I had not spared myself, either on stage or off. I had yet to learn to pace myself. Consequently, I was panic-stricken to learn that "Ballo's" conductor, Ettore Panizza, insisted on hearing me in the opera house the minute I arrived back in New York. Exhausted and unexpectedly stricken by stage fright for the second time, I was commanded to perform "cold," like an auditioner, on the bare stage, singing a role too-quickly learned and in which I should never have been cast. I peered into the blackness of the empty Met auditorium, sensing without seeing the threatening presences beyond.

I tried my best, but I did not sing well. Panizza didn't like me and I lost the part, which in a way was just as well since I was already a fairly big girl, hardly the type for a "pants-part" like Oscar. Nevertheless, it was shattering to be dismissed from a part before I'd even made my debut.

If Panizza had had his way, I'd have been relegated to bit parts and never heard from again. I faced operatic oblivion. Suddenly they wondered if they had made a big mistake. Nobody knew what to do with me; no one wanted to take a chance on me—except one. Erich Leinsdorf believed in me. He believed I could sing Sophie and he stuck with me.

Erich, who was just about my age, had come to the Metropolitan the year before to assist the musical staff and get experience helping prepare the German operas as an aide to the formidable director of the German wing, Artur Bodansky. When Bodansky suddenly died, Leinsdorf was left with the task of conducting some 55 performances in his very first season with the Metropolitan.

In spite of his youth, Erich had tremendous courage and confidence in himself and, luckily, it extended to me. If he hadn't been around, if he hadn't persisted, I would have been lost because there were people who claimed I was too young and too inexperienced to sing Sophie. Leinsdorf insisted I sing Sophie when everyone else doubted. He became my champion!

From the beginning I had the greatest admiration for Erich as a musician. His grasp, authority and understanding of the Wagnerian operas was amazing. And yet there were those who resented his very strengths and disciplines as a conductor. But Erich "knew"—he has always "known." His musical intelligence was extraordinary. His brilliance and maturity far exceeded his years. To me he was a colossus.

He watched over me. He took up the cudgels for me and there were still more hurdles to overcome. During the piano dress rehearsal for "Rosenkavalier," I was sent onto the stage for the second act in a wilted gown with droopy bows down the front panel. Leinsdorf took one look and stopped the orchestra. He grabbed my hand and led me straight to the Wardrobe Department and said, "I want you to make this girl the most beautiful new gown you can conceive." Then he went to management to make sure they backed him up.

These memories, unlikely as they seem—come to me now like flashes of a dream. I was out of my depth in all but my music and I was trying to learn everything at once. Luckily, I was so wrapped up in my work I didn't know how close I came to missing my whole debut until the crisis was past. Lotte Lehmann suddenly became ill and told the Met she could not sing the Marschallin that night. They were almost ready to cancel and substitute another opera when someone, Leinsdorf again I believe, thought of Maria Hussa in Chicago; so when I arrived at the opera house for my debut, I found myself singing with Maria Hussa, not Lehmann. It was the only time that lovely woman ever sang at the Met. Strange!

They told me that the newly decorated Metropolitan Opera House was resplendent on the night of December 7, 1940, but I was totally oblivious. I only know I was terribly nervous and excited, and concentrating with all my strength on what I had to do—and that's all I can remember. When you are as keyed up and exhilarated as I was that night, everything becomes a blur.

Stage nerves can affect you in strange ways. Sometimes I have been nervous for days before a performance, then perfectly calm when the curtain went up; or I have been calm beforehand and suddenly all hyper on stage. Usually the excitement and rush of adrenalin stirred up by performing creates a kind of euphoric amnesia. My debut was of the latter variety.

Despite all the drama that preceded it, mine proved to be the debut of the winter. Not only was it well-reviewed at the time, but in their books, critics Irving Kolodin and John Briggs described both mine and Leonard Warren's as uniquely splendid among those of other Americans of the period. The role of Sophie became peculiarly my own. Even today the personality of Sophie is stamped indelibly within me. From the first moment I stepped on stage as Sophie, I myself knew there was "something" that belonged; some "thing" that was so right, I can only think that I identified totally with Sophie in my own sense of wonder at the dream I was living. Every word Sophie sang in the opening lines of Act II was how I felt, and that's what must have come through. Even when Sophie chatters nervously without pause when she first meets Octavian, that's pure Eleanor Steber! I felt so strongly that Sophie and I were one. There was such perfect rapport between me and the experienced Risë Stevens as Octavian, and our mutual warm response to the Marschallins of Lotte Lehmann and Irene Jessner, that those first few years remain a deeply emotional experience; and not only for us apparently, but for those who witnessed those performances. Over and over people have told me that there never was a Sophie such as I was; that there was no one to match me!

The Presentation of the Rose: How I used to exult in those high, marvelous, long phrases with that great soaring line that takes Sophie up and over the high D-flat. A D-flat was not ordinarily easy for me, but Strauss's approach is perfect. I loved it. A real "high," you might say. Singing Sophie in the third act trio was a problem because she's competing with the Marschallin. What's so challenging about the writing is that Strauss, finally in this moment, has Sophie competing with the Marschallin for the love of Octavian, not only dramatically, but in vocal lines as well. Sophie starts as the second voice, and just at the end of the trio she ascends triumphant, both musically and emotionally. It's so brilliant!

When I first sang Sophie, I was asked to take the Marschallin's high B at the end and hold it while the Marschallin took the G. It added to the musical excitement for me and gave the climax of our trio a special sound. When I finally did the Marschallin myself, I again sang the Marschallin's high B as it was written, which again gave the trio a different sound.

"Rosenkavalier" continued in the repertoire without pause for 12 straight years. As a debut vehicle for me, it could not have been more fortunate and I will be forever grateful for it.

Nine years later when I started to study the role of the Marschallin, everyone was reluctant to see me leave Sophie behind. "I can understand why you want to move on," they'd say, "but when will we ever again feel such magic as there was between you and Stevens in the Presentation of the Rose?"

All I have written, of course, pertains to what happened through the years, but the night of my debut was also something special out front. In true, fantastic West Virginia style, all my friends and family from Wheeling came up to New York together on a train, this time a true "Eleanor Steber Special." And after the performance they threw a tremendous party for me and the entire cast at the old Savoy-Plaza. It was really great! Everyone I knew was there. And it was such a big deal that it kind of set me up as a prima donna that very first night. It was done up brown, you know what I mean? It was the pinnacle for a kid only seven years out of West Virginia.

Amadeus

I sang Sophie, Micaela and a whole slew of Rhine Maidens, Flower Maidens and Forest Birds that first season. They kept me busy with costume fittings, coaching sessions, and rehearsals daily, with performances every two or three days, but it didn't matter to me. I loved every minute of it.

Then in the spring of 1941 I sang a concert in Pennsylvania with the Scranton Symphony, directed by George Sebastian (later to conduct at the San Francisco Opera and eventually the Paris Opera). George and I hit it off immediately and, back in New York, he coached me in some Mozart arias, among them the mighty "Martern aller Arten" from "Abduction from the Seraglio." I believe it was through George that it was arranged for me to sing for Dr. Bruno Walter, who had come to the Metropolitan because of the Nazi takeover of Austria.

George played for me when I sang for Dr. Walter at his apartment. There was silence when I finished. I stood there holding my breath—forever it seemed. Dr. Walter looked at me curiously and asked in that soft, gentle voice, "Child, where did you learn to sing Mozart like that?"

I wasn't sure what he meant by "like that," but I told him about Mr. Whitney and how I had cut my musical teeth on Mozart with him, and about my work with George. Then, wonder of wonders, Dr. Walter immediately invited me to sing at a lecture he was to give for the Junior League between opera seasons. He asked for just one aria, Susanna's "Deh vieni non tardar" from "Figaro." It was so important to me that I broke away in the midst of a concert tour to rush back to sing this one aria for him.

I was seated at the luncheon next to *New York Times* music critic Olin Downes, my old "neighbor" from East 10th Street. When he politely asked me where I had studied, I instantly sang the praises of my maestro, Mr. Whitney.

"Do you suppose," he ventured, "that if I went up there he could teach me to sing?"

Without thinking, I shot back, "If you can give up six years of your life to work with him, maybe he could."

I was not only a rookie at the Met, but a pretty smart-aleck young girl to dare such a riposte to a man of Olin Downes' stature, but his question did seem ridiculous to me. Of course I have spent most of my life boasting about my years with my Maestro and, actually, I think Mr. Downes must have been serious because I'm told he did go to see Mr. Whitney sometime later. It's a wonder he treated me so well in print as he did in the years that followed.

How could I possibly have imagined the enormous importance of those first meetings with Dr. Walter?

The Metropolitan had already announced plans for a spanking new production in English of Mozart's "The Magic Flute" for the 1941–42 season, and Dr. Walter auditioned a number of young singers for his cast. When my turn came, I sang for him in the little dressing room on the second floor of the old Met which was used during performances as the leading tenor's dressing room. He had me sing music for the Queen of the Night (how I would have loved to do it, but I just didn't own a high F!), and Pamina's music as well. It was a bitter disappointment when he asked me to learn what I thought was the "small" role of the First Lady. What I really wanted was Pamina.

I didn't realize then that in Europe the First Lady is considered a premier role but as I learned it, I discovered what a perfectly beautiful role it is to sing. It was some time, though, before I realized how lucky I was. When I first started to learn the part I thought it too heavy for me; but Mr. Whitney had taught me not to "force" and I knew that if I sang correctly, my voice would project sufficiently. I soon became comfortable with the music.

In those early days nothing could keep me down. I was blooming with health, bouncing with energy. And the day I auditioned for Dr. Walter, especially, I must have seemed unbearably gay, gay, gay, as I always was. I giggled and chattered along excitedly as I stood before this great old man, one of the greatest maestros of all time. Serious and sensitive, he had known great tragedy and when he smiled, it was a very shy, sweet smile. He endured my exuberance patiently. Finally he reached out and touched my hand, murmuring softly, "Calma, cara. Child, you smile too much." I couldn't understand what was wrong with any kind of smiling. I know now that Maestro had lived so long and seen so much that he must have known the kinds of disillusionments which would be coming. But not me. Not that day! I was so full of it all nothing could hurt me.

The revival of "The Magic Flute" was greeted with enthusiasm. Even the English translation by Thomas and Ruth Martin survived the battering most opera in English received in those days. We had a strong cast headed by Charles Kullman as Tamino, John Brownlee as Papagano, lovely Czechoslovakian Jarmila Novotna as Pamina and Alexander Kipnis as Sarastro. Pinza sang this part later.

The ensembles were memorable, especially as they were composed, with one exception, of Americans. Completing the three ladies with me were Maxine Stellman and Anna Kaskas; the three boys were Helen Olheim, Mona Paulee and another Czech, Marita Farell (who had preceded me as Sophie). In these and subsequent performances, Americans James Melton, Nadine Conner, Josephine Antoine, John Gurney, Emery Darcy, Margaret Harshaw, Nicola Moscona and Mack Harrell demonstrated their increasing importance to the opera company.

My own comparative lack of operatic stage experience, common to most of us American youngsters in those days, my painfully naïve eagerness, and especially my distinctive West Virginia accent caused some little consternation during rehearsals. "Magic Flute" uses spoken dialogue instead of recitatives, and I had quite a few lines to declaim from my high rocky entrance. At one point I was supposed to tell Papagano, "This time, instead of wine for dinner, the Queen sends you pure, clear water." Simple? No indeed!

Dr. Walter asked me to repeat the line several times and then turned to consult with Felix Wolfes who was trying to help him make his multi-accented cast understood. Finally he motioned John Brownlee to the footlights and whispered with him. John listened intently, then nodded his head and climbed up the scenery to where I stood "on the rocks," if you will pardon the expression. "Eleanor," John said, "Maestro cannot understand you. Please, my dear, you *must* get the West Virginia accent out." And in his best Australian-cum-British accent, he illustrated. "The word is 'wahtah,' my dear, 'wahtah'—not 'waaterrr'."

I worked hard on it, but inevitably, like the centipede who began to watch his feet, on one Saturday broadcast I tripped over one line barely moments after I had also physically tripped up the steps leading to our scenic mountain. I informed Papagano that "Instead of 'wahtah' for dinner, the Queen sends you pure, clear 'wahtah'." Too little wine and too much 'wahtah' in any event. If I ever blew another line after that or again tripped my way on stage, no one tells the tale, at least not in my presence. It enraged me to make such stupid mistakes and it didn't do to jolly me about it afterwards.

As I began my second season at the Met, I was already chafing at the bit to sing bigger roles. I had an insatiable appetite for work and, irrational as it seems, I simply could not comprehend why I shouldn't sing *everything*. Although I certainly appreciated the privilege of working with Dr. Walter in any capacity, I had absolutely no inkling then where our mutual affinity for Mozart would lead. However, if there was one magic moment when my career turned a corner and hurtled inevitably toward my musical destiny, it occurred during my third season at the Met.

Dr. Walter, who could do nothing wrong at the Metropolitan as far as I was concerned, decided to bring "Le Nozze di Figaro" back into the repertoire. It had been revived in 1939–40 after an absence of 23 years, but quickly dropped. Now, Dr. Walter, who had worked closely with Ezio Pinza in Salzburg, revived it. In addition to Pinza in the title role, there was Bidú Sayao as Susanna, John Brownlee as the Count, Jarmila Novotna as Cherubino, Salvatore Baccaloni as Don Basilio and Irra Petina as Marcellina.

I had never seen the opera before I sang it, so I really didn't understand the magnitude and honor of the assignment when he gave me the Countess to sing. How could I imagine that this single role would change my life?

As a character, the Countess scarcely fit my psyche at the time – that lovely, somewhat disillusioned woman betrayed by her husband. It helped me to remember that she had once been the happy and vivacious Rosina of "The Barber of Seville."

I was simply petrified that first night when I went out to open the second act with "Porgi amor." I barely kept from trembling. Never mind that Mozart was supposed to be my second nature, or that I had known and sung the aria for years. "Porgi amor" is a perfectly awful piece to open up with: no preparation, no time to get your bearings; you simply start out cold with long piano phrases requiring supreme legato line and control.

The two big arias I knew well, but the rapid light recitatives and the extended ensembles were not all that easy. The Countess sings the second line to Susanna and most of it lay in my middle voice. With Bidù Sayao's faultlessly-placed soprano on top and Pinza and/or Brownlee below, the middle voice tends to get lost. The overall sound was marvelous, but it was not as easy to sing as I once might have thought.

This was also a period of musical counter-revolution against the abuses which had crept into the use of extravagant embellishment and cadenza among singers. Perhaps because this was a time when the conductor was dominant at the Metropolitan, there was a vigorous drive to purify the line and to return to the printed score. This affected me only because Mr. Whitney had taught me a certain amount of embellishment and appoggiatura in all my arias. My Metropolitan coaches immediately cut away all such decoration and ever pursued the pure vocal line. Downward appoggiaturas were permitted, but none from above. We lost, for a time, some beautiful ornamentation which Mozart had perhaps not directly written down in the haste of his composing, but which singers in his time were expected to add. Eventually I learned that embellishments moved in and out of fashion each season, but at that moment, having to wipe away the embellishments I was accustomed to was a tough adjustment. Today more than a few embellishments have returned, some to extremes — and so it goes.

I also found there was a tremendous amount of complication involved in the acting "business," and I was dealing with experienced pros. After performances, my husband often complained about the interplay on stage, particularly in the second act. Of course Edwin loved me and thought I could do no wrong, but he would tell me that I was allowing certain of my colleagues to upstage me or that I was singing into the wings. Perhaps I did hug the scenery a bit, but I doubt that anyone tried to upstage me purposely. I wasn't yet really stagewise. But I learned. I learned!

I became aware that something exciting had happened the night of that first "Figaro" after the third act "Dove sono," but what with that euphoric-amnesia I mentioned before that so often accompanies first nights, and my concentration on the Letter Scene with Susanna which follows the aria so quickly, the sensation slipped by.

It has always been my nature to concentrate solely on what I am doing, not on what I have already done. I was almost completely oblivious of what went on around me during performances. Only in later years did I realize any impact I might be making on an audience.

Miss Wonderful

I breezed into the Met each day open and eager for each new experience, and absolutely ravenous for every bit of coaching and rehearsal I could get. Everything and everybody at the Met was wonderful! The fact that I belonged there was almost beyond comprehension, but it was my world and I loved it all.

My darling friend George Cehanovsky, the most famous baritone comprimario of all time who sang longer at the Met and in more performances to date as I write, was there when I arrived. When we met over a romantic — yes, romantic — lunch a few years ago, he was 86 and still coaching Russian at the new Met. George remembered my beginnings in very flattering terms.

"Oh, my goodness, you were gorgeous young lady. You made great impression. We all talked about you and everyone predicted, without exception, that you would go far. We loved your smile. You were so happy at rehearsals — happy to be with the company, happy to sing. Never upset, never one unpleasant word with anybody. Nobody had anything but praise for you, and I do not remember one performance which did not come vocally right for you."

From a man who spent nearly every off-stage moment of his life for 40 years listening in the wings to every single person who sang during that time, it was a great accolade, and I cherish my lifetime friendship with this dearest of men.

As I gloried in my new life at the Met, it never occurred to me that anything about me or what I wore, or even my forthright enthusiasm for my new job and position in life, could be misunderstood. It's hard to believe, I suppose, that I could have arrived at the Metropolitan so totally guileless. I strode blithely through each day as if I were Parsifal after the Holy Grail. It never occurred to me to watch my step or walk gently. All I could think was, "My God, look at where I am!"

I had walked into the Metropolitan Opera House the very first season feeling very grand in a new mink coat (which my mother insisted I must have). I was thrilled with that coat because it made me feel like an honest-to-God opera star, despite the fact that, as mink goes, it was a very cheap coat. Never mind. It was mink and it was mine!

I was so enraptured with the whole business, I was completely unaware of all the flak I was creating. Now, with the clarity of hindsight, I can see I had done the worst possible thing. There I was, a young upstart soprano from nowhere, and already I'm waltzing around the Met flaunting a new mink coat. "Who did I think I was?" That was the impression I seemed to stir up in some quarters. But as far as I was concerned, I honestly believed I had to dress like that. After all, I was in the Metropolitan!

It was Constance Hope, then head of the Met Press Department, who set me straight. Connie, who had worked for both Grace Moore and Lotte Lehmann before becoming the foremost opera public relations expert of her day, eventually caught me coming in once and confronted me in her office. "Why on earth did you come in here flashing a fancy mink before you even made your debut? It makes you look as if you think you're already a great prima donna."

I thought about that for a while and finally decided that although I had no illusion that I was already a prima donna, I certainly was in the Metropolitan and that was a helluva lot farther than anybody in West Virginia was at that moment.

Since everyone was always wonderful to me face to face, I was never aware that I might be a topic of comparison with other artists, past or present. When Felix Wolfes told me, while we worked on Sophie, that I reminded him of a young Lotte Lehmann, I was flattered. Apparently he repeated the remark to other people. Then somebody else made some remark about "having a new young Grace Moore in the Company." Such comparisons are unfair.

Knowing nothing of the Grace Moore remark, and remembering how I had driven from Wheeling to Pittsburgh to see her movie, I went backstage with great temerity one day during a dress rehearsal of "Tosca" to pay my respects to Miss Moore. I knocked on her dressing room door and when she opened it, I timidly introduced myself and said I had come to express my admiration. She glared at me icily for a moment, raised an eyebrow and said, "Yessss? Thank you very much!" and shut the door in my face.

I simply could not understand why she should react this way to me until many years later when a young Lucine Amara, who was beginning to cover some of my roles at the Met, paid a similar visit to me as a senior artist. I could understand then why Grace Moore might have reacted as she did, for I became aware of a certain uneasiness when meeting a talented young artist coming along behind me. I hope Lucine found me a more friendly colleague at first meeting than I did Grace Moore.

Most of the time, however, I was too busy to notice what went on around me. I was rehearsing Amor in "Orfeo," Philline in "Mignon" and Ellen in "Lakmé," although I never sang any of them in performance. I had already memorized Violetta in "Traviata" and Mimi in "Bohème" and was eating my heart out because I didn't appear to have a chance to sing either of them.

I also sang a lot of Wagner. My roles so far were small ones of course, but I did sing a Rhine Maiden in both "Rheingold" and "Die Götterdämmerung," the Forest Bird in "Siegfried" and the First Flower Maiden in "Parsifal" with Kirsten Flagstad and the great heldentenor Lauritz Melchior. Melchior and I never really worked together on the stage at the same time except for a bit in "Parsifal," but off stage we were kindred souls. Over those first years we shared a lot of good times together, especially when the company was on tour. We both loved parties and enjoyed our beer and wurst. (Grace Moore, who was as big for parties as anyone, once supplied the entire tour train with champagne.) One day some years later, a huge package from Melchior arrived at my country home. It was the mounted head of a splendidly-antlered Alberta buck. It still graces a place of honor on the wall of my recreation room, and from its antlers hang all manner of tiny treasures, gifts and ornaments sent to me by fans and friends over the years.

I sang my first Micaela with Risë Stevens as Carmen. I did only four performances of that role the whole time I was at the Met, which saddens me because I really loved that part. I did get to do it later with Risë at the San Francisco Opera.

Until I started this book I was convinced I had actually performed the role of Ellen in "Lakmé." My memories of this role and this opera are so vivid, it's hard to believe I never got on stage with it. The records prove I didn't, but I certainly rehearsed it, costumes and all. It's really silly, but

I remember so distinctly that Maxine Stellman, Lucielle Browning and I kept making entrances singing, "O, j'adore quel tapage" ("I just love this excitement"). When I finally got to France in 1952, that line kept popping into my head whenever I didn't know what else to say; or, if that wasn't appropriate, I'd throw in "Pardon, M'sieur, je suis en mon premier voyage" from "Manon."

The Metropolitan presented gala Sunday Night Concerts at popular prices every week which were a blessing for all of us young Americans. We were all contract artists in those days (I got $75 to $150 a week) so the concerts were extra work, but we had regular opportunities to do single arias, scenes and sometimes entire acts of operas which we hadn't yet been given a chance to sing on stage, and in some cases, might never do. In my first Sunday night concert I sang Donna Anna's big second act aria, "Non mi dir," the merest taste of a role I felt I was destined to sing. On other occasions I sang several scenes from "Faust" with such rising American artists as Leonard Warren and Richard Tucker. I also did scenes from "Traviata" (the only stage preparation I ever got for this role) and arias from "Carmen," "Figaro" and "Ernani."

One Sunday night in March of my first season I was singing the "Jewel Song" from "Faust," which I had learned years before with Mr. Whitney. (In the true bel canto manner, Mr. Whitney had taught me everything in Italian. Even Agathe's aria from "Der Freischutz" became "Piano, piano" instead of "Leise, leise" and Pamina's aria from "The Magic Flute" I learned as "A lo so" instead of "Ach, Ich fuhls.") This meant that I had carefully restudied all of "Faust" in French with Jean Paul Morel. Wilfred Pelletier was conducting and I was happily singing along when Pelley suddenly looked up at me with alarm. His eyes cried out, "What are you doing, girl?" I instantly realized that I had unconsciously slipped back into Italian. I switched back to French and hoped that only Pelley and I knew what I had done.

I sang my first Marguerite in "Faust" in Havana, Cuba, with Lazlo Halasz before the start of my second season at the Met. Charles Kullman was Faust and I had Ezio Pinza as Mephistopheles.

I had studied the role on the Metropolitan roof stage in group classes conducted by stage director Lothar Wallerstein. We invariably had three or four other Marguerites, four or five Fausts, and maybe half a dozen Mephistopheles.

Marguerite was rewarding to sing in so many ways. Musically it's gorgeous, of course, but I loved acting her, this simple-minded, lower middle class girl who was, you know, more sinned against than sinner. I always think of Marguerite in the Kermesse Scene, this very religious young girl, walking away from the church and watching the rest of the boys and girls dancing and cavorting together and maybe cuddling behind the haystack. Why wasn't she part of it all? Why was she so sheltered and held away from everything natural and normal, so that when she was overwhelmed by Faust and the consequences of that alliance, she completely cracked up?

I sang "Faust" once again before I got to do it at the Met. Pelley, who was always such a warm friend and father-figure to us young Americans, had arranged for me to sing Marguerite in his native Montreal. Pinza was again Mephistopheles, but this time Richard Crooks was Faust. When I arrived for rehearsal at Pelley's studio in the Mount Royal Hotel, he jumped up and greeted me with such excitement I was overwhelmed. "My God, I'm glad to see you," he told me. "When I saw today's paper, I thought we'd lost you."

"What do you mean?" I asked. He spread out the newspaper and there on the front page was a big picture of me with a caption which read, "Victims d'une drame éternelle!" The paper was speaking of Marguerite. Pelley had thought I was dead!

My daylight hours in New York were spent chiefly with opera coaches. Felix Wolfes, a darling roly-poly little man with whom I did my first German parts, was a superb coach, but all the time we worked he'd munch candy, plopping one in his mouth whenever he could get a hand off the keys. We had wonderful times together. I coached other German roles with Herman Weigert, very erudite, cerebral and impersonal, just the opposite of Wolfes.

Most of my Italian parts I learned with Renato Bellini, again, brilliant in his field, but volatile, excitable and so attached to his cigarettes that he had to take frequent breaks to go into the hall to smoke.

Jean Paul Morel taught me most of my French roles. He was a sensitive, articulate musician who had arrived from France just as I landed at the Met. Whether it was just because he was young and French, I don't know, but for me he always held an especially appealing charisma.

Those four men who worked with me so closely could not possibly have been more different from the other. I learned so much just from the variety of their personalities, but I was also a good student. I took pride in good musicianship and I applied everything they gave me without question. I just learned. The instinct which turns good technique into theatrical electricity was already within.

There were so many at the Met ready to help a newcomer: stage manager Désiré Defrère, for instance. Defrère had a long and solid career as a singer, coming to the Met from the old Chicago Opera Company where he was the chief comprimario baritone during Mary Garden's great heyday there. While Defrère was chiefly stage manager, he also taught misè en scène to artists taking on new roles. I know I learned "Traviata" with him and, I think, "Bohème" and "Manon," operas for which I had no full company orchestra rehearsals, so I owed much to Defrère.

It was the same with my conductors—so many skilled and helpful men. I did one of the finest "Rosenkavaliers" of my life with Max Rudolf. I can still see the way his face lit up that night while he was conducting. He was much under-acclaimed as a conductor, and a fine friend and partisan on my behalf for many years.

There was genial Pelley, the rock-solid foundation of the conducting staff, and Fausto Cleva, coach and conductor, with whom I later made recordings; and Martin Rich, another splendid coach and under-appreciated conductor. I retain an overwhelming gratitude towards all these fine musicians who guided me through those early years.

Paul Althouse continued to watch over my voice until his death, but his influence on even the non-musical aspects of my career was much more significant than anyone knew. When I first came to New York from Boston, I looked like a young country "hausfrau." My long, darkish hair was drawn tightly back into a bun. I wore low-heeled shoes, plain suits with severe lines and very little makeup. Finally he sat me down and talked to me like a Dutch Uncle. "It's time we start getting you gussied up a bit, kid," he said. He told me to soften my hair, so I got a hairdresser, a permanent and an auburn rinse. Then Paul delivered me to Dr. Philip Hover, a dentist in his building, who gradually did a complete "Hollywood type" job capping my teeth. I was sent to Eddie Senz, then the best makeup man in New York, who showed me how to glamorize my public face.

Since hats were everything in those days, Jimmy Quillian steered me to Robert Dudley who created fabulous things for me for years, and someone else sent me to the first of many fine dress designers. When I could finally afford it, I posed for some glamorous photographs, the kind which showed me off in a plunging neckline and an enhanced romantic image amid dramatic lights and shadows. From then on, my appearance and public decorum became everybody's business and, naturally, everyone had a different idea how I should look.

Except for Paul's early efforts on my behalf, all this took considerable time and money. It was Paul Althouse, too, who used his influence to secure me an audition for concert management. There was so much to learn in those days—perhaps too much. Emily Coleman, whom I had not yet met, was watching, nevertheless. She wrote later in a *New York Times Magazine* story (1959) that "Steber and (Leonard) Warren had to create their major roles in the worst way possible—right on the stage of the Met, in full view of one of the most critical audiences in the world."

Without all these mentors in the studio, rehearsal rooms and in the pit, how could I have made it? I owe so much to so many!

Lehmann

Baritone Mack Harrell once told someone, "Steber has the greatest capacity for work of any woman I have ever known. She can do so many things at once." On the other hand, mother claimed I did too much. She constantly complained to my dad, "Eleanor's career is going too quick, too fast and too maddening—what with the Met, the concerts, the traveling and all those parties on top of it. I don't see how the girl stands it!"

It was a matter of "one man's meat," I suppose. I loved the work. I lived for it. It was all the other stuff—not the traveling, but the complexities of the "business," dealing with managements and publicists and family, and trying to find some way to satisfy them all, that wore me out.

My weight was a constant problem, and all the hard work didn't seem to help me. I came back from my first concert tour about ten pounds heavier than when I left, but I was young and active, so I was still firm and tight. I quickly discovered the health salon, the masseuse and other magic aids to the restoration of the figure svelte. But I'm not all that sure that a certain amount of weight wasn't essential to my well-being as a singer. I know of more than one artist who dieted strenuously—Callas, comes to mind—who never seemed to regain the early vocal body and sheen after losing a lot of weight. Weight may have troubled my vanity, but not my music, and that was what mattered.

That being the case, I could hardly have experienced the presence, much less shared the stage with Lotte Lehmann, unquestionably the greatest Liedersinger of our time, without longing to study with her. Yet although I sang with her regularly, I was as awestruck in her presence as the most adoring fan.

One night in January of 1943, one of the few times I did not sing Sophie with her, I attended the performance as the guest of Metropolitan executive Edward Ziegler. When I went back stage to see Lehmann after the performance, my impulse was to throw my arms around her and pour out my adoration; but I was suddenly overcome by self-consciousness and I stood before her, immobile and speechless, eyes brimming with tears. She comprehended at once, however, and she kissed *me*. I knew that I must find time to study with her. In my diary that night, still like a child at 28 years of age, I wrote: "She is a gorgeous, wonderful and great lady; I long to know her better — to worship at her feet."

Later that month I attended her annual Town Hall recital and again could speak of it only in my journal: "I am almost glad I had to wait until now to hear her in concert, for now my own experience makes it possible for me to at least glimpse her perfect gift. She is divine! Had I only heard her earlier, perhaps I might have realized sooner that miracle which comes from such complete sublimation of 'self' to the 'song'. Lehmann was so completely absorbed and surrounded by the music and the poetry, I felt as if I were in a holy place. I can hardly write of it.

"When we went back to see her after the concert, she was sitting like a little girl on the dressing table, signing record albums and programs, so dear and wonderful that again I fell mute. Once more she immediately understood, put her arms around me and let me weep some grateful tears."

I had my first lesson with Lotte Lehmann in New York the Thursday after that concert. There is simply no way to describe the impact of that winter's study with Madame Lehmann. We worked chiefly on Brahms' songs and Robert Schumann's "Frauenliebe und Leben," that simple, but so deeply moving song cycle which I would work on for a full 10 years before performing it in public.

I was in my third season at the Met when I worked with Lehmann. I was constantly learning new parts and struggling to find reasons for everything I was told to do; and although I never actually studied opera parts with Lotte, it was she who taught me to find my own special imagery in everything I did, in every song, every role.

She taught me how to create my own uniquely personal relationships to my songs, to place myself within them — an ability which grew as the years passed, so that I gradually became almost totally unconscious of myself and the audience and acutely aware only of the song itself.

That summer I felt so overwhelmed by the exciting revelations now enriching every piece of music I touched, that I wrote Madame Lehmann at her Santa Barbara home, trying to tell her what was happening to me. Lotte Lehmann is famous for her letters (as well as the author of half a dozen books), and replied immediately.

"I cannot tell you how happy it makes me to have you say that even in songs we have not worked together on, you have felt a change in expression. You see, that is what I am longing for: that you make *absolutely your own* what we are doing together."

"The way I am going as a Liedersinger is *one way*, completely different from other singers (and I don't say it is *greater*, only that it is *different*). My approach to the song (or the opera part) *is different* because *it is my own*. And if you understand completely this kind of approach, then a whole new world opens for you!

"Do you see, dear Eleanor, what it could be for you if you continue in this way? Everything which you do will be *living, breathing*; your words will be as expressive as your melody. You will become a 'singing actress'. Music and poem will float into *one* being. There is, however," Lehmann cautioned me, "always the danger of exaggerating the word. One has to be very subtle and to balance music with poem in the right way. I hope I can lead you further on. Certainly one cannot get it in such a short time. My God, it took me half a lifetime to develop my way! But *I had no one to show me*. I had to go quite alone on a path which seemed, to many singers, exaggerated, and was perhaps exaggerated before it settled down into my whole being. Now it is a part of me and cannot be separated from me any more. Even if I would not have success with my singing or would not find understanding, I know with all my heart and brain that what I do is right!

"I am terribly glad that you understand completely what I want you to understand. I had, years ago, *one* encouragement which meant much to me: Bruno Walter approved my way of approach so completely that this gave me the early confirmation that what I do is right!"

How much Lehmann's words meant to me! As a singer I have been characterized for my great exuberance. Now I understood that it was because I loved to sing! And it had been the same with Lehmann in her early years in Europe. We never knew *that* Lehmann here. But Felix Wolfes, who coached my Sophie, *had* known it, and that's why he said I reminded him of the young Lehmann. He knew her when she had that same kind of physical vitality and excitement in her singing that he saw in me.

In her own book, "Midway in My Song," Lehmann described her early difficulties with her voice teachers and vocal training, which was something less than the pure bel canto training I received from Mr. Whitney. During one of our sessions together, Lehmann quite unself-consciously said to me—her student—"Eleanor, I'd give anything in the world if I'd been taught the kind of breath control you have."

But the thing is, look what she did without it, within the limitations of her technique, through sheer musical passion—I mean it just poured out of her!

The parallels between us had been obvious, perhaps, to a knowledgeable Felix Wolfes, but I could not help being overcome by the generosity of this great and perceptive lady, so soon to retire and yield her stage to a younger generation just as the Marschallin retires in favor of the young Sophie. That Lehmann had long since reached the point "when the time of all the restlessness is past," made it possible for her to be completely selfless with a youngster like me who might have seemed threatening to a lesser spirit.

Lehmann was impulsive and always surprising. During one of her final concert tours, she found herself in Wheeling and took time to drop me just a short note, explaining, "I cannot sing in your home town without sending you my thoughts." Another time, when I was on tour, and knowing that my schedule permitted me no time to study with her while I was in California, she cautioned me against tiring myself by trying to finagle a long visit, then added, "But only to see you and talk to you will be a great joy."

What can I say? Even today it moves me beyond words. And yet I was always inhibited by my unyielding reserve, so different from that of other colleagues like Risë, from openly expressing my affection for her.

Although Lehmann completely stopped singing opera in the late 1940s and spent most of her time in Santa Barbara writing and painting, she sang a few concerts each year, and I tried never to miss her annual Town Hall recitals. Early in February of 1951 I attended the first of two scheduled for that year. These were always such happy reunions—with her and all the others of us who loved her. How can I describe the essence of Lotte Lehmann's art as I experienced it in those last days. Singing had become increasingly stressful for her. She told me that each time she returned to New York City, she became more and more nervous before each concert until finally she cried, "I cannot do it!"

Still, she walked out on the stage and sang that much more beautifully. She had reached that rare state of soul where song had become a pure, direct light shining through her; everything else had been burned away.

Two weeks after that first 1951 recital, I grabbed a plane in Nashville and rushed home in the midst of a southern concert tour. A friend had wired that this might be Lehmann's last New York concert. Although Lehmann really hadn't wanted it known, word had leaked out, so that the audience that gathered in Town Hall that Sunday afternoon was packed with her many friends and lifetime fans, all apprehensive and talking in whispers.

She made the announcement without warning immediately after intermission. There were cries of "No! No!" But she scolded us, thanked us for our love, and said her decision was irrevocable.

She sang so beautifully that day I couldn't really believe it was necessary for her to retire, but she could evidently no longer stand the anguish which intensified before each concert. For her final encore she said she would "try" to sing "An die Musik." I held my breath. It was a prayer—but she could not finish. She broke down just at the last and simply stood with her head bowed while Paul Ulanowsky played through the last line. It was heart-rending. I really could not take in all that it would mean.

"Die Zeit, die ist ein sonderbar Ding. . . ." "Time is a mysterious thing," as her Marschallin sang. Yet her art is as vivid to me today as it ever was. Time will never change that.

War and the Conductors

It has been suggested by opera aficionados with a strong European orientation that only the advent of World War II was responsible for the surge into prominence of American singers at the Metropolitan during the decade of the 1940's. That surge had started, as a matter of fact, during the late 1930's when Edward Johnson became the Met's new manager, and accelerated when he instigated the Metropolitan Opera Auditions of the Air.

As a simple matter of record, the roster hovered about five points either side of a 50/50 ratio of Europeans to Americans during the entire period. Considering that we lived in the presence of such artists as Pinza, Lehmann, Melchior, Brownlee, Alexander Kipnis, Giovanni Martinelli, Salvatore Baccaloni, Friedrich Schorr, Bruno Landi, Martial Singher and Gerhard Pechner—plus Bruna Castagna, Kerstin Thorborg, Karen Branzell, Irene Jessner, Jarmila Novotna, Irra Petina, Lily Pons, Bidú Sayao, Zinka Milanov, Jennie Tourel and Licia Albanese—the Americans who made and sustained their positions in the Metropolitan during that period had to do it on merit or go under. This becomes even more significant when you realize that every single conductor was European, either already settled here or escaping Europe just before the Blitzkrieg.

When you have in the Met such Americans as Richard Crooks, Jan Peerce, Charles Kullman, Leonard Warren, Lawrence Tibbett and Rose Bampton, Nadine Conner, Astrid Varnay, Patrice Munsel, Margaret Harshaw, Grace Moore, Gladys Swarthout, Helen Traubel, Risë Stevens—and me, to list the merest sampling, you had to be good to survive. Then we had Richard Tucker, Robert Merrill, and Jerome Hines, hardly passing fancies. Americans made it because we were good and we had staying power. Americans were then and are now the equals—or better—of any opera singers in the world. It's just been camouflaged by that mystique which surrounds the non-American artists who come to us fully seasoned, having gotten the kinks out of their craft in their own countries and out of our hearing.

With that off my chest—and I feel very strongly about it because I believe in our American artists—the attack on Pearl Harbor interrupted my life instantly and literally because I was to sing my first important radio concert with Andre Kostelanetz and the program, a big advancement for my career, was cut off the air by the news from Pearl Harbor. From then on each performance at the Met was preceded by our National Anthem, sometimes conducted by His Honor Mayor Fiorello LaGuardia.

Those Europeans who were already with us stayed, and a few more trickled in after hair-raising escapes like that of Gerhard Pechner who fled through the Balkans and through Asia to Japan, hitching his way to San Francisco with a dime in his pocket.

Aside from the general worries I shared with everyone else, the war didn't catch up with me personally until February 6, 1941 when Ed was reclassified and whisked into the Army with what I considered indecent haste.

I thanked God for my work, because I was totally unprepared for living alone, for coming home to an empty apartment after rehearsals, performances or from a trip. Fortunately, most of the time I was too busy to think, but I realized some years later that our enforced separation as my career shifted into a higher gear may have added years to our marriage. It certainly added a bit of spice at the time by creating some unusual and delightful opportunities for us to enjoy occasional romantic reunions despite Army regulations.

Like most draftees in our area, Ed was sent to Fort Dix, a desolate training camp set amid the sand and scrub pine of southern New Jersey. The first few weeks of basic training when no one was allowed leave were torture for us both. Suddenly, however, I found a way to see him; but first I had to sing in the final "Parsifal" matinee, after which a friend would take me to see Ed. The timing was crucial, so I cheated a bit and sang the First Flower Maiden minus the body makeup—fully two-thirds of my costume—so I could dash out of the opera house without delay. When we got to Fort Dix, my friend smuggled me in so Edwin and I could steal a couple of hours together in private.

Shortly before Edwin left, I had sung my first Met "Faust," conducted by the white-goateed Sir Thomas Beecham, a crusty, racy-humored termagant who thought nothing of singing, or shouting at singers, orchestra or audience (or all three at once) during a performance. He conducted a number of my performances that season.

Talk about busy! A couple of days after my first Marguerite, I stepped in to sing Micaela for an ailing Nadine Conner, then sang a concert for her in nearby Connecticut. Two nights later I sang Marguerite for Licia Albanese in Chicago. Once that April I sang Marguerite and the "Figaro" Countess on succeeding nights. This was to be the story of my life.

Three days after Ed left, I had sung in a "spectacular" presentation of Bach's St. Matthew Passion at the Met. The soloists sang in the pit with the orchestra and the chorus flanked the stage apron. The Passion itself was acted out in pantomime with full costumes and scenery, a kind of moving pageant. The ringmaster of this extravaganza was Leopold Stokowski, then the acknowledged superstar of musical histrionics. My colleagues included Jennie Tourel, Lucius Metz, Gerhard Pechner and Glen Darwin.

Immediately after the Met tour, I left on my spring concert tour, but was called back to New York quite suddenly when my management signed me up for a 13-week daily afternoon radio show. Between the two tours, I had been on the road for weeks so I was relieved to get back to New York.

"Your Home Front Reporter" for CBS was aimed at war-separated families, accenting news and features about servicemen plus "homespun humor" by Galen Drake. Tenor Frank Parker and I provided the music, along with an orchestra conducted by Dave Broekmann. It was a Manhattan version of my old Fur Trapper's Show where I'd first met Frank. We sang the kind of music I would be singing on commercial radio and TV for 25 years: everything from "Danny Boy" to "Smoke Gets in Your Eyes" and "When I Grow too Old to Dream," from "The Little Toy Soldier" to "My Hero" and daily duets with Frank. You can pack a lot of songs into 65 half-hour broadcasts.

It was a congenial and efficient crew which shaped the daily program with minimal rehearsal in a small closed studio. After the broadcast, more often than not, a bunch of us repaired to a chic watering place on East 52nd Street, the Barberry Room. The dark, thickly-carpeted interior was crowned with a high-domed ceiling inset with tiny white lights twinkling in competition with the human stars seated along the banquette. The glamour of it all appealed to me at first. Gradually, my loneliness at home without Ed, the pressure of the broadcasts, learning new roles, and dealing with the business end of things—with no one to turn to—all churned within me, and I began to look forward to the fun of these gradually lengthening "happy hours." My emotional ups and downs became more marked and closer together. But if, in the absence of my husband, I was beginning to burn my candle at both ends, I soon became aware of it.

Although eager for such rapid advances in my career as the broadcast seemed to provide, my mind was divided and torn; so between engagements, I contrived to arrange every opportunity to visit my husband at camp, even when it meant playing truant and leaving town in disobedience to the terms of my early Met contract.

For all these reasons, I decided to discontinue the daily broadcasts when the original contract ended. The Met had already added the Massenet "Manon" and Donna Elvira in "Don Giovanni" to my assignments, and I needed the summer to prepare a new concert program. The broadcasts, however diverting and profitable, were terribly confining. I not only needed more freedom to study, but I wanted to be free to go to Ed whenever he had leave.

As we started into the 1943–44 season, I experienced wild fluctuations of mood, chiefly about the Metropolitan. Whether my feelings were any different from those of other young singers in a similar position, I don't know. I never shared such feelings with my colleagues.

My diaries reflected these wide swings of the emotional pendulum. After my first day at rehearsal I wrote, "How pleasant to get back, the feeling is so much different this year—more relaxed and fun. It should be a good, good year!" Twenty-four hours later I agonized: "What a time! And such a turmoil! It is too wearing. I really must stop it, for it pulls me to pieces—particularly this feeling about others getting parts I think I should have. I certainly hope I can get over this. I must be a 'good girl'; not a 'mouse', just a 'good girl'." Then again, a few days later: "A long 'Rosenkavalier' rehearsal today. Stevens here—she really is a great girl and deserves the best of everything. Dr. Wallerstein is wonderful with me and makes my Sophie much quieter. Risë took me aside and told me that while it was right and rewarding to have friendships with my colleagues, I must put it aside when I get on stage. "That is your moment," she said, "and you must concentrate only on doing your very best for yourself." Then another entry: "General rehearsal of 'Magic Flute' tonight. We worked very hard and it is truly inspiring to work under Maestro Walter;

but I became quite incensed by people who were doing 'thus' and 'so'. I will feel better, I am sure, when I stop trying to run the opera house inside my head. I left frustrated and miserable. Nothing tangible, but it's very hard to contend with that place. Or is it me?"

I sang four new roles in two new operas that season, including Alice Ford in a brief revival in English of Verdi's "Falstaff." My long-time idol, Lawrence Tibbett, sang Falstaff in the first performance. He was a mere shadow of the giant he had once been, a gentle, troubled man, always gracious and friendly to me. Merely sharing the same stage with him moved me deeply. He did not return after the opening and Leonard Warren sang the remaining three performances. Critic Irving Kolodin felt the opera might have made it had Leonard been given the title role from the start. Leonard, of course, was quickly gaining the recognition Tibbett had won years before when he electrified audiences with his singing of Ford in that same opera.

"Falstaff" was fun for me chiefly because the extroverted and sometimes irascible Sir Thomas Beecham was in the pit. It takes courage to translate Shakespeare into opera. Our version, perhaps that opera's first conversion from Italian to English, may just have put opera in English back a good five years. We got our kicks from Sir Thomas who "helped" us by boosting the translation with interpolations of a few lusty, if not bawdy Elizabethan phrases. Some were hilarious, and we broke up more than a few times. And of course, Leonard was simply great as Falstaff. I was always sorry that "Falstaff" didn't go down well with the public.

Sir Thomas also later directed "Tales of Hoffmann" with the newly-arrived Martial Singher as Dapertutto and Ezio Pinza as Dr. Miracle. At one time or another, I sang Giulietta, the Muse and Antonia. I could have sung Olympia, of course, but the Met liked its dolls on the petite side. I sang Giulietta and the Muse as a pair and certainly could have sung Antonia as well at the same performances, but I never did; it was always either/or. I loved Antonia—musically so lusciously singable and dramatic that it was almost foolproof. But as happened with so many roles on which I spent vast amounts of study and rehearsal time at the Met, I missed out on future productions.

To this day, one of the most sublime musical experiences of my life remains a 1944 performance of Beethoven's 9th Symphony in Carnegie Hall celebrating Dr. Walter's 50th anniversary as a conductor. The New York Philharmonic was assisted by the Westminster Choir.

No one who attended that fantastic performance of the 9th (which I have always considered more as a great spiritual outpouring than merely a choral symphony) will ever forget how Dr. Walter, in a sublime state of exaltation, inspired a performance which electrified both artists and audience. When at last it was done, Maestro stood still and silent. We were all spellbound. Suddenly the audience couldn't stand it any longer. With a tremendous outburst, the audience rose, shouting, to its feet.

My mother was there that day and we recalled that we youngsters sang our evening prayer each night to the theme from the last movement of the Beethoven Ninth. The words we sang were:

> "All this day Thy love has kept us
> And we thank Thee for Thy care.
> Thou has warmed us, clothed us, fed us:
> Jesus, hear our evening prayer."

Mother exclaimed after that performance that it was as if the heavens opened to received this magnificent work, that the melody I had sung as a little child had burst forth into a grand "Alleluia"!

Bruno Walter was naturally one of the great influences in my life. I sang with Dr. Walter more times than I can remember, and recorded Mozart arias with him. His sensitivity and interpretive refinement impressed themselves into my being, and certainly it is no exaggeration to say that his musical decisions about what I should sing at the Met and with him in concerts changed the direction of my career as I had originally envisioned it and set me on the path which led me to become the first American acknowledged as a premier interpreter of Mozart.

Dr. Walter once told me that although as a young man he had been swept by enthusiasms for Wagner and the more dynamic romantic composers, he later decided that if there were to be just one composer he could live with the rest of his life—only one—it would have to be Mozart. A person had to mature, he believed, not only as a musician, but as a human being, too, in order to fully comprehend Mozart's infinite challenge. Certainly he brought that maturity, plus infinite delight and fulfillment as well, to every performance I ever sang with him.

If the aura about Bruno Walter was gentle and benevolent, that which radiated from Arturo Toscanini was volcanic.

Sometime early on, Bruno Zirato, long-time manager of the New York Philharmonic, called me and said that Toscanini wanted me to audition the Beethoven 9th. "Oh, my goodness," I said, "of course I can do the 9th, but that's nothing to sing for Maestro Toscanini."

Zirato repeated that this was what the Maestro wanted.

I persisted; Zirato insisted.

I begged him. "Let me do 'Traviata' or something like that." It seemed such a wasted opportunity to do the soprano part in a quartet for Toscanini. I should have known better.

Zirato turned down "Traviata." "Then let me sing from the 'Missa Solemnis'," I pleaded. That, while still Beethoven, would at least give me a chance to show him what I could do.

Grudgingly, Zirato agreed.

I got my way, but I couldn't have made a worse mistake. Maestro not only didn't choose me, he very nearly didn't forgive me. My managers told me later that Toscanini was absolutely furious because I had presumed to sing something other than what he had asked. He actually refused to pay attention when I sang and it was better than a year before he so much as mentioned my name.

At last, in November 1943 I was told he wanted me to prepare Marzelline in "Fidelio" for him and the NBC Symphony. This time I didn't argue. I was determined to make no mistakes so I studied the part with Herman Weigert and committed it to memory before I went, as I thought, to audition again for Maestro. I wanted so much for him to like me that on the way to NBC that day, I stopped at St. Patrick's Cathedral and knelt down to pray that I would sing well for him.

Jimmy Quillian played for me and I sang through the role without using my score, hoping Toscanini would notice; but all he said (with heavy Italian accent, of course) was, "Now, Meez Steber, you will sing eet again and I will conduct you."

I was in something of a daze when I left for I suddenly understood that I hadn't been auditioning at all—Maestro had already decided on me before I was even called.

The music business is full of stories about Toscanini's drive for perfection, his impatience and his stinging insults to faltering musicians, but I saw it for myself during our early rehearsals. I watched a colleague nearly destroyed right in front of my eyes. He made a minor error and got so upset when Maestro corrected him that he made another mistake. Each time Maestro stopped him he got more rattled. Maestro wouldn't tolerate mistakes and the singer knew it, so it got worse and worse. I felt so badly for him I wanted to escape.

Since I had already memorized the Marzelline, I felt somewhat insured against Toscanini's displeasure. This turned out to be true, but now I became fearful that I had made a terrible tactical misstep with the rest of the cast which included Rose Bampton and Frederick Jagel. As rehearsals started, they faced Toscanini with scores in hand. Midway through rehearsal, Maestro suddenly snapped his baton on his music stand and shouted, "How is it that Miss Steber is the only one who knows her music?"

Was I pleased with myself or reassured by being singled out as such a paragon? Not at all. Instead I felt suddenly guilty and self-conscious, imagining, as I often did, many possible repercussions for my bravura gesture of working scoreless. Instead of glowing in the warmth of the great Maestro's approval, I grabbed a cab after rehearsal and raced from NBC to Jimmy's 55th Street studio and told him what I had done. "And I'm sure," I moaned, "the others will think I tried to show them up by singing without my score." How naïve can you get?

The performance was splendid and only the first of Toscanini's many historic radio operas, but since he never found another occasion to use me, I was haunted for years by the uncomfortable feeling that I had somehow offended him. (So important was it to me that I still have the laboriously composed drafts of one letter—which I rewrote many times to make sure I got it right—to try and discover how Maestro felt.) To this day, I cherish at least two letters to me in his hand.

It was many years before I was able to accept the fact that it was his choice of operas rather than any faux pas on my part that precluded another chance for me to sing with him. This insecurity, which has persisted in me all my life, cast shadows now and then on events which I should have been able to enjoy in full sunlight.

I guess it was a good thing I had that little bit of self-doubt, because without it I would have been more impossible than I probably was. But the doubts were never musical. Never! I was never insecure musically, not even with Toscanini, and singing "Fidelio" was unforgettable.

Before the next Met season, I began my association with the San Francisco Opera Company, singing Micaela and Sophie, both with Risë Stevens, who had made California her permanent home after making the movie "Going My Way" with Bing Crosby.

Since Edwin was now stationed in South Carolina, I took Mother with me. For six weeks I alternated opera performances and a short concert tour on the West Coast, even taking time to fly down to spend a few hours sitting in the sun with Risë by her pool and taking a dip or two. For once I had time to enjoy a little sight-seeing, and discovered San Francisco's fabulous restaurants. I was awed by both the beauty of the San Francisco Opera House and the respect with which I was treated by the management. It came to me as something of a revelation, since the atmosphere at the Met seemed to me far more adversarial than benevolent.

Conductor George Szell came to the Metropolitan for the 1944–45 season. I had known him since his arrival in New York from Czechoslovakia, having met him at a party during which he played piano brilliantly. He was equally impressive and urbane as a conversationalist.

But at the Met I immediately got off on the wrong foot with him because I spoke before thinking. We were rehearsing "Rosenkavalier" and he made a suggestion about Sophie to which I responded quite innocently, "Well, I did so-and-so with Mr. Sebastian out on the coast." Szell went up in smoke. "Don't you ever tell me what another conductor says. Here, you do it my way."

I was stunned. Oh, that the stage would open up under me! I was now petrified that I had made an enemy of him, but his anger was transient, and on a later occasion he invited me to sing for him up in the conductor's dressing room. I was startled when he asked for something sung by Emilia in "Otello"—a phrase which carried me down to a low b-flat. Then he asked for the opening of "Per pietà, ben mio, perdonna" from "Così fan Tutte." Maybe I surprised us both because I had never really fooled around with music which lay that low. Perhaps he was thinking in larger terms of Desdemona and Fiordiligi.

George and I became good professional friends, although he was a difficult man to know. I can't help wondering if George could really be truly close to anyone. He was a strict, austere sort of person (yet once I got the distinct impression during lunch one day that he was angling for a more intimate sort of response from me). But he was a stimulating colleague and I had tremendous respect for him as a musician.

I continued to dream of singing Donna Anna in "Don Giovanni," but in 1944 the Met gave me Donna Elvira. I had Donna Anna so stuck in my mind as "my" role that I was not prepared to like Elvira. Yet I did. Elvira is not only just as important a role as Donna Anna, in a way there's much more dramatic meat in it. She has fire and fury and a good deal more pure animal passion then Donna Anna. My obsession with Donna Anna was well known to my friends, and someone once said that when

I sang Donna Elvira I was auditioning for Donna Anna. Not so. No, no, no, no! I sang Donna Elvira to a fare-thee-well, and when Donna Anna eventually came along, it was an entirely different characterization.

I sang my first Eva in "Die Meistersinger" that season. This is the lightest of the Wagnerian roles and it came just at the right time for me; yet while I loved singing the part, Eva as a person never held any particular emotional attraction for me. I never understood this because I felt strong personal identifications with most of my parts. Still, it must have been all right, because Francis Robinson, unforgettable and irreplaceable in the Met organization, said that mine was the most unforgettable Eva he had ever heard. You just never know.

A Taste of Honey

When I finally sang my first Violetta in "Traviata" with the Metropolitan, I had to sing it on tour. But that was all right with me because I got to do it in Boston—my town! That performance, with Jan Peerce and Leonard Warren, was an operatic celebration. It was such a successful "Traviata" I had to admit I was lucky I had been forced to wait nearly five years to sing Violetta. I had needed those valuable years of maturing in performance. And Mr. Whitney was there! It was always a great disappointment to me that he was unable to make the trip to hear me sing at the Met, but had to wait until the Met came to Boston.

After the performance I threw a party at the Ritz-Carlton which included my manager, my new press representative, Margherita Tirindelli, and Frank St. Leger, Edward Johnson's artistic director. *Newsweek* music editor Emily Coleman had also made the trip. A friend, both of mine and the other American Violetta, Dorothy Kirsten, Emily always kept a sharp eye out for a chance to tout American talent and she did a *Newsweek* cover story on the pair of us. The cover artist's colorful conception of contrasting American sopranos costumed as Violetta showed us each lifting a glass of champagne in a mutual toast. It was dazzling publicity for both of us.

What no one expected was the public outburst WCTU (Women's Christian Temperance Union) which expressed shock and rage that a national magazine "should so degrade two innocent young American girls" by showing us off with glasses of the bubbly in our hands for all to see. Letters to the editor continued for months, but it was too late. Champagne had long since become a fixture in my life.

I sang "Traviata" in Boston again the following season, a performance which baritone Robert Merrill, then new to the company, and tenor Richard Tucker remembered for reasons of their own. In one of his books, Bob recounts his tale with, I insist, considerable exaggeration. He claimed that I had nothing, or next to nothing, on under my filmy black Act IV peignoir and that he and Tucker had to make valiant efforts to protect my modesty. When Tucker came off stage during the scene in question mopping the perspiration from his brow someone heard him exclaim, "Good God, she has nothing on under that negligee!"

Not true. I wore a filmy nightgown under the negligee. I will admit that its neckline was very low and that when I fell over the couch with my head back, it became a degree more revealing than I had anticipated, but I knew exactly what I was doing and I'm sure it wasn't quite as bad as Dick said. Anyway, it never hurts to stir up a little excitement in the people you're singing with; just as I was sometimes excited—and should have been—by men I worked with (remember Franco Corelli's skin-tight white satin breeches in "Adriana Lecouvreur"?).

It was after that Spring 1945 Metropolitan tour that my career shifted gears again. Although I certainly had no complaints about my concert career, which was already as much as I could handle and kept me constantly on the move, my situation at Columbia Concerts changed. Bill Haensel, my personal representative, retired, and things just did not work out well between me and the two men who replaced him. I had become acquainted with James A. Davidson, a business manager who had done special tax work for Spiro Skouros and Lily Pons and who currently worked for people I knew like Lauritz Melchior, Helen Traubel, Jeannette MacDonald and Leonard Warren. He was already handling my finances, and when he established a concert management, I went with him.

I can't remember the date, but I do remember that I was in bed with a cold that earth-shaking day when Jim arrived to tell me that he had signed a five-year contract for me to sing 26 broadcasts a year—that's every other week—for the "Voice of Firestone" on NBC. What an utterly fantastic development for me!

I later learned that Richard Crooks, who had long been a Firestone regular, and an unexpected partisan of mine when we were both with Haensel and Jones Management (as well as my Faust in Montreal, if you remember) had given the negotiations a terrific boost by recommending me to the program's musical director, Howard Barlow, and the Firestone executives. There is no way I can possibly express my lifelong gratitude for such a generous act by that great American artist.

A few of my well-intentioned (?) friends and critics thought I might be compromising "my art" by singing the lighter concert music, sentimental ballads, popular standards and musical comedy so popular on the program. No such a thing! I was associated with such music from the beginning on my "Fur Trappers" program in Boston. To me there was *no unimportant music*. I was very conscious that on the radio, and later on television, I was being heard by millions of people. I gave them the best I could. I sang every song as if it were the most important piece of music I ever sang, and I meant it. I loved singing *anything*, and the Firestones gave me plenty of opportunity to sing oratorio and opera as well as the songs and ballads.

I sang for the Firestones for 10 years, sometimes sharing the program with their young Irish protégé, Christopher Lynch, with Leonard Warren and other Metropolitan colleagues. When the program moved to television, I moved with it, becoming the first woman to sing on national commercial television. I have never ceased to be grateful for all that my association with the Firestone program brought to my career and my life, and long after the program left the air I paid tribute to it from time to time by offering as a concert encore, Idabelle Firestone's "If I Could Tell You," the opening theme of every Firestone program. Harvey and Idabelle Firestone were wonderful to me and entertained me in New York or at their home in Ohio. It was pretty high living for a little girl from Wheeling, West Virginia, but I loved it and thrived on it.

Before I started with Firestone, during the summer of 1944, however, I starred on the Sunday "Coca-Cola Hour" with Percy Faith's Orchestra, and got a foretaste of how much more my career was going to affect my private life as time went on. I wanted to see my husband graduate in June from Officer's Training School in Florida, but had to leave before the ceremony to make it back to New York for my first rehearsal with Percy Faith. It upset me terribly because I was still very much in love with him. We had already been separated a great deal, because when the Army wasn't shipping him around, my work was shipping me.

Perhaps it was all this plus a deep desire to establish a permanent home for us to retreat to on that dream day when the war would be over, but this turned out to be the summer I found and put down a $50 deposit on my house, intending to rent. I had been house-hunting around Long Island, looking at everything from mansions to a glorified chicken house when I discovered a rustic, half-timbered house with a cathedral-ceiling living room, and great timber beams, all nestled in the hillside of a half-dozen acres in the Belle Terre section of Port Jefferson, overlooking the harbor. I named it Melodie Hill, but I should have called it "The Pause that Refreshes," since it was my Coca-Cola radio contract which made the purchase possible. Melodie Hill became the perfect retreat when I wanted privacy and an equally perfect stage setting for entertaining in style.

That year, however, I carried such a workload that I had little time to think about my new home. When it was over, I found I had sung 208 performances of all kinds within 12 months, an average of three a week, plus all the additional time spent coaching, rehearsing, and on fittings and travel. I had grossed better than $200,000—then equivalent to about maybe a million today.

A few of those 208 performances were in Mozart's "Abduction from the Seraglio" at the new music festival which had just been established in a once near-ghost town in Colorado named Central City. The Metropolitan had planned its first-ever production of "Seraglio" in English for the following season, and I had been told to learn the part of Constanza, a two-and-a-half octave dilly of a part which I had toyed with in my spare time since I first worked out "Martern aller Arten" with George Sebastian in 1941. The role had a clutch of high D's; up until then sustained, quality high C's had been my performing limit except for the perfectly-set-up D-flats in "Der Rosenkavalier."

The Central City "Seraglio" was cast chiefly with Met people and the production conducted by Emil Cooper, who was to handle it at the Met. A tall, handsome youngster named Jerome Hines was in it and made his Met debut the season following. Why I didn't put two and two together at the time and figure out that the Central City performances were an out-of-town tryout, escapes me. Perhaps I was too preoccupied with my own tussle with Constanza.

My chief problem singing this role proved to be the Central City altitude. The high D's were a struggle, and I worked and worked on them until I nearly gave myself laryngitis. It was the wrong thing to do. You don't get high notes by over-working. After I got through Central City—high D's intact but not the way I wanted them—I made a beeline immediately for Boston and Mr. Whitney, now 85, to get his advice before I tried the role at the Metropolitan. I became a student again.

"Don't *push* for the high notes, Steber," he admonished. "Keep the rest of your voice light and lyric and when the time comes, the high notes will be there. The same for the bottom of your scale."

He was exactly right, of course, and I should have known it for it was what he had taught me. I had simply become so involved and anxious,

I had forgotten that basic principle. When I returned to New York, I restudied the role as he had instructed me and the high D's were right where they should have been. I also found that once down from the mountains, I could carry long phrases which had given me unprecedented difficulty in the high altitude. I was so delighted when I discovered this that I rushed over to Jimmy Quillian during a Firestone rehearsal and cried, "Oh, Jimmy, I could sing this whole show in one breath. I've got so much breath now I don't know what to do with it all."

The Metropolitan premiere of "Seraglio" proved to be a solid plus for me, but the critics in general felt the opera was strictly in the "featherweight" class and that the English translation suffered from the variety of accents among the cast. Irving Kolodin declared that whatever its deficiencies, the opera "might have lasted in the repertory with a new conductor and . . . cast . . . of Steber's quality." Nice for me, but no help to the opera which died after four performances and was not heard again until the 1979–80 season at the Lincoln Center house.

New Worlds to Conquer

Back in Boston, just before I came to New York, there had been plans for me to study in Italy for at least a year on a Beebe Scholarship. The war canceled that dream. But in 1947 music had already risen like a phoenix from the ashes of war. When I was invited to sing the Countess in "Figaro" with the Glyndebourne Opera Company at the very first Edinburgh Festival in Scotland, I jumped at the chance.

The Glyndebourne Company had been founded by John Christie down in Sussex, where he built an opera house right on his own estate. I never actually performed in his Opera Theater, but we rehearsed there and lived in the manor house with the Christies, so I was able to savor the full flavor of this unique establishment. I was already acquainted with Audrey Mildmay (Mrs. Christie) who had sung Susanna to my Countess in Montreal during the war with Sir Thomas Beecham, and I more or less assumed this had something to do with my Glyndebourne engagement.

Tales of post-war austerity in England were so horrendous that I sailed for England laden with canned (or "potted" as the British say) food. All the artists, including me, had to get ration books for food and sugar, which we turned over to our hosts. Their wealth made no difference; the scarcity of food was classless.

Between rehearsals I explored the countryside. One day I switched from foot to pedal-power and cycled along the Sussex roads to get a first-hand view. Suddenly I saw a car coming straight at me down the "wrong" side of the road. I panicked and tried to wheel over to the side—but which side? Just then I reached an intersection, lost my bearings and crashed into a hedgerow. I picked myself up and hightailed it back to the Christies where Audrey gave me bloody hell and told me I could have been killed. Properly chastised, I promised never to do it again. I never did.

Rehearsals were great fun, especially with my favorite Count, John Brownlee, in the cast. John was always very special to me. From my first rehearsals of "The Magic Flute," John had always given me constant support and guidance. He was my friend. And he helped me not only by his good advice, but by his example. I learned simply from observing his impeccable style, both as a man and as a performer. John was probably the finest gentleman I've ever known, and I loved him dearly. The Manhattan School of Music was blessed when he became its head.

Reassured by his presence, I rehearsed with Carl Ebert and an exciting cast which included a young Italo Tajo as Figaro, Giulietta Simoniato as Cherubino and a lovely Italian soprano, Elena Menotti, as Susanna. A delightful Scot, Katherine Lawson, was Marcellina. Walter Susskind conducted.

We traveled as a company to Edinburgh by train, and I must say that as my first overseas experience, the festival was perfect. Then, of course, you never know how any particular engagement will affect the rest of your life. One of the first people I met in Scotland was the young German impresario who had organized the Festival and would continue to manage it for some years. His name was Rudolf Bing.

When I was not singing, I heard performances by other great artists at the Festival, including cellist Pierre Fournier, violist William Primrose, and the mighty pianist Artur Schnabel. When I went backstage to pay my respects to Mr. Schnabel, whom I had never met, I was stunned when he told me he had already heard me sing in America and paid me great compliments about my Mozart. His praise took my breath away, not only because he was set so high in my estimation as a musician, but because three friends from conservatory days, Ruth Culbertson, Leonard Schore and Florence Kirsch, were his students, as was Victor Babin who would appear significantly in my life two decades later. (It was Ruth Culbertson, by the way, who played for me when I was a student in Boston and who added grace to my vocal line, especially in Mozart, by suggesting I take great care not to rush the last beat in a phrase. A small thing, perhaps, but it makes all the difference.)

I returned at last to New York to the old merry-go-round and added two new roles to my repertoire. After six years of singing the First Lady in "The Magic Flute," I was finally awarded Pamina. Now I was again faced with that matter of spoken dialogue, this time under a much brighter spotlight. Special measures were called for and I called for my friend, actress Helen Mencken, whom I had met through Lamb's Club Shepherd Bert Lytell and his wife Grace – Helen's sister. She worked informally with me on my lines until one day she decided "I won't be happy with this until I can hear you in a theater."

Judith Anderson's "Medea" was, at that moment, the hottest ticket in New York, and was playing at the National Theater just up the street from the Met. Helen arranged with Miss Anderson for us to use the stage between performances so it was against a classic Greek background that she coached my Pamina. This was the first, but not the only time I would turn to an actress from the legitimate theater to help me prepare my part. I'd learned my lesson well from Mother back in my "Irish Maid" days: always study with the best.

Everyone seemed pleased with my Pamina, including Irving Kolodin who described it as of "lovely sound and musical excellence." I had been so long with "The Magic Flute," however, and so well acquainted with Pamina that I took over the part with comparatively little excitement. It was more like a natural progression.

What *I* was looking forward to was my first Massenet "Manon" later in the season. For me, if for no one else, this turned out to be a project fraught with difficulties and uncertainties. I prepared the part carefully, privately coaching it with Jean Paul Morel. Jean always gave me such a lift, not simply because he was a vibrant, exhilarating individual, but because he worked with such conviction and authority. I always had the feeling he was constantly trying to find the best both in himself and in me – there was *never* any compromise with the music.

I studied the role dramatically with José Rubin, one of the Met's temporary Broadway draftees, so between Jean and José, I worked as hard on the role as circumstances permitted. We rehearsed the general misè en scène on the roof stage (that drab and dusty loft at the top of the old Met), but I never got on the Met stage with it until the night of the performance. I had no orchestra rehearsal whatsoever.

Returning home from the Met the day before the performance, furious and frustrated, I complained to everyone within earshot, "Never again will I do a new part at the Met under such circumstances. No artist should have to perform a part without at least one full rehearsal. I have enough repertoire to carry me through. I shall not attempt to do any new roles again. The hell with them, *all* of them!" (Famous last words.)

Paul Engel had made me absolutely fabulous costumes for "Manon," but I woke up in a cold sweat and all-but hysterical the night before the performance, trying to figure out how I was going to manipulate my immense tomato-colored cape around the stage in the St. Sulpice scene. I nearly fell apart the afternoon of the performance because I kept imagining myself falling flat on my face in that gorgeous costume in front of 3,500 people—all because I never got a chance to practice with it on stage.

It was shocking to think what we had to do in those days, especially the Americans, because we had as yet no regional opera companies or, for the most part, conservatory opera schools or even access to the provincial European houses in which to learn our craft. But, my God, what experience! Think of Roberta Peters, for example, making her Met debut as Zerlina with no rehearsal at all; and Astrid Varnay who, at 23, sang Sieglinde in "Walküre" one day and Brünnhilde a week later with absolutely no experience in them whatsoever. We had to invent! We had to be alive and flexible and imaginative to do what we did.

George Cehanovsky, who had sung Brétigny in every "Manon" since 1927, claims he saw no signs of my inner tumult. "She had all the material for this part," he told a mutual friend, "and I was not conscious she had no stage rehearsal. You see, in those times, when an opera was already in performance and a new artist comes, one, two, three roof rehearsals and you do! Never had benefit of stage rehearsal. I know. I also made my debut in this opera and I never even saw 'Manon' before general rehearsal, and I had to follow Lawrence Tibbett as Brétigny."

What would I have done without extraordinary people like George Cehanovsky on stage to help me? George was a very special person and a man of great elegance. As I sang my first "Manon" he seemed always close by, offering a hand, easing me into advantageous positions, whispering a helpful suggestion now and then. He was of inestimable help and encouragement to me then—and always. As usual, George was modest. "But, of course this would be my business as old artist," he told our friend, "and the performances were always fine. If there had been something she did not do right, I would have remembered it even today. It was so natural, her performance, that I thought, 'My goodness, she *is* Manon!' And about singing—she was splendid. When she came to the end of aria 'Adieux, ma petite table,' I had tears . . . she touched my soul. And, oh my, she was gorgeous-looking lady!"

With a man like that by my side, how could I fail?

Twenty-four hours can make a world of difference in outlook, and the day after the performance I was singing another tune: "My first Manon! Oh, what a glorious thing to do and how well it went! After that one spasm of nerves in the afternoon, I settled right down and was as cool as a cucumber this evening. My costumes were glorious. I received loads of roses and afterwards, a little party. Everyone seemed delighted. Herbie Fields just loved it. Even Jim Davidson was quite bowled over."

I would be remiss in dismissing "Manon" without mentioning the controversy evoked in some quarters by my gigantic red cape. There were endless yards of material in this "infamous" red garment, and despite my earlier fears I had managed it without mishap, climaxing the passionate St. Sulpice scene by sweeping the cape around the shoulders of des Grieux as I urged him to escape the monastery with me. What could be more natural? Manon seduces him and envelopes them both in the red cloak of passion—fantastic!

Besides matters of vocal technique, the most frequent question I am asked is how I prepare roles, as if it were some mystical process with a secret key which I could reveal to the world, if I wished. Preparing roles is a craft. There are no "old" or "new" roles; only the mating of music and drama, whether the composer be Mozart, Puccini, Strauss, Wagner, Verdi or Barber. There is little difference in the procedure of learning any role, be it Donna Anna, Arabella or Vanessa. There is only the individuality of the artist and her unique persona; that's where the mystique comes in.

Music is rehearsed with a coach, presumably as written by the composer and according to the tastes of the musical director; the misè en scène with the stage director whose imagination is inspired or limited by the set designer and production concept. All these are crafts, the hard labor of making opera.

In my own experience, I had seen very few operas before I performed in them. Consequently, I brought no preconceptions to my roles and came to understand and project them with a completely fresh outlook. By the time I got a part on the stage, I had absorbed each character thoroughly into myself; I had become the Countess, Donna Elvira or Tosca. If audiences saw parallels or differences between mine and other interpretations they witnessed, it was in their perceptions. Audiences and critics are the only ones so preoccupied by comparisons. Similarities do exist, of course, because of the precrafted framework of any given opera, differences because each artist approaches a part in his or her own way.

When it comes to roles such as Arabella, Constanza, Vanessa, and Marie in "Wozzeck", all of which I created for their Metropolitan premieres, I assume history will always be colored to some degree by what I did or brought of myself to each part. So, in a way, I set a bit of new "tradition" which will endure long after the source has been forgotten. And so it goes.

Knoxville, Summer of 1915

My love affair with the musical poem "Knoxville: Summer of 1915" began sometime during the 1946–47 opera season when my manager thought it would be a terrific idea if I commissioned a major composition for voice and orchestra from one of America's top composers. It seemed a simple proposal with many inherent advantages for both the composer and me.

I think the choice of Samuel Barber was the brainstorm of a young man named David Hocker, who had an interest in both of us. David worked on my behalf in the Davidson office and he was also Samuel Barber's friend. I loved the idea. As an American, I felt a special pride that a major piece of music was to be created just for me by an American composer, and I felt a pleasurable curiosity about what he might conceive for my particular voice. I was now financially secure enough to afford the fee of $1,000, a not insignificant figure in 1946.

The "business" of my career had become so complicated, it made me nervous. I left everything I could to my managers. Consequently, all the arrangements with Sam were handled by third persons while I got on with my work. I was, and in a sense still am, in the dark as to precisely how things happened. According to musicologist David Ewan, Sam completed the score on April 4, 1947. Sam himself mentioned to more than one person that the work came quickly once he began it. He said he was still working on it, possibly completing the orchestration, when he received the unhappy news of the death of his aunt, the great contralto Louise Homer, which occurred on May 6.

When Sam announced the score was ready, I invited him, conductor Dimitri Mitropoulos, David Hocker and a few others to spend the weekend at Melodie Hill to hear it. Sam played it and I read through the entire 18-minute work at sight. There was instant celebration! I was enraptured, and so was everybody else, including Mitropoulos, who begged us on the spot to premiere it with his Minneapolis Symphony. But this could not be.

Sam was at this time one of a number of young composers and conductors in residence at Tanglewood, Massachusetts, at the festival Dr. Koussevitzky had established (while I was still in conservatory) as a summer home for the Boston Symphony and a training ground for young talent. And Dr. Koussevitzky, I learned, already had an option on the premiere performance.

We had to move quickly because I was to leave for the Edinburgh Festival in August; so, together with my husband and David Hocker, I drove up to the Berkshires where Sam had arranged for our welcome and entertainment. It was my first visit to Tanglewood. After a perfectly wonderful Sunday afternoon concert we were entertained by the Koussevitzkys. I stood, awestruck, in the presence of this great man whom I had worshipped as a conservatory student. I had never before even seen him face-to-face, much less spoken to him.

In the midst of such emotions, my memory of that day remains somewhat confused. The house was packed with young professionals like the young Leonard Bernstein, Lukas Foss and Gian-Carlo Menotti, and everyone was talking about this dazzling new work Sam had written for me. Dr. Koussevitzky beamed at everyone, and I can still remember my relief when he said, "Yes, I tink dees is very good idea," and invited me to sing it with the Boston Symphony the following spring. I felt like a New England Conservatory student who had achieved the absolute pinnacle of opportunity.

After we left I began to feel that it had been settled so neatly that perhaps Dr. Koussevitzky had set up the whole thing before I came on the scene, and that we had just been going through some public formality. But I was so excited about the whole thing, the thought slipped from my mind, and "Knoxville" became a labor of love.

"Knoxville: Summer of 1915" struck strong nostalgic chords in all three Americans involved in its creation. The author of the text, James Agee, had written it some years before as an emotional memory of his own youth in Knoxville, and it was first published in the *Partisan Review* in 1946. Sam had long been familiar with Agee's writing since he had already written the song, "Sure on This Shining Night" to an Agee poem back in 1938, and the two were good friends.

Sam later recounted some of his personal reactions to the Agee lyrics in some New York Philharmonic program notes in June, 1977: "When I had found 'Knoxville'. . . it struck me as very like my own childhood in West Chester, Pennsylvania. Agee and I were the same age and of similar background; we both had backyards where our families used to lie in the long summer evenings, and we each had an aunt who was a musician. I well remember my parents sitting on the porch, talking quietly as they rocked. And there was a trolley car with straw seats and a clanging bell called 'The Dinky' that traveled up and down the main street. A lot of odd coincidences. Agee's poem was vivid. It moved me deeply and my musical response that summer of 1946 was immediate and intense. I think I must have composed 'Knoxville' in a few days."

My own reaction to "Knoxville" was unequivocal. I felt at once that it belonged particularly to me, because I also lived in a time when we lay on the grass on quilts and I can remember the "frailings of fire that breathes." Even today, the line: "The stars are wide and alive; they seem each like a smile of great sweetness and they seem very near. . ." stirs me each time I step outside my home to wonder at the night sky over Melodie Hill.

Every word that Agee wrote means something special to me: My Mother, too, was a musician, and *my* parents were good to me. But what tears me apart are those penultimate phrases when the child cries out that even his loving parents "will not, will not now, not ever. . . tell me who I am." That always wrenches my heart because it recalls my own anguish as a teenager when nobody could tell me who *"I"* was. The whole concept of the piece—Agee's words and Barber's music—still arouses profound emotions in me. Agee's words were not only beautiful in themselves, but they conjured a haunting nostalgia for my own growing years. Wheeling is not so far from Knoxville, and everything in the poem (for it is a prose poem) was part of my life and is rooted deep within me.

Sam, in the previously-mentioned program notes, comments that "with 'Knoxville' you have to know the words and even so, I'm not sure that they would mean to a foreigner what they mean to an American."

I agree! "Knoxville" is so American, so much a part of our private language that I doubt Europeans can ever hear it as we do. I remember playing the record for a musically-cultured German lady who said she couldn't understand why anyone would write or sing so rapturously about such a mundane thing as a family lying on the grass. I tried unsuccessfully to explain that there is a special quality about such words for Americans, a quality that goes beyond their actual meaning to evoke a whole way of life. The very sound of the text, certainly for generations of our time and place, recaptures a sense of continuity, of childhood, of being loved and protected.

The clarity of the "Knoxville" text must be credited, in part at least, to the composer. It was Sam's discerning eye and ear which enabled him to cut and lift bits of the original text faultlessly, yet without changing an existing word, and join them in seamless sequence. The opening phrase, as a matter of fact, was picked out of the middle of an Agee sentence, and it is this delicate perception which crystallizes the poetic aspect of the piece. The original work, which may now be found in the prologue to Agee's Pulitzer prize-winning book, "A Death in the Family," is somewhat more rambling. Whatever the shape of its origin, Sam distilled the best of it and set it to unforgettable music.

The world premiere of "Knoxville: Summer of 1915" was set for April 9, 1948. Shortly before, I flew to Boston with James Agee (an elusive, but compelling personality for whom I felt a warm, although quite secret, attraction). We had publicity photos taken with Koussevitzky. We were all happily anticipating the event when someone inadvertently dropped a bombshell.

A few days before the performance, in a casual conversational aside, tossed off so carelessly that I have forgotten who it was, I learned that "Knoxville" had *not* been written for me, and that the speaker had seen and heard the music before I ever commissioned the piece. I was stunned. I felt betrayed!

Can you imagine how I felt? I was supposed to have commissioned an "original" piece of music, written specifically for me, to the tune of $1,000 and it wasn't written for me at all. Apparently it was part of an informal arrangement previously made between Sam and Dr. Koussevitzky, who wanted a piece to perform with contralto Carol Brice. Sam must have reset it for soprano. I simply paid for it and got the first performance.

Breathing fire, I furiously confronted Sam (who may have been unaware of what I had been told) and he tried unsuccessfully to reassure me. Nevertheless, with the premiere close at hand, I had to calm myself. When the chips were down, I was a responsible performer and certainly had no question whatsoever about the value of the music itself. I shoved my anger to the back of my mind and went to rehearse with the orchestra.

The suggestion that only the native-born American understands "Knoxville" became manifest, when two friends who witnessed the first orchestra rehearsal observed that, clearly, Koussevitzky himself seemed all at sea with the piece, finally vacating the stage in frustration and leaving it up to the concertmaster and me to work it out with the orchestra. As it turned out, Koussevitzky also had something else on his mind.

We had all counted on the premiere of "Knoxville" to make a terrific splash in the press, so we were nonplussed when, on the evening of the first performance, the Boston Symphony announced Dr. Koussevitzky's retirement and named Charles Munch as its new conductor. Newspapers and magazines were full of it and my little "Knoxville" fell unnoticed by the wayside.

Musical history has long since vindicated us all. Never in the wildest reaches of my imagination could I have envisioned that "Knoxville" would become the timeless success it remains today. Nor can I conceive how anyone else could have introduced it to the world. It has been the most perfect piece for me, in every respect.

"Knoxville: Summer of 1915" is eternally linked to me, although many fine artists are performing it today, including my own students. My love for the piece remains steadfast, despite its uncertain provenance. This was resolved in part, however, by Sam's own words in those 1977 program notes, which a fan brought to my attention. During his interview with Sam, Philip Ramey had asked if the character of the text had dictated the score's restrained orchestral setting.

Sam is quoted as saying: "Originally, I had a much fuller orchestration than the one which was published. I had begun 'Knoxville' before Eleanor Steber commissioned me, with no particular singer in mind. I suspected that what she really wanted was a big, whooping thing to do with Koussevitzky and the Boston Symphony, but of course 'Knoxville' is not that kind of piece. Since I didn't hear that first performance, being in Rome at the time, I can't say how it went, but the Boston critics gave it terrible reviews. I do feel," Barber added, "that Koussevitzky hadn't the faintest idea of what the words meant, at least not unless someone sat down with him and carefully translated the text into Russian. . . Anyway, after hearing a fine performance in Minneapolis by Steber and Mitropoulos, I decided that the piece didn't need a big orchestra and, in fact, was better off without it."

"Knoxville," Sam concluded, "is one of those pieces which either moves people very much or leaves them entirely cold. For me, it's a tender remembrance which, for good or bad, seems to have its own little niche." Sam dedicated the "Knoxville" to his father.

Time and my own love for both the music and text have given me a more philosophical acceptance of the circumstances of its creation which not even the hard truths revealed in the program notes can dislodge. The real trouble was that it happened the wrong way 'round. If Sam had come to me himself and said, "Eleanor, I have a piece I think is right down your alley and I'd love to have you do it," I would have jumped at it. Then I could have said, "Well, Sam, it's great and I'll get my managers to arrange a deal with you."

Instead, the whole business was conceived behind the scenes and it made for some very bad feelings at the time. Those "bad feelings," now faded into the mists of history, can be laid to the mechanics of the music business.

Musically, Sam and I were ideally matched. He continued to compose his songs and operas until his untimely death, and I continued to sing them. As always, "all the rest is dust and ashes."

On the Road

From the moment I left on my first concert tour, I took to life on the road. I loved the challenge of winning each new audience and of meeting new people. I reacted to leaving New York with the same lift of the spirits as a kid leaving school for vacation.

When I went on the road the national network of local concert organizations was at its zenith, and although it was not specifically in the contract, it was understood that all artists were expected to be entertained by local sponsors for whom, particularly in the war years, concerts were the highlight of the social season. Nobody "insisted," of course, but such cooperation was strongly suggested.

While many artists felt that such social commitments were intrusive and avoided them wherever possible, I thrived on it. I loved it all! I loved meeting new people and I loved all the special attention. However, I always tried to give as good as I got. There were a few artists who vanished immediately after performances. I never did this. I never wanted to. I never held myself aloof from anybody, and the result is that I have kept a huge number of friends all over the country. I am still in touch with people I met on my first concert tour.

Full of high spirits and almost unbearably "up" after a concert, I was always delighted at the prospect of a reception or party. I developed a talent for remembering people, their names, interests, and details about their lives. I could meet dozens of people and be able, when I left, to call everyone by name. During my foreign tours, people were astonished and delighted when I called them by name, whether they were Yugoslavian, Greek, Indian, Japanese, or what have you. This was an important part of my public life and my success, as well as my happiness.

Of course, not every party was great. There were poorly organized receptions where no one knew what to do. There were hostesses, pretentious and otherwise, who didn't realize that singing a concert is vigorous physical work, often leaving an artist famished for food and a moment or two of privacy. And there were times when I had to do a little fancy footwork to avoid the unwanted attentions of an amorous husband or committee member. But the most insensitive were the hostesses who held back refreshments, suggesting that I "sing a few numbers," notwithstanding the fact that I had already completed a two-hour concert. But these were the exceptions; on the whole I enjoyed myself immensely.

Jimmy Quillian, who toured with me the first 15 years, loves to tell how, when I'd start out from New York, I'd be carefully counting calories at each meal, but that when I'd been on the road for a few days my determination would flag, and I'd end up saying, "Oh, what does it matter. I'm *hungry!*" So much for self-discipline.

At first we traveled everywhere by train, and I used my time to read. Once, when Jimmy's seat and mine were in different parts of the car, he heard me laughing uproariously, and came dashing up the aisle to find out what was so funny. I was in the middle of the current runaway bestseller, "The Egg and I," and it brought a rush of vivid memories about the time I spent at my Uncle Charley's farm as a kid—so like "Ma and Pa Kettle," and me playing up in the hayloft with Cousin Cecil when I was 10 or 12.

On my tours I refused to sing some of the hackneyed stuff my management thought appropriate for America's small town audiences. Ward French, head of Community Concerts, thought my programs were too sophisticated. I never believed this, and I refused to "sing down" to anyone; so, although I sang a lot of light music on the radio, in my concerts I always programmed liberal doses of French and German art songs, as well as English and American composers, plus Mozart and Italian songs.

Bill Judd also thought I should have sung more opera and fewer art songs, although he admitted that Nelson Eddy, who was world-famous for his light operetta movies, also sang a very strict recital program. His fans had to wait for the encores to hear songs from his movies. So I wasn't unique. I eventually gave in and added some arias and included a group of Puccini heroines, which proved to be very popular.

At one point during all this program hassle, I remember submitting a program to a concert chairman in a university town and had it turned down several times as being "too intellectual." After a lot of correspondence, I got fed up and dictated a program to my secretary which included every "gumdrop" I knew.

When I walked on the stage, anyone in the audience who knew anything about me was wondering, "What the dickens does Steber think she's doing?" Before I sang a note, they were bored, my accompanist was bored, and I was bored. We all struggled grimly through it and I thought it would never end. But I never allowed it to happen again, nor did anybody ever fuss at me about my programming after that. My judgment has been confirmed by a concert career which has spanned almost 50 years.

Music critic Byron Belt recalls a time before he came to New York when he was chairman of the concert series in Evanston, Illinois. We met when I rushed out to cover for Eileen Farrell who was indisposed. Her ready-printed program included numerous popular works by Wagner, Puccini and Verdi. When Byron got a look at my program it really rocked him, and although he was a great admirer of mine, he was really worried because I had included the "Seven Early Songs" of Alban Berg, which even Byron had not heard at that time.

"Berg?" he questioned. "In Evanston?"

"Don't worry," I said, "people will love them."

"And," Byron admitted later, "damned if they didn't."

Bill Judd used to book logically-routed tours so that artists could loop out and back with no wasted time, and a day or two between concerts to rest. When he discovered I was using two-day layoffs to fly back to New York to get my hair done, he gave up.

Most of the time I used layover days to work on new music. Once, when we were in Kansas City during the mid-fifties, Jimmy located a department store which had studios and a small stage on the top floor, and engaged it for a few hours. After working with me for a while, Jimmy took a break and went into the hall for a smoke, and was accosted by the studio receptionist who said that a "Mrs. Strickler" would like him to step into her studio.

Jimmy suddenly realized that Mrs. Thomas Strickler was the voice teacher of President Harry Truman's daughter, Margaret (now a noted mystery writer). Mrs. Strickler begged Jimmy to bring me in to "meet little Margaret."

That was okay with me, so we stopped in at this tiny studio and were introduced to Margaret, whereupon Mrs. Strickler said, "Oh, Miss Steber, would you listen to little Margaret sing?" I was tired and hungry, but why not? I think Margaret sang "Una voce poco fa" with Jimmy playing for her. No sooner had she finished and I had murmured a few encouraging words when Mrs. Strickler asked me to sing for Margaret. I pointed out that I had been working out strenuously for the past few hours and begged to be excused. I said my goodbyes as graciously as possible and started to leave the store.

Although I knew I had been perfectly correct, nevertheless I felt a little guilty for refusing to sing for them. So I stopped by the store's record department and bought two volumes of my "Firestone Favorites" album which I autographed for each of them, and sent them back to the studio.

The world of politics and politicians often crosses with musicians. I sang many times in Washington for Congressmen and Presidents of both parties. Although I have never been an "activist," I have always been fascinated by politics. I had a strong conservative heritage; but more than that, a fervent love for my country which grew even more passionate in future years when I began traveling through foreign countries.

In the fall of 1940, the charismatic Wendell Willkie was challenging Franklin D. Roosevelt for the Presidency in a highly-charged campaign. As the results came slowly in those pre-automatic voting machine-and-computer days, Jimmy and I boarded a train somewhere in Upper Michigan and went immediately to the club car to listen to the election returns. We had a drink while we listened. After a long while, Jimmy suggested we should try to get some sleep, but I wouldn't leave. I wanted to hear what happened.

I adored Wendell Willkie, and I grew almost desperate as he fell further and further behind in the running. Jimmy went to bed, but I stayed on until the early morning hours, heartsick at every discouraging return. When we got off the train the next morning, tears of disappointment kept flooding into my eyes. Jimmy was concerned about how I could possibly sing the big concert we had that night because he knew I was upset, sleepless, and a little hung-over. He needn't have worried because it turned out to be one of the best concerts on the tour.

When we were alone again on the train, he hemmed and hawed and finally screwed up the courage to ask me, "Eleanor, how in the world did you manage to do such a gorgeous recital tonight with almost no sleep?" The tears came again, and all I could manage was a whisper. "I did it for Wendell Willkie." And anyone who knows me knows that was God's own truth.

Although there were times on the road when I was bored and lonely, when there was nothing to do but read or see a movie, most of it was great fun. I don't know how it was for others, but a few went on record with their reactions to my life on the concert stage.

Cornelia Otis Skinner, the world-famous monologist and my favorite Long Island neighbor, once told a reporter, "Eleanor has a completely contagious love of life. She has a child-like esprit, a personal simplicity, and a love of singing I have never known in anyone."

My long-time friend, Emily Coleman, the music and dance critic for *Newsweek*, wrote once that, "Unlike most singers who make their living at it, Steber loves to sing. She has serenaded cab drivers all over the world and diners in cafés everywhere. She warbles indoors, outdoors, and always at parties."

That reminds me that I have often felt that the word "amateur" is much misused and maligned. Instead of being applied exclusively to non-professional performers, it should be applied to me; for "amateur" really means "one who loves," and that is how I feel about what I do.

My friends were not always prepared for me. I remember one night in Mississippi with my friend, Hattie Pearl Lea. Jimmy had been entertaining us hilariously after a concert in my hotel suite until I finally got wound-down enough to sleep. Hattie Pearl returned to her room.

About 5 a.m. I awoke, ravenous, and called her. "Hattie Pearl. I hope you're not too sleepy," I insincerely apologized. "I'm hungry." So poor Hattie Pearl dragged herself out of bed, and within minutes we were dressed and driving toward the beach in search of food. She meekly munched bacon and eggs, and glanced somewhat askance at me, I am sure, while I wolfed down spaghetti and meatballs while we watched the sun come up.

I come by my appetite honestly. When I was still in grade school, my family occasionally visited Atlantic City on "the family plan." Food was served to us as a family, and since my brother and sister were finicky eaters, there was always plenty of food left on their plates. Rather than waste already-paid-for food, my parents invariably turned to me: "Eleanor, now you clean up those plates!" The habit persists.

I have always enjoyed the rewards of my career, and the pleasure of important and accomplished people; but somehow or other, I never quite fell into the trap of being impressed with "status" for its own sake. Most of my best and closest friends have been people from middle class backgrounds like my own, who have loved me for what I am, through good times and bad. I think immediately of Ellen Martin, without a doubt my dearest friend, and darling Bobby Barker, a Port Jefferson boy who came into my life when he was 14, and is still close to my heart.

During the Korean War, Bobby was in the Army, and I had momentarily lost track of him, although when he was home he had always had carte blanche at Melodie Hill. I was singing with the Birmingham Symphony. Unbeknownst to me, Bobby was stationed nearby and had a weekend pass so he could attend my concert with a couple of buddies.

I swept onto the stage that night in a spectacular gown with a train almost 20 feet long, which immediately slipped off the stage and followed me along, drooping over the edge of the apron. When I got on the stage, the microphone wasn't working. It didn't worry me but I saw the conductor was concerned. I tried to reassure him, calling over, in full voice, "That's all right. I don't need the damn thing." Of course the minute I opened my mouth, the mike went on and my voice boomed throughout the hall. That got a laugh, I can tell you.

I still didn't know Bobby was there. After the concert while I repaired to my dressing room, Bobby got on line with a lot of other people to see me. He says he felt kind of self-conscious, in his olive-drab uniform in the midst of elegant Birmingham high society. When I finally saw him I let out a big whoop, pulled him inside my dressing room, and shut the door. For a few moments I forgot the crowd waiting outside. I sat down with Bobby and his friends, opened a bottle of champagne, and enjoyed old home week with my pal. Bobby was always part of my life. He took care of Melodie Hill when I was alone, and often took care of me. I could not have two better friends than Bobby and Ellen.

Ellen, in later years, often traveled with me, both in the States and in Europe, and in these past years stayed with me at Melodie Hill whenever she could. Neither Ellen nor Bobby ever asked anything of me, never wanted me to be anything but myself, and never wanted anything more than for me to be happy. They are best friends, in different ways, and always good companions.

Hollywood

There was never enough time. I was scheduled to sing my first fully-staged production of "Madama Butterfly" in no less a setting than the Hollywood Bowl. The performances were set for the first week in September of 1948, and although I had done tremendously exciting outdoor concert performances with Dimitri in both Philadelphia and New York, I had never prepared the opera dramatically.

I had to prepare the role alone, outside the Met, and without anyone else in the cast, except the stage director. I worked with him on the misè en scène at every opportunity. He seemed pretty good, but without anyone to play to it was all vague and confusing. Once again I was involved in something which had to be done in a rush and with little stage preparation.

If the uncertainty upset my equilibrium, it also stirred up the old juices. On this occasion, as on so many others before and after, the very stresses which upset me seemed to spur me on. Being ready for anything was my stock in trade, and I cherished my reputation for flexibility and teachability in my craft. I soaked up instruction like a sponge, which turned out to be a particularly good thing in this case.

I succeeded in getting Butterfly under my belt dramatically because I found a marvelous Japanese girl, Agnes Miakawa, who had studied at the Paris Opera and had sung the role there herself. She put me through my paces and got me routined in the part as best she could in a few short days. She also taught me how to get into my costume properly. Our costumes came from the vaults of the Old Western Costume Company, which for years had supplied most of the production companies on the west coast. Maybe it still does. My bridal costume turned out to be a rich white satin kimono which swept the floor at least four feet behind me. I was rather thrilled when someone told me it had originally been worn by Ginger Rogers in one of the dream sequences from "A Lady in the Dark."

It's fortunate for me that I didn't know that the Hollywood Bowl production was conductor Eugene Ormandy's operatic baptism of fire. Since it was his first "staged" opera, it's hard to know what Ormandy expected. Everyone knew he liked to conduct from memory, but it's one thing to conduct a symphony orchestra and another to correlate all the components, i.e. singers, staging and scenic adjustments (invisible choruses, and whatnot) of an opera. Ormandy found he was hard put to keep track of his own problems in that huge place, let alone worry about us singers. All he could hope was that Jan Peerce, Richard Bonelli and I knew what we were doing.

The full stage rehearsals at the Bowl turned out to be pretty wild, endless affairs to say the least. Ormandy started and stopped over and over. All told, I ended up singing one full stage rehearsal plus an orchestra rehearsal starting early one day and lasting well into the evening, a public dress rehearsal the next night, and the actual performance on the third night—all in full voice.

When I was safely through the whole business, I wired Mr. Whitney back in Boston saying, "Thank God for you. Without what you taught me, I could never have done what I did the past three days."

That Ormandy, who is now in his eighties and in the process of retiring as I write, also lived through this frantic initiation to opera may have been due to his skill and derring-do, but also because he was blessed with a saving sense of humor.

When I first sang in the Bowl, Hollywood was still a cohesive social community, where everybody knew everybody else. There were stars a-plenty at the performance and the festivities which followed. The next several days were nothing short of dazzling for an old movie fan like me. Jeannette MacDonald and Gene Raymond threw a huge reception for me in their gorgeous big home—which seemed to cover a whole mountain top. There were at least 300 people there, many of whom I had watched for years on the silver screen.

Not the least of these was Nelson Eddy, with whom I had just recorded songs from "New Moon." But the most miraculous coincidence in all this started back during my initial trip from Wheeling to school in Boston. After changing trains in New York, I had ventured, like any other truly sophisticated traveler, into the club car. I was sipping my beer when this great, handsome, tow-headed giant in evening clothes blew in along with a similarly-dressed companion. I recognized him at once, for he had sung a recital in Wheeling, although he hadn't yet made a movie. I ordered another beer for courage and got half way through it before I dared approach him. I introduced myself with a confidence I didn't feel and told him that I, too, was a singer and on my way to Conservatory. He asked me a couple of polite questions and wished me luck—all of which, I am sure, sent me into Boston already up on cloud nine. Later I sent him an invitation to my graduation concert. Of course he didn't come, for he had already become a big movie star, but he wrote me a kind note.

Now, 15 years after that first casual meeting, he was at a reception in my honor. When I mentioned how much my mother wanted to meet him, he swept her right off the floor, hugged her and gave her a big kiss. The whole thing was almost like a movie.

I had an exciting time in Hollywood. The Leonard Firestones entertained us and we spent time with Dick Powell and June Allyson, Walter Pidgeon and George Murphy. Character actor Edward Arnold was a good friend of Gene Raymond and Maestro Ormandy, so he also put out the red carpet. We were in the midst of all the Hollywood glamour I had ever envisioned.

Of course I was interested in making movies! Who wouldn't be? Grace Moore, Gladys Swarthout, Lily Pons and Risë Stevens had become instant international superstars (although that term hadn't been invented yet) by making movies. And if it had been possible, I would have jumped at it.

After considerable dickering, one of the studios had offered me what was called a "starlet contract" similar to those given to so many contract players in those days. However, there were too many drawbacks. There was no guarantee, for instance, as to exactly what the studio would do for me. They would give me the standard salary guarantee (a pittance compared to my concert and radio fees) and they would "permit" me a mere six weeks a year for concerts and opera; the rest of the time I was expected to vegetate in Hollywood awaiting their pleasure.

They also insisted that I must lose some more weight, although I was down to a size 14 when they talked to me. When I made my debut at the Met, I had been what you might call "fulsome"—and I became so again; but getting down to size 14 was as small as I was going to get. So, as much as I wanted to make a movie, I had to say no. I've never regretted it, however, because the career that lay ahead of me was the one I was born to live.

Changes in the Wind

When Edward Johnson announced plans to retire at the end of the 1949–50 season, we all knew that it would mark the end of a unique era at the Metropolitan—for me, for my colleagues and the growing millions of opera lovers who had become attached to the Met via radio during the past 15 years.

Edward Johnson personified something more than "management" to me. Born in Canada, he had made his career as a tenor chiefly in Italy, where he was known as Eduardo di Giovanni, before returning to the North American continent and the Met where, among other roles, he was particularly acclaimed for his Pelléas. After the untimely death of Herbert Witherspoon, he agreed to take over the Met's artistic management.

He was a handsome, clean-featured man with prematurely white hair that suited him perfectly; a genial impresario with happy, smile-wrinkled eyes who was accessible to, and understanding of, his artists as only another member of the profession could be. There are some who claim he ran a loose ship, but whatever it was, it seemed to me largely a happy one. Even the audience felt a bond with their highly-visible manager as he strolled benignly through the halls, smiling a welcome to everyone, the perennial "nice guy," never without his white gloves, cane, and glistening top hat in hand.

Despite my deep, personal affection for him, I could never bring myself to address him as anything but "Mr. Johnson" or, in private, the Italian "Eduardo"—never the casual "Eddie" which came so easily to some. Mr. Johnson had a keen interest in the Company's young Americans, particularly the Auditions of the Air winners for whom he felt especially responsible. We were his youngsters—"Johnson's kids," some called us.

He cared about us; he encouraged us; he looked out for us. It was Johnson who sent me to Renato Bellini to coach all my Italian roles. He sent me to Grace Christie, a former dancer, so I could spend two years with that extraordinary woman learning body control and movement. He arranged the classes with director Lothar Wallerstein to make us more stage-wise.

Congeniality permeated the atmosphere while he ran the Met. While most singers were too busy and traveled too much to enjoy friendships outside the Met, our working rapport at the Opera House was absolutely marvelous. I discovered some years later that this amazed European singers. In Vienna, for instance, while I was preparing "Frau Ohne Schatten," one singer turned to me and exclaimed, "You are so generous, so free with your smiles, with yourself! Are all American prima donnas like you?" And I replied, "Yes, we are. We love each other." And we did! Those 10 years with Mr. Johnson, we all loved each other—and him. He never failed to visit me before each performance, and I always felt free to go to him for advice about anything. I'm not quite sure I always got a definitive answer, but I certainly left feeling happier.

With the arrival of Rudolf Bing in the Opera House for what was supposed to have been a year of observation and study, the atmosphere changed, not only for the singers, but for Mr. Johnson himself, whose authority was subtly undermined by Mr. Bing's presence and public statements.

When Mr. Bing officially took over the following season, the "happy family" broke up in a battle of wills between the new manager and his new company. Dozens of artists simply vanished, and those who remained became preoccupied with the task of simple survival. The Opera Company, which had become almost 60 percent American, once more began to call heavily on the pool of European-born or trained singers.

However time will judge Mr. Bing, he certainly had a way of making himself felt; so much so that some folks today seem to have the impression that the Met management simply leapfrogged from Gatti-Casazza to Rudolf Bing. But in spite of them, the Americanization of the Metropolitan during Mr. Johnson's régime continues even today in the house at Lincoln Center.

When I first met Mr. Bing in 1947 at the Edinburgh Festival, he asked me to return the following season to sing Donna Elvira in "Don Giovanni," but I explained that since I had already sung Donna Elvira at the Met I would prefer to sing Donna Anna. He wouldn't hear of it, even when I explained that returning to Edinburgh would mean giving up

Firestone broadcasts and part of my concert tour. I couldn't make those sacrifices for anything less than Donna Anna. My firm refusal may have set up some sort of unconscious antagonism between us.

However, finesse was never one of my strong points. No! That's my father in me: honesty to the point of fault, and I have been far more blunt about some things than my father ever was. Oh, I tried. I really tried throughout my career—God knows I tried to be politic, but I just never seemed able to carry it off.

But Mr. Johnson, with the approval of Fritz Reiner, had given me a crowning gift his last season—the Marschallin in "Der Rosenkavalier." It was to be the opening night opera—the only opening night I ever sang, *and* it was to be televised. That was a real innovation in 1949.

So, after nine years of Sophie, I began all over again on "Rosen-kavalier." Starting in June of that year, I took the ferry each weekend from Port Jefferson harbor across Long Island Sound to Westport, Connecticut where I coached the role with Maestro Reiner.

I will always have very special feelings about Sophie, not only because I felt so strongly I was Sophie, but because the emotional environment and the women with whom I sang during that period were uniquely warm and dramatically intense on the stage. There was a magic in our "Rosenkavaliers" which I no longer feel in today's performances. But I approached the Marschallin with a sense of fulfillment and rightness; for did not the Marschallin describe herself as having been once like Sophie?

I had just turned 35 as I prepared the Marschallin, a fact few knew since my official age was always given as two years younger. Even 35 was not young as far as the libretto was concerned, but it was young in a Metropolitan tradition calling for a somewhat more mature and matronly demeanor in the role. Reiner, however, felt he had considerable evidence that the Marschallin was approximately 32 and Hugo von Hofmannsthal's introduction to the opera seems to validate casting a Marschallin young and attractive enough to inspire the passion of a very young man.

As usual, I had no chance to get the "feel of the part" on the stage, and had the added strain of singing my first performance of it for the opening night audience. However, only critic Irving Kolodin of the *N.Y. Sun* thought I was too young for the part; but if Kolodin doubted that the Marschallin was a part for me, no one else did. Reviews included such lines as: "She surpassed herself. . . with the delicacy and feeling with which she sang and acted. . . her Marschallin was aristocratic and bittersweet. It had style, grace and tremendous emotional impact." (Coleman, *Mirror*)

Or, ". . . a salute to Eleanor Steber. . . It seemed to me she was exquisite in it . . ." (Chapman, *News*) Finally, Olin Downes of the *Times*: "Miss Steber's Marschallin is beautifully conceived; has tenderness and charm. . . ." and Robert Bagar of the *Telegram* noted: "She gave to the whole poise, serenity and charm, all qualities you might expect in a nostalgic aristocrat. . . her voice was lovely and sensuous and big enough . . ."

There was a lot of pro and con discussion about my age, something that wouldn't happen in this new era of young Marschallins. Always the flak bothered me, regardless of any disclaimers I made at the time. It irked me that people had so many preconceived ideas of how the Marschallin should look and act, that so many apparently closed their minds to what I was trying to do. I may have been the youngest Marschallin at the Met, but I would have bet any anything that I wasn't the youngest to sing the opera, nor do I think anyone would have quibbled about my age if I had sung it in Europe. In telling me I was too young, my critics were trying to claim that you can't do a role unless you have had the life experience. That's a lot of rot!

No one knows the kind of soul-searching I did to put my mind in that of this woman who had taken a 17-year-old lover. Nor did I have to live in poverty and degradation to understand Marie in "Wozzeck"; but I have to *feel* her and *know her in my heart* to do Marie or the Marschallin, or any other role.

The same is true of Manon, of Violetta. Were people trying to say you can't sing "Depuis le Jour" from "Louise" unless you have "lived in sin" on the left bank in Paris? No! But you've got to turn yourself inside out in order to take the role inside of you. In her autobiography, Lotte Lehmann wrote that she had lived the life of every character that she had sung. Lillian Nordica said the same thing. And it's true for me too.

I have learned each role as Eleanor Steber. When I have learned it, using all the techniques at my command, gradually the role takes me over. When I finally get it on stage, I become that character. At the same time, part of me is wholly aware of what my character is doing, because to become emotionally lost in a role is to fail to project it beyond yourself.

There were many, many times on the stage when I was unaware of "me"; step into the wings, go back into my dressing room, yes, certainly, I am completely out of it; but on a stage, although conscious, never conscious of "self." When it works—and of course it doesn't always—something "happens" and when it does, you transcend your mortal self.

So, in that season of my first Marschallin, the old order passed away. Rudolf Bing came to the Met and, for a time, nothing changed but the atmosphere since the 1950–51 season was already set. Losing Mr. Johnson, however, was a terrible emotional wrench, especially for me as one of "Johnson's Kids," who had grown up under his guidance in an American-oriented Met. There would not again, in the lifetime of my career, be another whose kinship and understanding of singers would provide such concern and constant support.

Town Hall

While all the turbulent changes were under way at the Met, I was working on a tremendously exciting project of my own. To set the scene, I must go back to the summer of 1944 when I sang my first concert with Dimitri Mitropoulos at the Robin Hood Dell in Philadelphia. I had never met the great Greek maestro, but as a student I had heard him when he first came to the U.S. to conduct the Boston Symphony.

Our first program was standard summer fare, but Maestro and I hit it off famously. Since then we had done concert versions of "Madama Butterfly" and "Tosca," and I had sung twice with his Minneapolis Symphony, including a performance of "Knoxville."

We were an unlikely pair: Dimitri, solitary and private, and me, full of laughter and love of good times. It became my honor and joy to make music with him and to know he was my friend. I would have done anything to please him.

In early April of 1949, Maestro and I met by chance and mutual delight in the lobby of the Hotel Washington in Seattle. Over lunch I happened to mention that although I had been in New York for 10 years, I had never given a Town Hall recital and was considering one for the following year. His eyes lit up.

"Elinor," he cried, "let us do it together! I have not played a recital since my days in Greece and I would love to do one with you. I'm sure we two could find a unique program to do together."

Imagine my joy and astonishment! How could I conceive anything more perfect? We agreed upon it then and there. At once we decided to do the seldom-sung "Geistliches Lieder" from the "Spanisches Liederbuch" by Hugo Wolf, and Claude Debussy's "Cinque Poèmes de Baudelaire."

But we had more difficulty settling on our third group. Dimitri proposed Arnold Schoenberg's "Buch das Hängenden Garten," but after I returned to New York and looked at it, I realized that it not only lay rather low for me, but that it was so very atonal it might put off our audience.

Mitropoulos then became excited about a new piece he had discovered. "Ballad for the Railroads" was composed by Ernst Krenek who had recently arrived from Vienna and was now teaching on the west coast. This "Ballad," Dimitri said, was á continuous work for voice and piano and had not yet been performed publicly. He thought it was a distinguished work, and that settled it. Dimitri's opinion was good enough for me.

When I received the manuscript, I fell in love with it. It was "my meat" as "Knoxville" had been. As I worked on it, I was transported back to my Grandmother's house, where as a child I had lain awake and listened to the rattle of the trains passing behind the stables. I could again hear the clanging of the safety gates, the roar and vibration of the train passing over the crossing and gradually fading until the last long, lonely hoot as it reached another distant crossing. The romance of these iron monsters was vividly woven through this music.

But the music was a challenge, believe me! Suffice it to say that Krenek was Schoenberg's pupil. Many times I had to sing a vocal line which had no apparent connection with what had been written for the piano—in one instance, a whole sequence where I sang a vocal line which lay half a tone above the scoring for piano.

We completed our program plan sometime in mid-winter when Dimitri called to ask if we could drop the Debussy and substitute another piece which had very special memories for him: Marc Delmas' "Du Rêvè au Souvenir," sort of a French "Frauenliebe und Leben." Dimitri had played it years before for Katina Paxinou, whom I knew as a great Greek actress but who had been famous as a singer in her younger years in Greece. (I met this impressive woman in Athens in 1955 at a reception given by the Secretary of Cultural Affairs, and we greeted each other as friends through a shared experience.) From both of them I felt a great attachment toward the Delmas work and sensed that I had won a special place in their mutual felicity toward it.

During the opera season I spent every spare moment coaching with Paul Ulanowsky, the noted pianist who always assisted Lotte Lehmann. I memorized, polished and perfected this program toward the day when Dimitri and I would finally rehearse together. I was aware, of course, what an extra chore it must have been for Dimitri to add his own preparations to an already heavy schedule.

Seldom in my life have I felt so consecrated to a task. I even worked with composer Ernst Krenek, who came to New York to add his insights to my preparations. I was so lifted by all this and the prospect of sharing the stage with Dimitri Mitropolous that I anticipated almost a divine fulfillment.

April 5 finally arrived. Houletar, my current couturier, had created a ravishing gown of navy blue satin, and to celebrate I had my hair styled in a new short cut which required no fuss. I was well prepared musically and utterly at ease in the knowledge that Dimitri would be with me. Seldom had it been so serene backstage: no nerves, no jitters, no uproar of any kind. I had nothing to do but go out and make music with Dimitri.

The audience was wonderful and called us back over and over — 14 times, I was told — and I felt grateful and full of wonder at how lucky I was to have done such a program with this magnificent Maestro. Throughout the big party and the happy hours which followed it, I felt very, very proud.

I was caught totally off-guard by the violent outburst our collaboration inspired in the press. We were both shocked numb, and shattered, because it had never occurred to either of us that we could be so dreadfully misunderstood. The critics simply took me apart! I awakened to learn that I had been "presumptuous," an upstart American tackling the sacred precincts of Hugo Wolf. They castigated the Krenek, one of them so lacking in background and research that he cited the half-tone higher-than-the-piano passage as evidence of my "often merely approximate" pitch.

There were punishing comments by all the critics, most relating to our choice of music. One, damning by faint praise, wrote that "Miss Steber and Mitropoulos performed. . . with the utmost devotion and insight, yet it proved. . . sadly disappointing." All found it a program little suited to my gifts. Nor did they fail to strike at me by comparing my comparative professional American "innocence" to the musical sophistication of Mitropoulos "who accompanied her, and against whom even her splendid musicianship could not stand, in spite of all his efforts at subservience." Perhaps this last stung the most, for Mitropoulos had not acted as my "accompanist." He was my colleague. My Maestro!

When Mitropoulos personally went to the *Times* and took critic Virgil Thomson to task for his comments about the program and claimed sole responsibility for its content, Mr. Thomson then scolded Dimitri, insisting that he "could ruin Steber" with a program like that. This dismayed Dimitri who came to me as a penitent, feeling he had done me some terrible disservice by encouraging me to sing it, particularly the "Ballad of the Railroads."

But he had not done any such thing! I had agreed with him from the beginning, for I felt that my first Town Hall concert in New York with Dimitri Mitropoulos deserved to be special. I also felt responsibility as an American to prove that I could handle anything as well or better than any European who came down the pike, and I am convinced that one of the reasons the program was received as it was, was because I was an American. If a European singer had done that concert, critics would have been hypnotized by the continental mystique and there would have been gasps of wonder all over the place.

Perhaps the Krenek "Ballad" was too avant-garde for us to have done at that time. That the audience didn't really comprehend it didn't occur to me at first, because I was so deeply immersed in it myself. Later on, of course, after I got to thinking about it, I realized that I had been so caught up by the personal challenge it presented to me that I failed to understand that the audience would not hear it as we did. I honestly loved the "Ballad of the Railroads" and I eventually did it again under different circumstances.

Composer Ernst Krenek thoroughly approved my performance (even suggesting he would assist me himself in a future concert) and wrote me enthusiastically: "It was a wonderful performance and I was touched when I noticed how faithfully you remembered every little detail we had worked out together. You and Maestro have done a magnificent job and I am very happy about it." He added some healing balm: "I heard many enthusiastic comments so I hope you were not upset by the few sour notes in the press. These people never had much comprehension of, and no sympathy for, my music and that's just that! It does not impress me one way or the other."

Was our Town Hall program too far off the beaten musical track? Well, in retrospect, maybe; but to do anything with Dimitri—I didn't see how it could miss. Was it possible that people, including my own personal following, felt let down because I hadn't given them what they wanted and felt they had a right to hear from me? To judge from their ecstatic reactions to my future New York concerts, that's very possible.

All this philosophical calm came long after the recital. The next day I left for Atlanta and I remember that Edwin and I were still so upset when we boarded the train that we began talking about giving up the whole business to go join Albert Schweitzer in Africa.

When I returned to New York, the critical furor had abated somewhat and I talked it out with Dimitri. He was all for remounting the horse which had just thrown us, and invited me to sing Honegger's "Cristoforo Colombo" with the N.Y. Philharmonic. That would have curled their hair!

Dimitri and I were great companions with a very deep love for each other as musicians and friends, but I listened to my very strong instinct at this time and said, "Dimitri, they don't like us to be together, so I don't think I should sing with you this year."

So we put off the whole thing for a few years until we got together again to do the Berlioz "Les Nuits d'Été," which made a history of a different sort.

Twist of Fate

My modest little apartment on 11th Street had quickly become inadequate, so that when Edwin was released from the Army in 1946 we went apartment hunting, and finally found one in a converted town house at 1025 Park Avenue. The house had originally been owned by Reginald DeKoven, composer of the "Robin Hood" of Boston days, and the floor we occupied had served as DeKoven's private studio. Our immediate neighbor in the penthouse above was Leonard Bernstein.

The dominant feature of the apartment was our large living-cum-music room with a handsome stone fireplace at the north end, a grand piano at the south end, and casement windows with cozy, cushioned window seats along the far wall. The walnut-beamed ceiling added intimacy to the large square room. Between the fireplace and the grand gold crescent couch which faced it was a massive round glass coffee table which housed my growing collection of autographed first-performance conductors' batons. Paul Althouse had such a personal collection displayed vertically in a glass wall case, and he urged me to gather my own.

Although the living and business areas were not so commodious, the Park Avenue apartment provided the setting I wanted for my rising status as an opera/concert/radio star. For that it was perfect. When I was not singing, I was caught up in a continuous round of entertaining, cocktail parties and dinners. We were often at Broadway shows, the opera or the symphony and parties where the champagne flowed like water, as did the martinis and manhattans. It was heady stuff and I adored it. If I worked hard at my profession, I still played just as hard as I had in Boston, except that now the stakes were higher, and it sometimes worried me. My diaries are full of such entries as: "Went off my diet tonight, dammit. When will

I ever learn? I have not the will to resist when others are enjoying themselves. Limited myself to cocktails before dinner this time and stuck to soda water afterwards. Perhaps I will improve."

No matter how gay the party or how late the hour, I was back at work the next day. On the few occasions I was not up to it, I'd call Frank St. Leger, Mr. Johnson's assistant, to say that I was indisposed, had a sore throat or offer some other acceptable excuse. Most times, however, I made rehearsals no matter what. If I felt somewhat under the weather, I was sometimes not the only one. The strange thing was that often on such days rehearsals went better than usual—the old adrenalin, I presume.

Unquestionably I had a ravenous appetite, not only for my work and its rewards, but for the trappings, aura and ambience, if you will, of "stardom." I came in at the fringes of an era which was fabulous for real glamour, for "stars," and all that "star" meant: the entourage, the parties, the lovers and all the fixings, including my golden spotted dalmatians. That's what I wanted and, for the most part, what I got, although in those days we were all pretty careful to keep our "acts clean" in public. Stardom represented something that's been in my nature all my life: wanting to be loved, to be admired and to know that I counted for something in the world.

But Edwin had different dreams of what I should be. He had great ideas for my career and an ever more grandiose lifestyle because he felt the symbols of success were so important. So, of course, as the exchequer grew, so did the dreams.

Everyone, but *everyone*, worked at developing my public image. That's the way things were done in those days, similar to the way the big movie studios handled their stars. We didn't "let it all hang out" as they do today. We created careful and, one hopes, beautiful images as stars. I hardly needed encouragement. This had always been my dream. I got all the life I could handle, and more. Certainly I had no complaints about income and God knows I was busy. I just wanted to experience everything I saw—just *everything!*

My first full year under the direction of Rudolf Bing was a good one. I was averaging between 150 to 200 performances of all kinds each year, 25 to 30 of them at the Metropolitan where I was scheduled to sing not only Pamina, Donna Elvira, Marguerite and the Marschallin, but got one of my few opportunities with a Verdi opera and made the most of it when I sang my first Elisabetta in "Don Carlos."

During the next three seasons I scattered a few more performances of it, but after that, my Elisabetta, like Micaela and Manon, got mislaid and forgotten. For me, the early 1950s at the Met are characterized by the thunderous public disputes between Mr. Bing and some of the most famous old hands (and my old friends) on the roster. The Bing régime became known as one in which controversy and notoriety superseded the conscientious professionalism of the majority of artists. I fared better than many of my colleagues, although I remember it as a time of great uncertainty.

"Don Carlos" was a good opera for me. It was just a twist of fate that I sang it so seldom. That "twist of fate" was an attack of acute appendicitis, the first illness to knock me out of action since I had my tonsils out in grade school. I'd had no warning symptoms at all and I was stunned by it. I'd grown to feel almost invulnerable to ill health, barring singer's throat and an occasional bout with asthma, all of which I considered occupational hazards.

On January 5, 1951 I awoke in Doctor's Hospital. Since I had been scheduled for a broadcast performance of "Don Giovanni" that day, news of my emergency surgery was broadcast nationwide to explain why I was not singing. I was overwhelmed by the outpouring of communication from all over the country.

With the leisure to reflect, I took time to fill some of the blank pages in my diary. "I am swamped by flowers and cards," I wrote. "It begins to look as if there's more glory in being sick than in being a workhorse. It's nice having so many people concerned about me, although I don't think I'll try anything so drastic in the future.

"Both my current and past Metropolitan managers, Johnson and Bing, sent me flowers (yellow roses from Mr. Bing) and called, as did an unbelievable number of my conductors, colleagues and business associates. An incredible number of friends and fans have written and called. The cumulative effect of all this attention, together with all the time I've had to think, have given me a chance to get my concentration off my work for a moment. This is the first time since I left Wheeling for Boston that I've been able to look around and see where I am."

Not then, however, nor at any time did I ever seem to know how good my work was in relation to my time. I was driven by an anxious desire to excel and was very seldom satisfied with what I had done because I always knew I could do it better. Recognition never reassured me very much.

However, I found those first days of recovery rewarding. I got glimpses of how fulfilling the past 10 years had really been. I received so many evidences of affection that it seemed finally that all the hard work, the anxieties and, sometimes, the tears had not been wholly in vain. I began to believe that I really meant something to a great many people. This was a wonderful discovery, for in losing myself in the whirl of my career, I saw I had lost perspective on my life as a whole.

Only the night before my appendix rebelled, I had been walking with Edwin along familiar New York streets almost in tears, asking, "Where am I going? What is there for me to go on to? What is my goal?" And suddenly, like an answer from God, the next night I lay under the big light on the operating table. Was it cause or effect? My ailment was real enough, but perhaps the provocation had been my own inner dissatisfactions. Psychosomatic? Maybe.

I recuperated at a leisurely pace (they treated appendicitis seriously in those days), and was ordered not to perform for the remainder of January. But toward the end of the month I returned to Paul Althouse to work myself back into vocal shape. It took only this single step to the front lines—the hectic beat of New York City and the urgency of starting over—to rouse tiny prickles and stirrings of discontent.

I began to feel apprehensive, without knowing why, unless I was simply low in energy. In one way, I would have been delighted to retire from the whole scene; but then I'd see stories about my colleagues, hear what they were doing or feel someone was getting an assignment I thought should be mine and the old gnawing began. Weren't those the same things that had been going through my mind before my appendix stopped them? And I thought I had it all figured out! Does one ever?

I decided that hard work was the solution and that the first thing to do was the very best job I could with the Marschallin. And I did. If it is true that when in doubt one should do what one knows best, I made the right decision. In my case, this was to make music.

When I returned home from the hospital, my husband had presented me with a magnificent antique sterling silver tea service purchased at Vardis and registered at Harrod's in London. I was overcome at first; it was pretty impressive. Then I became uneasily aware under the surface that the tea service, like everything else, was a gesture from Ed, but a gift *I* would pay the bill for. Edwin had become a wine connoisseur as a Chevalier du Tastevin and a member of the Gourmet Society. He began building a collection of expensive wines, and both our city and country homes boasted more and more elaborate purchases, particularly antique furniture, rugs and art.

For me an "entourage" was no longer a symbol of success; it was necessary to keep things going. There was always at least one secretary, a personal PR representative, a manager and an accountant, plus a maid in the New York apartment who usually accompanied us to Melodie Hill. When we could get one, we had a permanent major domo of sorts in the country to maintain the house and grounds.

Gradually, as we worked into the 1950s, life began to have a hollow ring to it. There was so much going on, so many people, many of them not even my friends, and so much "politics" that while I loved my work, the joy began to drift away. I was carrying on in an emotional vacuum. My husband had long since ceased to pursue any independent career of his own, involving himself totally in mine and joining the Davidson office in an undefined capacity which was rarely comfortable for him or anyone else. As early as 1947 Jim Davidson began to urge me to step out on my own and leave Ed behind. Then others started pressuring me to leave him until I finally had to command both family and friends to keep hands off my marriage. I fought a losing battle. There were almost daily crises and I constantly found myself uneasily in the middle, juggling wounded egos and walking a precarious emotional tightrope while trying to patch differences and keep everything in place.

I often felt both manipulated and maneuvered, like an inanimate object, a commodity discussed, debated, packaged and sold. This stirred up some of my early Wheeling memories of feeling trapped and helpless to determine my own life. I began to wonder sometimes just for what or for whom I was working so hard. One night after a conference with Ed and Jim Davidson and another long discussion with Ed about my future, I reviewed the substance of our "conference" and what "we" had decided. "This year the personality of Steber must be set, finally. This means analyzing and choosing the lovely, the fine, the beautiful and positive points of the personality spiritually, vocally and physically. Edwin assures me he will spare nothing to provide me with the best designers, the best publicity, the best representation he can find and, if I will do certain things, he feels I can finally take the place that I have been striving for and just missing these past few years.

"I must at all times act like Eleanor Steber, 'the lovely, beautiful, glamorous opera, radio and concert artist. . . America's great lyric-dramatic soprano', 'the Metropolitan Opera soprano who has enough glamour to start a new Golden Age of Opera all by herself.' (So *they* have written about me!)"

Then, in parenthesis and with dark underlinings, I concluded that while I wanted to believe such accolades and, indeed, enjoyed them at a superficial level, they were in conflict with my inner vision of myself. I never related to what I saw in the mirror. Even as I was growing up, all I could see was my damned droopy eyes, a funny face and pouty lips and straight, straight hair; yet in my imagination I saw myself as someone very beautiful. But the closest I've ever come to it was when I was costumed and made up for roles like Manon, the Countess or the Marschallin. I just never thought I was beautiful and if someone said I was, I wondered why.

I had no confidence in my own "self" at all. Oh, I believed in my voice and what I could do with it, thank God, but that was all. But I had never been taught to decide things for myself, never even allowed to pick out my own clothes as a child. Mother brought home material and clothes from my Aunt's dry goods store and I wore what mother thought best. She decided everything. Mother was the real prima donna; I copied her.

But I hardly gave a thought to all that back in 1949. All I knew was that everyone was trying to shape me into a different personality. Certainly no one suggested I should find out who *I was* or that I should just be myself. Even Edwin, way back in Boston, had urged me to contain my natural exuberance and "act like a lady." I kept trying to please everyone, but all it did in the end was create these terrible angry conflicts within me. I was pretty mixed up. I looked around and began to wonder where in the dickens *I* was. I mean, where was I in all this business. Which of all these people was I supposed to be, and which, if any, was *me*!

The other thing that kept popping up was a creeping concern about my lusty social drinking. "Why," I'd ask myself, "is so much importance placed on this silly fetish, fad, habit or what have you, called *drinking*? Why it should be so important to me I cannot understand, when I know I am an artist from whom people expect a dedicated way of thinking."

I was still in my early thirties when these conflicts nudged themselves increasingly to my attention. I was a strong, vigorous and determined woman, and when I became concerned about my drinking then, I'd simply knock it off. New régimes, which included every variety of discipline, self-imposed and otherwise, were my constant companions. So was rebellion. I took a stab at every new diet which came along. My most steadfast mentor in this quest was Diana Ross, whose health salon on West 55th Street was my home away from home. I recorded each new diet, each half-pound variation in weight as conscientiously as I listed my concert engagements and the gowns I wore at each or diagrammed my stage directions in my notebook. I fought an unending battle against each pound, each inch I gained whenever I broke the slightest bit from my strict regimes.

What held me together was my music. It seemed that no matter what kind of turmoil went on around me, I could turn it off instantly when I started to work. My saving grace, then and always, was my ability to shed emotional baggage whenever I had to sing. It was as if nothing could touch me when I walked into the opera house, rehearsal hall or concert auditorium. Once in a theater—any theater—I was a free soul.

Mother once told me that singing gave her greater satisfaction than any human emotion, including sex. Knowing myself to be a much more passionate woman than my mother, I rejected this. And I continued to resist as well as resent the idea, really, because I didn't want to think I was so like her. But when it comes right down to it, it's been the same for me.

I was always so in love—not with people so much, but with what I was singing and the roles I was portraying—that my only true identity lay in my work. All my emotional vitality went into that, no matter how I felt off stage.

I don't mean there was no nervousness or tension about singing. Of course there was; but if I could be quiet and prepare in my own way, once I was in my own dressing room I thought only of what I had to do. This was my private world, the one place I kept all to myself.

Wild, Wild West

I could not see it then, but the whole structure of my life as I had come to rely upon it had begun to crumble. To begin with, I had come to an angry parting of the ways with my manager Jim Davidson.

My years with him had never been entirely smooth, although certainly I had him to thank for my initial Firestone contract. The "Knoxville" business, of course, had left me wondering, and I felt Davidson's behavior about and toward my husband was degrading and insulting.

In many ways Jim had proved an efficient manager for those five years, and he had wonderful people working for him. He was very clever to a point, but he was also a manipulator, too much a wheeler-dealer. I finally decided he was not representing me properly when I discovered that he was attempting to subvert my position with Firestone to bring his other clients onto the program. I had no intention of compromising my Firestone contract, so that when Jim dragged his feet, I gritted my teeth and called Chuck Ryan out in Akron and made my own deal, maintaining the terms I had enjoyed in previous years, Mr. Davidson's new tactics notwithstanding. Jim was furious that I had successfully negotiated my own contract and we agreed to sever our relationship.

For a while Edwin took over all the business of my career and negotiated my return to Columbia Concerts, then headed by Arthur Judson. Bill Judd was assigned to handle my bookings and he became, in effect, my business manager, and a lifetime friend. It was a great relief to be back in the fold of Columbia Concerts, and with my health renewed and my business affairs settled, I finished the 1950–51 opera season, went on tour, recorded the official Metropolitan "Faust" with Eugene Conley

The Steber family (left to right): Mrs. Ida Nolte Steber, a boyish Eleanor, sister Lucile, William C. Steber, and brother Bill.

Steber just before graduation from the New England Conservatory in Boston.

Homecoming special in Wheeling after winning the Metropolitan Opera Auditions, courtesy the B&O Railroad. (Photo: Cress-Wheeling.)

(*Above*) Steber celebrates with tenor-coach Paul Althouse and her "champion," conductor Erich Leinsdorf, following her Metropolitan Opera debut. (*Below*) Unbeatable *Figaro* trio: Steber, the Countess, John Brownlee, Count Almaviva, and Bidu Sayao, Susanna.

Eleanor and husband Edwin Bilby
during World War II.

Steber with idol, Lawrence Tibbett, and New York Mayor Fiorello LaGuardia.
(United Press International Photo)

A young Steber poised on the brink of fame.

After the first of four Met premieres, *Abduction from the Seraglio,* Steber and general manager Edward Johnson share congratulatory smiles.

The Voices of Firestone: Steber, composer Idabelle Firestone, conductor Howard Barlow.

Now a prima donna, Steber presents vocal scholarships to officials of her alma mater with adored teacher, William F. Whitney (with goatee), proudly looking on.

(*Above*) Steber at Metropolitan Opera Opening Night with movie star Jeannette MacDonald, left, and satirist Cornelia Otis Skinner. (*Below*) Conductor Fritz Reiner signs a baton for Steber's valuable collection of first-performance conductors' batons.

Steber signs first post-WWII contract with Wieland Wagner to sing Elsa at Bayreuth.
(United Press International Photo)

Steber and Carola (the horse) ride
through a park in Florence, Italy,
rehearsing for *Girl of the Golden West.*

As *Charley's Aunt* on Broadway with Darryl Hickman.

Kicking up her heels backstage with bosom buddy from *Così* and *Arabella*, Blanche Thebom.

Giving her all in a Met performance of *Manon Lescaut*. (Photo by Sedge LeBlang)

for Columbia Records, and got to work on two new roles: Fiordiligi for the Met's new "Così fan Tutte," and Amelia for a summer production of "Amelia Goes to the Ball" in Central City, Colorado.

Following my annual homecoming concert in Wheeling, I left everyone behind, for once, and flew west alone to begin "Amelia" rehearsals. I was unusually lighthearted, even for me, and eagerly anticipated a happy time free from all family and business obligations.

I had flown all night to be on time for the first rehearsal and, although I had worked on the part in New York with conductor Tibor Kozma, I didn't feel as prepared as I would like to have been. I soon discovered that there had been no rehearsing to speak of before my arrival, so everyone was in roughly the same state.

During that first grueling five-hour rehearsal, Kozma began to scold the young chap playing Amelia's lover for mistakes I knew were at least partly mine. I don't mind being called for my own errors, but my sense of fair play is always outraged when my faults are ignored and a lesser known artist is chastised in front of the whole company. I stood it as long as I could, then stopped the rehearsal, stepped to the footlights and asked Mr. Kozma not to blame someone else for my mistakes. The chorus and other soloists grinned and all but cheered. Mr. Kozma was somewhat less delighted.

Any conductor's arbitrary verbal lashings at defenseless supporting players inspired outbursts of indignation from me on several occasions when I felt I was the only one in a position to speak up, all of which won me friends in the ranks and a reputation for some "temperament" among a few conductors.

The atmosphere in Central City was relaxed and informal. After dinner that night, I continued to work on Amelia with the cast and Maestro Taussig for almost three hours, and then we all took off for the Gold Coin, the oldest saloon in this former ghost town, for a whopper of a stein of beer.

Dress rehearsal the following day was performed in the afternoon before a packed house of Gilpin County residents and went quite well. Because of my limited preparation, I played Amelia almost on sheer inspiration, but I seemed to have done a rather comical job. The audience loved it and while there were some rough spots, it really *went*.

When it was over, I met some of the company for cocktails. We sat around and gaffed a bit and before long it was too late for dinner at the Teller House, so it was off to the 'Old Fashioned' (a popular old-time saloon). Rick Ricketson began to ply us with champagne, and before long the evening turned into a rousing party crowded into my suite which, I might add, had once housed the legendary Mae West.

Well, that certainly was not the most appropriate sort of evening before an opening performance, particularly at that altitude! But party or not, I arose early the next day, ate a hearty breakfast with some of the company, and threw myself into the jolly spirit of this rehabilitated mining town.

To my delight, the "Rough Riders," a brilliantly-costumed band of riders representing the original denizens of the old West, rode into town that afternoon. I wanted to join them, but the directors asked me not to for fear that the horses might get skittish and I would be hurt. I could understand this, but I was disappointed. I settled for parading around town in my own Frontier Suit, adding something, I hoped, to the local color.

After the performance, which went well, I swaggered on down to the Golden Nugget where I was finally "prevailed upon" to sing. Prevailed upon? Hardly. It's almost harder to stop me than to "prevail upon me."

The night life in Central City was exhausting but exciting, and the fun didn't stop any of us from spending our daylight hours hiking into the mountains and exploring the territory. On July 17, my birthday was celebrated with friends at a local country club. Then back to Central City for a party I threw for the cast, with sandwiches and cakes topped off with champagne brought by Vera Gibbs of the Metropolitan Opera Guild. The kids in the company surprised me by singing "Happy Birthday" from the balconies looking down over the Teller House patio. How wonderful to celebrate amid the camaraderie of my "partners in crime"!

I was enjoying a freedom I had never known—out from the shadow of the Met and the watchful eyes of husband and family. There in Central City I could laugh as boisterously as I pleased without a disapproving glance, stride freely around the town, wear what I chose, or regale an appreciative audience with my slightly bawdy jokes, and laugh as loudly as I liked. I loved it and so, apparently, did everyone else. It was a revelation!

During those two weeks of performances, except for a few matinees, I spent my days horseback riding, exploring and being entertained and living in unaccustomed close fellowship with my singing colleagues. After the evening performances, we regularly trooped off to the Golden Nugget or the Gold Coin where I joined the gang, delivered a few arias for the crowd, sang a few duets with the boys, and danced with everyone.

Amid the rollicking fun and laughter of one such evening, we were eating dinner when I looked up and was startled to discover a pair of dancing Irish eyes in a friendly Irish face, piercing into mine with unmistakable intensity. Unsought and unexpected, our eyes met with the sudden electricity which sets up a buzzing in the ears, turns knees to water, the heart into a kettledrum, and sweeps away the heartiest appetite. For once I left my steak untouched on the plate.

I was transformed in that moment. No more prima donna, but just me, a girl named Eleanor, caught up in an all-absorbing emotion which brought time to a standstill. I was romanced, courted, and kissed with strength and tenderness I had never known. I was swept off my feet through an ecstatic evening colored and magnified by the beauty of the Colorado night.

Everything about that night remained so vivid and I was filled with the wonder of it all, an extraordinary idyll! The night was magical, an almost full moon above, scudding clouds, romance in the air and champagne in our veins! And somewhere along Bear Creek Canyon stood a post with two stones upon it, and further down, if one were to look, one might find a broken champagne bottle and two glasses—a pledge to the night!

Does it all sound like a scene straight out of a movie romance of the thirties and forties? It was what I had longed for. I never lost a yearning for the romance and adventure I had lived vicariously in the movies and books. And it was an element of excitement which had been almost totally missing in an almost passionless marriage, more and more dominated by my career.

While only for the briefest moment did I consider the interlude more than a delicious kind of private dream I had lived out, it had awakened something in me which was to change the course of my life forever.

My father always said I led with my heart, and I'm sure I tried to give as much of myself as I could to anyone who won my affections. But that something in me which made me a performer always gave me a kind of subliminal awareness that I was simply caught up in a sequence of personal soap operas.

In later years, I more consciously enjoyed the momentary diversion of role playing almost as a game, completely disassociated from the serious commitments of my real life. That came later. But for a moment in Central City, the heavens shook and the emotional blinders dropped from my eyes. After 20 years of constant study, work and the do-or-die urgencies of performance, I fell victim to one of those soul-shaking infatuations to which the unguarded heart is so terribly vulnerable.

Così Fan Tutte

I returned to New York determined to pick up life as if nothing had happened. My husband and I escaped for a few days to Atlantic City, but as an attempt to recapture days long past it was about as successful as placing a band-aid on a compound fracture. Then Ed, who had remained in the Air Force Reserve, was called back to active duty during the Korean War. Although he was assigned to nearby Mitchell Field, it was obvious he could no longer manage any part of my career. So I signed on Martha Moore Smith, former public relations director for the Cincinnati Symphony, to join me as a personal PR representative.

In October I set out alone with Jimmy on a concert tour which would take me back west to the home country of my secret Central City passion. However much I debated seeing him again, wisdom had nothing to say about it. Our brief reunion, however sweet and exciting, was deeply disturbing, and emotions I had never before encountered kept me off balance. My little battle of conscience seems so naïve in retrospect. No matter how often I rebelled against my strict moral upbringing, and I did, I was tormented by guilt.

Those few who were truly close to me, surely including my husband, knew that something had thrown me out of orbit, for I was not only burning my candle at both ends, but in the middle as well.

While entrained from Chicago to Duluth I poured out my secret infatuation to Jimmy, then cried myself to sleep. I woke the next day to wild, blustery weather, well suited to my mood and fancy. I had expected to be in dreadful spirits, but strangely arose gloriously relaxed, alive and in love. Rehearsing songs like "Passigiata" and "Le Balcon" filled me with such sheer ecstasy I could hardly stand it. The concert that evening was wonderfully received, probably because I sang it right out of my love.

During that tour, I poured everything into my songs. My pent-up feelings continued to spill over and out of control. I finished the tour in Charleston, West Virginia and went home to spend a few days with my parents. During that brief refuge in the home of my youth, everything boiled over. Distraught to the point of hysteria, I was unable or, probably unwilling, to tell my family what was bothering me. Instead, I pretended a gaiety I did not feel, drank too much and eventually cried myself to sleep.

Riding back to New York on the train, I realized my emotional stability and physical well-being were seriously threatened, so I made a tormented decision to put an end to my "Central City affair." On the train, I wrote the letter which I thought would slam the door on it forever, although I couldn't have been more mixed up and driven by terrible emotions churning within me.

While I was back in New York, my family gathered its considerable forces together to help me, without knowing what was wrong. In a letter of passionate concern and unsparing bluntness, mother urged me to see a doctor and unload some of my career. She thought my work was getting me down, instead of holding me together as it was. "How you did such a bang-up concert in Charleston with so little rest," mother wrote, "all on nervous energy, was all Lucile and I talked about as we drove home."

Mother minced no words. "You have done yourself enough honor in these 12 hard-working years. Now you must throw off everything that is wearing you down and promise not to drink even a glass of sherry until you build up your nerves. We know the burden you are bearing and we cannot stand to see you going on and working as madly as you are.

"Who cares about a bigger house? Who cares about 'prestige'? Who will care about Eleanor Steber if her health cracks?" Reassuring me that the family stood ready to strengthen and help me gain my heart's desire, mother wrote with the ferocity of a lioness defending her young. Her last lines held something of a threat as she made it clear she wouldn't hesitate to intervene instantly in my behalf if she felt it necessary. "We are still very strong," she declared simply, "in every way."

Daddy, who hardly ever wrote me a letter, added his a few days later. "Darling, Miracle Daughter," he wrote, "I am worried and truly in distress about you. It seems to me you must be in a bad state of mind about something you cannot tell us. I fear that you may be approaching a nervous breakdown or physical collapse over something in your private life. Perhaps the life you are living, your music, I mean, has been entirely too strenuous for you; but I am inclined to suspect that there is something more than your career that is causing you to seek escape. You talk in riddles."

"Eleanor, dear," he concluded, "I am unhappy because you are unhappy. You're a wonderful daughter and you have accomplished marvelous works, but these works, this success mean nothing if you are not happy."

I had no answers, but there was one sure cure-all — work — and I had a load of it ahead of me. I was scheduled for seven major roles with the Metropolitan and two of them were brand new. (Of the seven, I would have orchestra rehearsals for only two.)

I was assigned to work with conductor Fritz Stiedry on both Desdemona in Verdi's "Otello" and Fiordiligi in the Met's spanking new production of "Così fan Tutte." I had learned both roles during the earlier months of 1951, in spare moments between all my other chores.

Now I had to do my dramatic homework as well. I knew that, as a new production, "Così" would receive the full treatment with plenty of rehearsal and Mr. Bing had already announced that the great actor, Alfred Lunt, would stage the production. "Otello," on the other hand, was an ongoing production which would get routine preparation. It was only my third Verdi role and I wanted extra help.

Way back in 1945 I had walked into Sardi's restaurant one night, and was talking to a group of people when I heard a distinctive male voice proclaim: "My God, here's the greatest Mozart singer of them all!" It was José Ferrer, then performing Iago to Paul Robeson's "Othello" on Broadway. José's wife at that time was Uta Hagen, the production's Desdemona. Both José and Uta were avid music lovers.

I made a point of attending their "Othello" as soon as possible and was received backstage with open arms, after which we all went out and had a gay old time together. So, naturally, when it came time to coach Desdemona, Uta Hagen was my natural choice. Uta was playing "St. Joan" on Broadway as I prepared my Desdemona, but she seemed delighted at the chance for us to work together. We had shared an immediate rapport when we met, and I felt I'd known her all my life.

Before we began to work on the opera itself, she insisted we read through the full Shakespeare text together so I could get my basic insight from the source. Then she put me through my paces, working on Desdemona, scene by scene, coaching me chiefly on the character, emotional reactions and development of Desdemona, leaving the specifics of action to the province of the Met's stage director. When the Met began stage rehearsals, she came to watch. I discovered that my sessions with Hagen had given me a serenity unusual to me in a new role.

After rehearsals she ran to meet me. "I am amazed that anyone can encompass a role so completely in such a short time. You are now doing instinctively what I would have told you to do if I had directed you myself. You've not only taken and used everything I gave, but you have gone way beyond it."

Coincident with all of this, we rehearsed and opened "Così fan Tutte" on December 28, 1951. This delectable opera in English brought together a happy cast of good companions including Blanche Thebom as Dorabella, John Brownlee as Don Alfonso, Richard Tucker and Frank Guarrera as the lovers and Patrice Munsel, Despina."

We had all greatly anticipated working with Alfred Lunt, but I suspect that either he came to us expecting to set his stylistic imprint on a production which had already been blocked for him, or that coming from the legitimate theater and the logical procedures of dialogue, he was somewhat non-plussed when faced with the need to devise directions for repeated musical phrases and recapitulations. There was no little confusion until John and Blanche, who had done "Così" together at Glyndebourne, worked it out. Even so, I sometimes felt we should have had traffic signals for a few of those moves we made.

What Alfred Lunt gave us was style—highly imaginative and detailed 17th century style, smoothing and polishing our movements, adding finesse and grace. He himself added to the charm of the production by appearing on stage before the performance as the lights dimmed. Dressed as a servant, splendidly turned out in salmon velvet knee britches and towering white wig, he ceremoniously lighted the ersatz candle-footlights with a long taper. Then with a low bow, he gestured to Dr. Stiedry that the performance was his.

What a delight this opera was! I loved the pure vocal deliciousness of it, and no matter how many times I sang it, I was amazed that I had been able to encompass it so well; it had seemed such an impossible task when it was offered to me the previous year. In a very special way, I think Fiordiligi gave me more pure pleasure than any other role.

Everything about the opera was just great: the duets, the trios, quintets and, of course, Fiordiligi's two big arias, especially the famous "Come scoglio," one hell of an aria which I always looked forward to with great zest because I had it so well in the voice that it always felt fantastic to sing.

The first two performances bridged the old year and 1952 by five days. After the second performance I was relaxed and thoroughly happy with it. Not only did it seem to play better than the first night, but I felt more comfortable in my own performance.

I purposely avoided reading the reviews because I didn't want anything to spoil this wonderful feeling and I went along quite happily until the following week when I glanced through a weekly news magazine without thinking. The whole review was about Alfred Lunt's marvelous staging, and referred to the singers only incidentally as Dresden dolls brilliantly manipulated by Mr. Lunt. Our singing was ignored, and our names mentioned only in passing.

We were all furious, particularly since we knew how much the production owed to Blanche and John. We loved Lunt, but we hadn't forgotten a few digs like the day he described us as "looking like bowls of rancid oatmeal." We huddled together before the Saturday broadcast matinee like mischievous kids and decided it would serve everyone right if we just walked through our Dresden Doll act without singing. This gave us back our sense of humor.

I had really lost mine, however, the first day I read the review and very nearly got myself in the soup. The story so outraged me that I flew to the phone to tell Mr. Bing just what I thought. Fortunately he was out, so I ended up pouring my wrath on poor Ann Gordon in the Met public relations office. The outburst blew itself out, like most of my tempers, in a matter of minutes, and by evening I was wondering what I had gotten all steamed up about. "Così fan Tutte" fell into its proper place as the highlight of the season.

As we moved further into January, I began to suffer increasingly severe attacks of asthma which had been a familiar, but relatively minor problem until all the emotional conflicts started building up inside of me. My continued upset chose this point of physical vulnerability to burst out.

Still, throughout the month I sang at the Met every three or four days, adding the Puccini "Manon" to my schedule as I prepared for my first Desdemona, which was scheduled, wouldn't you know, for a broadcast matinee on February 9. Suddenly someone discovered that the last performance of "Così" was scheduled for that same evening. Alfred Lunt came backstage during a January "Così" bemoaning the fact that I wouldn't be singing the final performance of "his" opera because of the matinee. "That creates no problem for me," I told him. "I'd be perfectly willing to do both performances if the management will permit it."

I had nearly done it before when I was brought in to sing Donna Elvira one night after I had sung "Meistersinger" at the matinee, and a number of times I'd done "Fausts" and "Figaros" on succeeding days, which I thought was actually much harder. However, this may have been the first time anyone had "volunteered" to sing two major roles, including a debut role, on the same day.

Mr. Bing dutifully came to see me and said, "Look, my dear, this is entirely up to you."

"Oh, I can do it," I assured him (although if the operas had been scheduled in reverse order, I might have decided otherwise).

The day of what came to be called my "double-header," Uta Hagen arrived at my dressing room with a bunch of mimosa in her arms and a little package which she left on the dressing room table, demanding I open it before the performance. Bubbling with as much anticipation as if she were going on herself, Uta said, "I don't know if mimosa is considered a good luck offering for opera, but it certainly is for the theater. I'm so nervous and excited, I can't stand it. This is going to be a long day!"

While I was dressing, I opened Uta's little box. In it I found the beautiful moon ring that she herself had worn in every performance when she had played Desdemona on Broadway. Her note ended: "This now belongs to the new Desdemona."

My Desdemona was an unqualified triumph. If I had sometimes found the New York music critics equivocal in their judgements as I grew up musically in their musical hearing, they showed no such equivocation now.

Virgil Thomson, whose attack on my 1950 Town Hall recital had shattered me, now found my Desdemona "perfect from every point of view." Louis Biancolli of the World Telegram described it as "beautiful in every respect." The other reviews were equally rewarding.

Between my debut as Desdemona and the evening "Così," I rested in my dressing room, downed a good-sized steak and a bit of champagne from Sherry's restaurant on the parterre level of the old Met, and then proceeded to sing Fiordiligi to a fare-thee-well, a performance which prompted cheers and outpourings far exceeding anything that had greeted any of my earlier performances.

This feat, which was witnessed by two sold-out houses, won all the public and press acclaim we had failed to win for the "Knoxville" project and Town Hall. Many people like Uta Hagen, friends, and my loyal and vociferous members of the Eleanor Steber Music Club, attended both performances. Critics and public were dazzled by the tour de force. For once I had had a challenge that was big and exciting enough to suit me, and I reveled in it.

Playwright Noel Coward, who came back to visit after the "Così," understood completely. He said, "My deah, you should do it every day, and I want always to hear your second performance!"

We made a big thing out of it, of course, for its news value; but I never doubted I could bring it off. I'm always "up" and ready to sing again after every performance, something which seems much easier to me than to do back-to-back performances on succeeding days where I have to get myself up again after an overnight letdown. But two was enough. I slept well that night.

Mixed Bag

The much-publicized operatic double-header had been more nearly a catastrophe than the public knew, since two days before the big event I had suffered the worst asthma attack of my life. Whenever the tensions in my marriage worsened, so did my asthma; the parallel increase in my smoking simply added to the problem. (Yes, I smoked — had since I was a kid. Nothing I liked better than smoking a corncob pipe on the back stoop in Wheeling.)

Yet, it never occurred to me to cancel a performance (or stop smoking) because of it, for I had an unshakable faith that it would never interfere with my singing. So I tossed off my two operas in one day, rested for 24 hours, then set off for Washington to sing at the National Women's Press Club dinner, a prestigious event which was to honor President Harry Truman and his cabinet.

Another attack of asthma hit me at about six o'clock, but I steadfastly refused to cancel, demanding and getting a shot of adrenalin and a canister of pure oxygen which I inhaled in my dressing room. I got through it splendidly. The only casualty was my gown, which split a seam when I took a last huge breath to carry me through the climax of the "Fledermaus" Czardas.

As I boarded the train back to New York, the asthma flared up again and I was racked by convulsive spasms. During the endless four-and-a-half-hour trip, I struggled for every breath.

Once in New York I was rushed to the doctor, who treated me not only for asthma but for a mild pneumonia which had apparently aggravated the asthma. With stopgap treatment I got through a couple of Met performances and a Firestone broadcast, but on February 27 they put me into St. Clare's Hospital where the then-new miracle steroid ACTH was dripped into me intravenously for a full week.

When I left the hospital I was bloated from the steroid, with the moon face which was typical of such treatment. Against medical advice I taxied directly to the Metropolitan to sing Desdemona. That was the night my Otello, Ramon Vinay, got so carried away with his own dramatics that he threw me down on my "ACTH" so hard I bounced. Oh, Dr. Stiedry was furious with him!

After the performance, armed with my own supply of ACTH, I boarded a midnight train and headed out of New York. I had sung the "Otello" March 3. On March 4 I sang a concert in Weirton, West Virginia and two days later another in Durant, Oklahoma.

With every mile that my train sped south and west, my asthma diminished. While it never completely left me, it also never recurred with the ferocity of those 1952 attacks. Forever after I have carried little pocket inhalers which instantly clear any wheezing or incipient asthmatic spasms. It was a wonder I missed so few rehearsals, and those only in the early morning of bad days before I could "clear my pipes." I never missed a performance because of asthma.

So absolute was my speedy recovery on this road trip that the night after my Durant concert I raced to Kilgore, Texas to fill in for an ailing Nelson Eddy. To get to Kilgore we had to take the only chauffeured vehicle available, bizarre as it was—a comfortable black Cadillac hearse. I slept like a babe as it sped through the night.

Back home, my friends and doctor persuaded me that emotional tensions and my marriage problems were triggering my asthma. I was willing to try anything, so I agreed to talk with a psychiatrist to see if we could get to the source of my difficulties. Whether my visits to the psychiatrist accomplished anything or not, I don't know, since cortisone had already considerably relieved my symptoms, but I knew we had problems, whether they were responsible for the asthma or not.

Despite all the symbols of success, my marriage with Edwin had been disintegrating for years. Our occasional attempts to recapture romantic evenings with intimate dinners accompanied by our cherished wines invariably ended in arguments so terrible, and about which I remember little or nothing, except that my dalmatian, Beppo, frequently hid under our bed during our thunderous outbursts.

What had happened to those two idealistic innocents from Boston who little more than a decade before had shared their dreams, music and poetry? Edwin was going through tortures of his own, which he was unable to explain either to me or to himself, and there were times when he suffered blackouts and found himself inexplicably in some strange part of New York. I was at my wits end to know what to do about either of us.

It was in the darkest hour of a night in this period that I ran from the house and walked through the darkness for blocks, ending at the East River Bridge where I gazed down and contemplated release in the dark waters.

But there is always tomorrow; always another chance. Surely something good would happen; *must* happen! And if I succumbed to the lure of oblivion, I would never know what might have happened on that tomorrow; nor, in my own egocentricity, would I be there to witness the effect of my demise. I don't know how consciously I thought such things through at that moment, but finally I did turn around and wearily trudged back to my life.

My schedule stopped the sessions with the psychiatrist, which was just as well, for I became impatient with all the brooding introspection and issued myself an ultimatum to stop feeling sorry for myself and get on with my life. And so I did, through a concert tour during which the same questions nagged at me, hopelessly begging a solution.

Toward the end of the tour I wrote: "Tonight's concert went vocally well, but I am mentally and emotionally quite exhausted. As I sang my songs I felt empty and unreal and most unlike myself. I seem to have no real drive this year to take me through my concerts. They practically sing themselves, but without inspiration they become merely routine, and to me, to be just 'routine' is a terrible comedown."

It was time to recharge my spiritual batteries, and I knew it. I also knew that if our marriage was to endure, Ed and I had to have a chance for complete renewal away from New York and the pulling and tugging of those around us. So with Ed scheduled to be released from the Air Force in mid-July, we planned a real vacation in Europe doing all the things we had ever dreamed. We set sail on the SS United States full of hope that this extended trip would cement our future together.

That summer of 1952 was a real "Rhine Wine Journey." We visited every vineyard and *cave* from the Rhone Valley all the way up one side of the Rhine to Wiesbaden, and back down the Moselle side. We enjoyed a two-day visit with Eugene and Gretel Ormandy in their chalet in Switzerland, overlooking both the French and Swiss Alps. We were there on Swiss Liberation Day and saw the bonfires being lit on every mountain top, a custom since the days of William Tell.

We stopped at Lake Como, and spent five days in Venice before driving back to Salzburg where we saw the world premiere of Richard Strauss's last opera, "Die Liebe der Danae" and a unique performance of "The Magic Flute" in the Grand Riding School. We heard Hilde Gueden in a charming performance of "Don Pasquale" and a dynamic Verdi "Requiem" conducted by Victor de Sabata.

Back in early January Mr. Bing and his new artistic director, Max Rudolf, had asked me to prepare the "Lohengrin" Elsa for the 1952–53 season. This surprised me because I hadn't anticipated singing any additional Wagner roles. I considered it carefully, unaware that even back in 1945 Lotte Lehmann had told a mutual friend that she thought Elsa would be ideal for me. Anyway, I began work on Elsa in New York with Herman Weigert, and when I arrived in Salzburg, coached some more with Prof. Heinrich Schmidt, assistant to Wilhelm Furtwängler at the Vienna State Opera.

After Salzburg we stopped at Bayreuth, where in the post-war renaissance the two Wagner grandsons had begun to create whole new concepts in production. I was all-but speechless at meeting these direct descendants of the great composer. Then, at Herman Weigert's suggestion, they invited me to audition for them in the historic Festspielhaus.

Once again in totally unfamiliar territory as I stood alone on that huge stage trying to see something or someone in the darkness beyond me, I shook with almost terminal stage fright, which became embarrassingly evident when I forgot the words in the middle of "Elsa's Traüm," of all things, and floundered around until I picked them up again. I was certain it was a total disaster, but they must have heard something they wanted, because they immediately invited me to return to Bayreuth the following summer to sing Elsa.

What a tremendous lift to my flagging spirits! I was to become the first American to sing Elsa at Bayreuth since 1894 when New England's Lillian Nordica had sung it there. And what a coincidence, because although our careers were separated by nearly 60 years, we had both learned our craft in Boston.

The whole trip, which was to have been the honeymoon Ed and I never had, and which I hoped might bring us close together again, only drove us further apart. We were just going through the motions. The only congenial moments of the trip were those devoted to the delicious cuisine and delectable wines served to us throughout Europe. To my chagrin, I embarked for New York 20 pounds heavier than when I had left. Nevertheless, the new sights and the change of scene had refreshed me, and I was eager to return home and lose myself in work.

Back at the Met, after a whopping big fall concert tour during which I did a concert almost every other night, I sang a season of all-German opera, assuming one remembers that Mozart was German. I began with my first "Lohengrin," staged by Dino Yannapoulos; once more having to debut a major role in New York. For once, however, I felt lucky, even under those demanding circumstances, that I could get Elsa locked securely under my musical belt before I had to face the tribunal at Bayreuth.

I also sang Eva again. I felt particularly good about Eva this time. "In the first place," I noted, "I made no mistakes!" (I never could rationalize the smallest musical error on my part, no matter how inconspicuous to others. *I* would know I'd muffed it, and *I* wanted it right!) "Last night," I continued with satisfaction, "I was never even aware of the prompter, and I felt like Eva for the first time in all the times I've done the part. And I—even I—knew I was in excellent voice. The 'quintet' was like a dream and the rest of the cast was marvelous. Mr. Reiner was in rare conducting form. All told, an A-1 performance and the applause from the sold-out house was terrific!"

The Met gave no quarter, even after such a long evening's work, and the next day I was back from 10:30 a.m. to 5 p.m. working on "Così fan Tutte." "Così" remained one of Mr. Bing's best productions. What a delight! But how we missed Alfred Lunt to brighten our days with his inimitable presence.

With "Lohengrin" set for Bayreuth, other European engagements were worked out for me, and at last I could look forward to singing in Vienna.

My annual January negotiations with the Met in early 1953 were discouraging. The next season was still very much up in the air. Once again, in spite of all my successes, I was beset with the doubts, fears and frustrations which always bedeviled me about my position at the Met.

I had now been singing at the Metropolitan for 13 years and, with a few exceptions in the beginning, always in major roles; yet even the year I sang my two "Otello/Così" performances in one day, the Met was paying me only $500 to $700 a performance and it didn't seem as if they were going to budge much beyond this for my next season. Firestone paid me $2,000 for each half hour on the air, and my concert fees ranged from

$1,250 to $2,500, chicken feed today, but substantial then. The failure of the Met to grant appropriate financial recognition of my value to the company was the source of lifelong aggravation to me. It was always concerts and radio appearances which maintained my income in the six-figure bracket.

Yet neither then nor in the future did I speak out. I never voiced my dissatisfactions in public. I wouldn't have dared. I might have lost my job and, no matter what, I didn't want that. The Met was my home; it was where I belonged! So I kept my mouth shut and did as I was told.

In the meantime, Dimitri Mitropoulos again urged me to sing with him and the New York Philharmonic. My self-enforced musical separation from Mitropoulos had been terribly painful, but nothing had broken the special bond of affection and profound musical affinity between us. Once again we began to hunt for something special we could do together.

We settled on a little-known cycle of songs, "Les Nuits d'Été" by Hector Berlioz, set to poems of Theodore Gautier. The only orchestration was in the hands of Thor Johnson in Cincinnati; a single phone call to Thor, and the score was ours. Not only were the songs perfect for the range and timbre of my voice, I was acutely attuned to Gautier's poetry and Berlioz's soaring long lines. The orchestration was lush. "Les Nuits d'Été" has won broad popularity since I first sang these songs.

The song "Au Cimetière" will always be my favorite, however, for when I visited Vienna later that year, I wandered into the cemetery where Mozart is supposed to have been buried. No one knows where he lies, but I found the monument erected in his memory. At that time it was all overgrown and uncared-for; and suddenly the line "Connaisez-vous la blanche tombé" sprang into my mind as I stood in the soft twilight and heard the cooing of the mourning dove which had also caught Gautier's ear. When I finally recorded these songs, this piece evoked the most extraordinary feeling within me.

"Les Nuits d'Été" proved a miraculous welding of music and artists, music and text. The performance was scheduled for Easter Sunday, April 5, 1953. Arthur Judson, still head of Columbia Concerts, attended the final rehearsal. When it was over, this tough-minded, intimidating man approached me. "Now," he declared, "I concede that you are truly a great artist!" I cannot tell you what this meant to me. Mr. Judson was just not given to making such statements.

"It can hardly be a coincidence," wrote one reviewer after the concert, "that the best of Steber's singing is done under the guidance of Dimitri

Mitropoulos. Their complete understanding of what they want to do seems to give Steber an extra something. She appears to be freed from all restrictions and draws freely from a wide range of vocal resources. I have seldom heard her in such extraordinary voice. One would not think she had just finished a heavy season of opera and concert work. Even though singing with a symphony orchestra, she kept her shifts of emphasis delicate and restrained. She made fine use of exquisite coloring. Critics used adjectives like 'languorous' and 'hypnotic shimmer.' Her ease and beauty came not so much from her technical know-how as from the obvious love she felt for these songs."

Our Town Hall alliance was truly vindicated! Dimitri and I had once more joined forces to create an historic musical moment. I cherish the memory of this and all the music we made together. Within the year we recorded the six songs which comprise the cycle, plus three additional Berlioz songs, and it's comforting to know that after all these years, ours remains the definitive performance of this luscious music.

Dimitri must have felt much as I did, for after this experience he sent me a photograph which he inscribed: "To the singer of my heart." I treasure this as I do a letter from him at this same time in which he said: "I really feel each time I do music with you that I enjoy being alive. You are such a generous person and such a serious artist that it is a real pleasure for any musician to work with you. . .so enjoy yourself and keep yourself well, for what you have to offer the world is very precious."

Is it any wonder that my memories of this fantastic man and the music we made together are still so vivid?

Agitato

I returned to New York realizing that except for my music, life had become meaningless. I stood at the absolute peak of my success as an artist with all the engagements, acclaim and money I could want. I was working my head off, yet I was coming home to emptiness. The Park Avenue apartment had become the symbol of it.

The enchantment which began in Central City had turned me around so completely that I began to regard my entire life in an entirely new light. I was shocked to realize that I had reached 37 years before anything had ever touched the depths of me as a woman as that brief encounter had done.

It wasn't that I had been so terribly innocent, but I had gone straight from my rather protected home in Wheeling to school in Boston and had married the man I fell in love with in my first semester. For 20 years we had stuck together, always friends, but also always less and less lovers. Now we were living in two entirely different worlds.

I realized that our only chance lay in Ed's building a life and career for himself, but he had no interest in it. In addition, the conflicts between him and the rest of my staff grew worse daily. Now I realized I had to force the issue. So, early in 1953, I decided to close the Park Avenue apartment, make Melodie Hill my permanent home and live in a hotel when I had to be in New York. It was a painful decision, but to a degree, it worked. After I sang "Les Nuits d'Été" with Dimitri in April, Ed got started at his first new job and I went on tour with the Met singing "Così" and "Lohengrin." I was still torn between my impossible romance and my loyalty to Ed, despite the fact that he was becoming more and more irrational. I sang my tour performances quite as usual that spring although my home life was a shambles. I drew heavily on the support of my friends in the company. It took a near-catastrophe to snap me out of it.

We were closing the Met tour at the end of May with "Lohengrin" in Toronto. I was happy with the performance, but tenor Brian Sullivan, who was singing Lohengrin, became so furious about something he had done, hadn't done or imagined he had or hadn't, that he refused to come out for his curtain calls. Who knows what got into him! Anything could set off that black Irish temper of his.

But the audience kept yelling for him, and finally someone went back and pulled him out. He came out for his bows in his dressing gown, a towel slung around his neck. He looked more like a prize fighter than a Wagnerian tenor.

It was an evening already fraught with rather hyper emotions at the end of a long season, with most of us tired and eager to get home. We were all dressed, packed and ready to leave for home, but we all made an appearance at the big reception thrown for the company in a private suite by our hosts, the Canadian sponsors of the Metropolitan tour. As a party, it was delightful and relaxing, but unusually sedate.

The company had chartered a plane to fly us back to New York, so when they announced it was time to go, I headed for the bathroom to fix my face. The hotel was old-fashioned, (the Prince Edward, if I remember correctly) and as I walked through the door I caught my heel on the high marble door sill, pitching forward onto one of the brass handles on the antique bathtub. When I came to, I was lying over the tub, bleeding. My fur coat and hat were soaked with blood. I was a mess. I washed and looked at my bloody face in the mirror. I could see a thin, clean split right down the center of my forehead. I called for help, and Mabel Krug, an old Toronto friend, called a plastic surgeon she knew. He came immediately and sewed it up so beautifully that in time it became barely visible. Of course I didn't make the charter flight to New York. I stayed in Toronto all the next day and Brian Sullivan, God rest him, stayed right with me, comforting and reassuring me with a gentleness I will never forget.

Instead of returning directly to Manhattan, I got a flight into MacArthur Airport on Long Island and went directly to Melodie Hill to prepare for my trip to Vienna. It was all terribly hectic, even for me. I had my hair restyled to cover the offending scar, and the day before I left for Europe, they took out my stitches. Bloodied, but unbowed, I took off.

Auf Wien

When I arrived in Vienna on the third of June, I had expected my European representative, Martin Taubman, to be my only ally in the "city of dreams" I had waited so long to visit. I was happily astonished, then, to find a number of American opera colleagues and other friends waiting to welcome me.

During those first few free days, I managed to catch a performance of "Rosenkavalier," and two operas new to me, Strauss's "Arabella" and Alban Berg's "Wozzeck." I also caught performances or rehearsals of "Tannhauser," "Fidelio," "Tosca" and "Così fan Tutte." Then, on June 8, I had my first rehearsal with Dr. Karl Böhm for our concert performance of "Die Frau Ohne Schatten" in which I was singing the Empress. I had come to Europe hoping that my appearances in Vienna and Bayreuth would add new dimensions to both my artistry and my reputation (which, of course, they did), but I did not expect another cataclysmic event before I had sung my first performance. I was gazing aimlessly out into the auditorium during a pause in the final rehearsal at the Konzerthaus and I thought I saw a familiar face. "What on earth," I wondered, "could Paul Strauss be doing in Vienna?" Paul was a young American conductor who had for some time been a protégé of Dimitri Mitropoulos. He had often been present when Dimitri and I worked together. Paul had been to several parties at my house. I remembered him particularly at one after the Lewisohn Stadium "Tosca" and another following our notorious Town Hall recital.

When at last I caught his eye, we recognized each other for sure. He was as surprised as I. We met after rehearsal with the usual "What are you doing here?" and I discovered he was touring Europe as a conductor with the American Ballet Theater. We chatted about our work, home and Dimitri. Then, with that festive impulse of old friends meeting unexpectedly in a foreign land, I broke a date, and we went together to the Balkan Inn where we ate a sumptuous meal and sipped delicious red wine.

We talked and talked! It was that most wondrous of adventures when two people respond to each other so spontaneously that sentences tumble all over each other and they disclose their innermost thoughts to each other at first meeting. We joked and jousted with words; we confessed a little and explained a lot, delighted with what we discovered and finding such beauty in each other that we were quickly bound in a bond of deep affection.

All-but oblivious to our surroundings, we strolled along as we talked and eventually found ourselves sitting outside the Sacher Stübe, sipping cognac. Realizing at last that I must have *some* sleep before my debut in Vienna the following day, we said good night, and I wandered dreamily into my hotel, clasping to my heart the big bunch of roses Paul had thrust into my arms somewhere along our way. As I climbed into bed, the memory of that delicious night filled my being and lifted my spirits.

I didn't see Paul the day of "Die Frau," although I was so excited about the concert, it was impossible to rest quietly in my room. I was tempted to call and ask him to walk with me during the afternoon, but I hesitated to disturb him in case he was studying. So I didn't call, but during the course of my walk, I wandered into the lobby of his hotel with a vague hope of bumping into him. It became just like a movie comedy, because at that very moment, he was calling on me at the Sacher Stübe.

That night, in high spirits, I joyfully sang for Vienna—for Paul. How could it not go well? There was a confusion of general rejoicing backstage afterwards. Dr. Böhm seemed pleased with my performance and George London, always a tremendous favorite in Vienna, was ecstatic. I was elated for many reasons, not the least because I adored the way the part sat so beautifully for my voice.

After the performance we had a big venison dinner at my hotel and Paul came back to my suite afterwards, quite a feat in those days when it took some doing to get an unannounced guest past the concierge.

I was awakened the next morning by calls from Martin Taubman and Paul who told me I was already the "talk of Vienna." The critics were ecstatic and I should have been more than satisfied, but I was not. My performance was not as relaxed as I felt it should have been and I was annoyed with myself because I had used a score for the last part, although I had memorized the rest. It was just my usual day-after-performance insecurity. Certainly no one else gave me reason to doubt myself because there were immediate proposals about my returning to sing at the Staatsoper the following season.

This was the first of many such overtures about singing in Europe. If during the months and years that followed, I wondered why a number of these offers vanished in the mists of time, I was usually too busy to give it much thought. Years later, however, when I met some of the people who had tried to book me for European engagements only to be told I was unavailable, did I begin to realize that a great many such opportunities had been "cut off at the pass" by intermediaries.

I was always handicapped in my European dealings, both by language and because I had no one there truly protecting my interests, even though in addition to the regular commissions, I also paid the expected "finder's fee" to my various European representatives for any performances they secured for me. Perhaps I didn't offer enough or someone else offered more. But in 1953 I knew nothing of all this, and for the 10 days or so that I was in Vienna, it was more than a city; it was my private paradise.

Because of Paul, I had become involved with the Ballet Theater Company, attending their premiere in my favorite black taffeta with the brave decollétage. Then on the night before my Vienna orchestra concert Paul and I went to a huge party thrown for the entire Ballet Company up at Grinzing. Paul wasn't much for dancing, but I was, and had a beautiful time waltzing with the boys in the company. It was a happy party, with lots of champagne and when we all started singing I lost track of time.

But someone was watching out for me. Rudolf Bing was also at the party and knew I was singing the next night. He did keep track of the time, and eventually he drifted over to Paul and murmured, "Have you forgotten she has a concert with Ormandy tomorrow? Don't you think it's time to take her home?"

Thanks, boss!

The concert with Ormandy came off beautifully before an audience filled with good friends from the Met cheering me on, including soprano Hilde Gueden and Frances Yeend, George London and tenor Svet Svanholm; and another former Auditions winner who came after me, mezzo-soprano Mona Paulee. And there were messages from home: from President Eisenhower, no less! – from family, friends, and amazingly in those early post-war days, fresh "American" flowers flown in from my fan club.

Life was so beautiful for that brief time in Vienna! But Paul had to move on with the Ballet Theater and I was due in Bayreuth for "Lohengrin" rehearsals. We said our reluctant and lingering goodbyes, but we both fervently believed our parting was merely temporary.

My college and operatic German had sufficed admirably in cosmopolitan Vienna, but the Bavarische Deutsch, the Franconian dialect which confronted me on my arrival, threw me for a loss. I feared my difficulty in understanding it would do me in for sure. (While it is true that my family's origins are German, German was never a true second language for me. My grandparents came to America because they wanted to become Americans as soon as they could. They spoke only English – although with slight German accents. And, of course, in post-World War I America, German was not generally taught in the schools, so I missed it there as well.)

In Bayreuth, the artists were traditionally housed in private homes and I was delighted with my big, modern apartment; but what a time I had communicating with my landlady, Frau Geyer! I was relieved that first evening when dramatic soprano Regina Resnik, a New Yorker from the Met, turned up at the party which introduced me to the famous artists' hangout, "Die Eüle," a family tavern near the Festspielhaus. Later, Astrid Varnay, the American Wagnerian artist, who was to sing Ortrud with me, joined us.

It was all strange and new and a bit frightening. I found myself completely on my own and carrying, I felt, much responsibility for the future of other American Elsas at Bayreuth. "And," I thought unhappily, "I have no Paul Strauss to lift my spirits after rehearsals."

The next morning I met my conductor, Joseph Keilberth (almost no English) and despite my apprehensions I responded at once to the strong personality of this quick, discerning and thoroughly knowledgeable man. I sensed at once we could work well together.

I was scheduled to start immediately with both musical coaches and a language tutor – all of whom spoke a German I could easily understand. Yet I remained anxious. I was terribly nervous, and almost unhappy, wondering why I let myself in for all that terrible uncertainty when I could be comfortably at home. (An old refrain.) I *did* have confidence in my voice and I knew that eventually it would turn out well. Regina Resnik was a darling, and while I must admit I am quite overshadowed by her very good knowledge of the language, she was wonderful to me, and it was a joy getting to know her better.

By mid-June I was deeply involved in the thorough preparations given to Bayreuth productions. June 24 was a tough one, I remember. I had another session with my coach Herr Korn, and later met with my Lohengrin, young Wolfgang Windgassen and Maestro Keilberth to sing through the love duet. It went well, although I felt my voice was still none too good. The weather was not the best for someone with my bronchial difficulties, and my asthma was giving me some trouble – nerves and asthma again!

After another strenuous rehearsal the next day, still feeling uneasy, and a stranger in the town, I strolled down to Die Eüle that evening. I sat alone sipping white wine and gradually began to enjoy a sense of being among the people. I felt comforted to realize, finally, that they were after all much the same as I. From then on I felt much more "gemütlich" toward Bayreuth.

At work, however, I never ceased to feel that I must always be a little quicker, a little sharper to merit the approval of my directors and co-workers. Suddenly I understood that perhaps this was the way many European artists felt when they came for the first time to the Met; strange to our city, to our ways and our language. I was reassured by this thought.

A day or two later I had a long talk with Wolfgang Wagner (with Herman Weigert translating for us). It was hard not to be intimidated by Wolfgang: so energetic, so quick, and snapping out his sentences in that devilish Franconian accent – I was petrified that I could never comprehend, much less digest the deluge of instructions I was daily getting from him and everyone else. Happily, Maestro Weigert filled me in after this conference with everything I had missed and assured me that either he or Astrid Varnay (his wife and long a famous artist in her own right both at the Met and Bayreuth) would be close at hand if I needed them.

Not until some time later did I realize that I was enjoying something I hardly ever had – the longest, most comprehensive rehearsal period of my life. This once I was given all the time, direction and opportunity to polish every aspect of my role in a disciplined atmosphere – to get it all thoroughly into my system before having to sing it in public. I worked a month on Elsa. As my German improved, I delved deeper into her character and gradually began to slip into the world of "Lohengrin." By the time the opening was upon us, I had a profound appreciation of these preparations in which all details of the production were so totally integrated.

The first performance was scheduled for July 23. Amidst all this, my publicist, Martha Smith, called to say my husband had peremptorily fired her. I told her she was rehired and that I would take care of it when I came home. Edwin, whom I had asked not to come at all, arrived anyway, and my parents came just in time for the opening night. It was an especially moving experience for them; not only were they to hear me sing in this historic opera house, they were on a pilgrimage of sorts, having waited a lifetime and traveled 4,000 miles to return to the home of their ancestors.

When the curtain finally went up, I felt almost as if I were singing in a trance and the performance a dream. Afterward, with the cheers of the Bayreuth audience still ringing in my ears, I was escorted to the huge banquet given to celebrate the opening. When I entered the banquet hall to an ovation and was seated at the head table with Wolfgang Wagner on one side and Wieland Wagner on the other, I was still in my dream.

This spare and starkly staged "Lohengrin," with two American girls singing Elsa and Ortrud, won terrific reviews which were later translated and published at home. Unfortunately, however, there are always people surrounding some artists who cannot seem to let any performance be! I was always particularly vulnerable to this destructive sort of nit-picking because I was so gullible.

It would never occur to me, nor, I think, to most artists, to criticize the work of another singer, because we can always imagine ourselves standing in their shoes. But I have found that non-singers in our business are often careless, if not self-serving, with their pronouncements. People began coming to me with little "confidences," telling me first what this person said and then what another person said. Somehow or other it never occurred to me to doubt them, or their motives, but I always listened seriously to everything I was told and considered it all, the bad with the good. This played havoc with my self-confidence.

After the heights to which the dress rehearsal and first performance had taken me, I was overwhelmed by so many conflicting comments that I didn't know what to think. I remember writing to Paul that "according to most reports, it was a colossal success. But the whole thing has been spoiled for me because of little whispers that 'they' were disappointed with the size of my voice (whoever 'they' were).

"Not only that, but I have been led to believe that there has been some talk calculated to belittle my achievement. It is hard to accept, but I am afraid that I have been persuaded. Martin Taubman said that in contrast to my overwhelming success in Vienna, he was afraid I had been put upon. Edwin and others have told me the same.

"My own impression," I wrote, trying to sort it out in my mind, "was that I portrayed my role as I was directed. I felt that I sang it with the same technique and beauty of voice for which they had engaged me. That the opening performance was a letdown over that of the dress rehearsal may be true, this happens; but it was magnificently received by the public. But for me, the harm has been done.

"Incidentally," I added, "Dimitri was here and very happy with my performance. Knowing me, he knew I performed as I was directed. His was the single sane and logical voice in the whole place."

I wish I had been able to enjoy doing my job. Why can't people let well enough alone? Why must they always try to stir things up? (I wish, too, that I had been aware then that the newly-revived Bayreuth productions so deviated from earlier, more traditional stagings that it took the "cognoscenti" some time to adjust their old built-in prejudices. Ah, well, I didn't know—and so I was sorely agitated.)

Troubled though I was by this, and by Ed's presence, I always put on "a good face" in public. Fortunately, my instinct is to enjoy the experiences of the moment and in pleasant surroundings and I can easily be caught up by jolly companions.

There were still some constraints and perhaps suspicions among the local populace toward Americans in those postwar and "cold war" days, but I think I did my bit to enhance friendliness with the local residents as I tootled around Bayreuth on a bicycle dressed in a colorful dirndl, always with a great big smile and a "Hi" for everyone. Pretty soon people were smiling back and calling out to me as I rode by.

The food and drink in Bayreuth was fabulous. There was the potent "Goldwasser" ("one drink and you're set for the day!") and, the great Wurtzburger beer! But the food itself...oh, my! Yet I remember one meal which wasn't quite what I had hoped.

Mother and I had bumped into Dimitri Mitropoulos on the street one day and I invited him for dinner that night. I immediately sent my wonderful "zimmer mädschen" and cook, Frau Lisa Meidel, to the butcher for some rehrücken (saddle of venison) because I knew Dimitri loved it.

While it was cooking, we worked on a luscious spread of gherkin salad, potato salad and other delectable side dishes. When Frau Lisa finally presented the pièce de resistance, it looked like an old boiled shoe. "Frau Lisa," I gasped, "what has happened to that meat?" I started to remove it from the table, but Mitropoulos commanded me to leave it, declaring that it was just exactly as his own mother had prepared it.

I couldn't understand. As soon as I could, I slipped into the kitchen to find out what had happened to that gorgeous piece of meat. Frau Lisa shrugged and said that of course she had simply put it in a pot as usual and boiled it. "But you're supposed to roast it in the oven!" I cried. "But there *is* no oven here, Madame," she replied.

If I deserved *my* reputation for robust appetite, Dimitri's was worthy of something else, despite his lean and oftentimes gaunt appearance. In Bayreuth, as on many other occasions, he was always first at the table and totally absorbed in the food, and utterly oblivious of conversation until the meal was finished.

I still remember when Dimitri came to Melodie Hill the day Sam Barber came to play "Knoxville." I had cooked two lovely ducklings — something I did beautifully in those days. When the music was finished, Dimitri was ready to eat. He hated waiting for people to have cocktails (never took more than a sip or two of brandy himself and deplored the cocktail hour as a total waste of time), and paced back and forth like a lion, urging us again and again, "Come on, come on, let's eat." At last we sat down to eat and, before I knew what had happened, Dimitri had polished off one whole duckling himself, leaving the remaining duck to be shared by four of us.

While still in Bayreuth, I had a couple of free days between "Lohengrin" performances, so Ed and I took my parents on a short trip up the Rhine. When we returned to Bayreuth, it was rather late, well after that night's opera had rung down. Hungry and tired from our trip, we stopped at "Die Eüle" for a bite to eat.

The visiting opera lovers had vanished, and the townspeople had taken over the place, sitting around one big table and eating with great gusto while my family and I sat watching from a table off to the side. All you could hear was a terrific clatter of knives and forks against the plates and certain happy gnawing sounds. Then, as they finished eating, they leaned back and began to sing.

Mother stood it as long as she could, then decided she had to join in. Mother spoke a serviceable Plaat Deutsch which everyone understood, so over she went and started singing old German songs. Pretty soon mother had everybody singing with her and *she* was directing *them!* Even my shy father got himself up and sang the "Jaeger Song" in German. So there were my parents at the center of the party while Edwin and I sat by watching.

I'm my mother's daughter, however, and there was no possible way I could sit listening to others perform without getting into the act myself, so eventually I joined them. When I finally offered up Brahms' "Wiegenlied," in my silkiest pianissimo, the crowd grew silent, and the evening closed on almost a reverent note.

What a gorgeous evening! When it broke up it was about four o'clock in the morning—and *that* didn't go down too well with the powers-that-be, let me tell you, because I was scheduled to sing Elsa the next night. No matter what those "powers-that-be" might have thought about my late night at Die Eüle, who is to say when music reaches most deeply into human hearts—in the magnificence of the Festspielhaus, or in the intimacy of a cozy cafe? If it is the commitment of your life to make music, must you choose between them?

Some years later I received a letter from Frau Lisa saying, "All of the people here, "Die Leute" of Bayreuth, want to know when you are coming back. They have never ceased talking about you and your mother and father that wonderful night at Die Eüle."

Those were the bright times. Within myself, however, as I fulfilled my daily commitments, I was becoming a fragmented soul. I was boxed into tight little compartments which must have puzzled people who saw me frequently. As Steber-the-singer I applied myself diligently to my schedule of performances, and the Steber-in-public ate and drank and laughed with the crowd. Privately, however, I was two other people. The new spirit which Paul had lit within me burned with a hot white light, while at the same time, my conscience was tormented because I knew I must make some immediate decisions. An end to my marriage now appeared inevitable, but the concept was so foreign to my upbringing that for the moment I found it unacceptable. I mulled it over and over.

Rejecting even the idea of divorce, I decided that only in a last emergency could I take such a drastic step. "Edwin is an honest human being and loves me very much," I wrote Paul. "He has surrounded me with so many things necessary to my career and has built such a protective financial base around me that even if I should have to stop singing, I could live comfortably. He has devoted his whole life to the building of the fable I am supposed to be. So must I ever remain Galatea to his Pygmalion!"

I recalled how earnestly I had tried to live up to the precepts of marriage which I had been taught, including a willingness, even eagerness to have a child, to give up the career itself perhaps. Now, suddenly I realized that I could never *again* be that paragon of wifely virtue. By now I hardly knew who I was, but I did know I was no longer that young girl who had married the idealistic young man in Boston. I understood at last that somehow Steber must be Steber, serving the gods of music and art, passionately grateful they had blessed me with the talents I had been given. Somewhat melodramatic, perhaps, but that's the way I am. However, momentarily at least, I struck a healthily pragmatic glimpse of clarity when I considered my ten-day idyll with Paul Strauss in Vienna: "Perhaps it will pass," I wrote, "leaving a sweet memory which will quicken a bit when we see each other again, only to fade in the face of the demands of our careers; or perhaps it will remain a fire in our hearts to feed our spirits and become a brilliant inspiration to all that we do. But, 'wie shön es war'"—how lovely it was!

What a difference it might have made if I had been able to hang on to this thought permanently, because my instinct was correct. At its best, love has never been an end in itself to me; it has been, instead, a fountain spring to my art. At that moment, however, I was still chained to a Puritan conscience, while my yearning for an unattainable ideal of love drove me to the limits of my strength.

Shortly before Edwin's arrival, I had determined to carry on our marriage, but the undesired reunion shattered my decision and confirmed our differences. Not only had he arrived uninvited, but within hours the situation exploded and we had become two terribly torn-apart people. As if a film had dropped from my eyes, I saw the full extent of the charade we had been playing out. I wasn't living *my own life*, but one scripted for me by Edwin and others who really didn't seem to know the first thing about what kind of person I really was. Yet now, through all the confusion and anguish, one clear beam shot through and shone crystal clear: I had to have the freedom to be what I was and was meant to be!

Disaster

When Jimmy Quillian, who had accompanied my concerts for 13 years, decided he'd had enough of the road, my old friend Edwin Biltcliffe, of Boston days, joined me in mid-tour and remained with me, with very few exceptions, until he retired.

When Biltcliffe and I returned to New York after completing this first tour together in the winter of 1953, my husband and I were all but completely separated. Ed had finally secured a job managing the Springfield, Massachusetts Symphony and I was living in a New York hotel. Although I knew divorce was inevitable, I vacillated, unable to initiate the final step. Melodie Hill remained the only place we both still considered home.

One evening in my hotel as I leafed casually through the pages of my diary, I was dismayed to find that the few entries for the past year graphically documented the deterioration of my marriage—a bitter witness. They convinced me my course was right, and the fact that I was finding such peace and quiet pleasure away from him was further proof that the path I had chosen was right for me. If only Ed could find a rewarding life in his new job, I thought, everything would be all right. It was not to be.

It all blew apart during the long New Year's weekend which followed my debut as Rosalinda in "Die Fledermaus." What was supposed to be a quiet family reunion at Melodie Hill with my husband, my parents and a few good friends erupted into a ghastly melodrama, and late Sunday afternoon I fled to my New York hotel.

I was operating now on pure nervous energy, trying not to think. My performances at the Metropolitan had started before Christmas, and by the latter part of January I had sung a couple of Donna Elviras, plus my Fiordiligis, Rosalinda and the Countess in "Figaro" with "Traviata" to follow. At the same time, I was coaching two new roles, and now I had to manage many of the details Ed had formerly handled. I had to locate an apartment where I could practice, and make a new city home for myself. I worked numbly, trudging from one appointment or rehearsal to another.

On the 26th of January I'd had an exhausting day rehearsing at the Met, then with a coach, and ending with a massage at Diana Ross's. I returned to my hotel and struggled with my accounts until Maestro Rescigno arrived to help me polish Donna Anna, which I was scheduled to sing soon in Chicago. We finished rehearsing about midnight.

After he left, I had a couple of drinks to relax, and started packing for a single out-of-town concert the next night. Tired and depressed, I took time out to call Paul Strauss, who was conducting in Oregon. We had a happy conversation which so elated me and filled me with such happy hopes for our future, that I puttered merrily about all night, organizing my belongings for a new move, sipping as I worked. Before I realized it, it was 7:00 a.m.

Everything might have worked out all right if I hadn't had a special stage rehearsal of "Figaro" at the Met that morning for George London, who was scheduled to do his first Count Almaviva of the season.

I caught a little sleep, but when I awoke, I was still feeling my drinks and it was too late to cancel out of the rehearsal. I made it to the Met all right, but when I got on the stage, I got lost in the scenery. I couldn't remember my entrances or a single word of the text. I tried, but I was gone. I walked off the stage and called my secretary, Pat Young (actor Roland Young's widow), to come and get me.

Within minutes of the rehearsal's start, and before I called Pat, Bill Judd had already received an S.O.S. from Max Rudolf. "Max was very kind and sweet about it," Bill told me later, "and he didn't find it an easy call to make; but he didn't mince words. He told me to come and get you."

Normally you couldn't get me to cancel a performance. I sang many times when I was ill, had bad throats, asthma, or hangovers; but I'd sing! And sometimes, perhaps, I shouldn't have. Certainly, I should have skipped this rehearsal.

Bill Judd didn't give me a chance. I was scheduled to fly to Washington that afternoon to sing at the White House. Without a word to me, Bill called them to say I was indisposed. When he reported what he had done, I gave him hell because I thought, quite mistakenly, that I could have recovered sufficiently. Bless the man, he took my wrath without a murmur. He felt he was there to protect my interests, and he believed he had done it—as he had.

I never returned to my hotel. When I left the Met that day I moved in with Diana Ross. Pat Young returned to pack up my things and helped me settle permanently into Diana's quarters near the City Center on West 55th Street.

Living completely alone had just not worked. Nothing had prepared me for it. Growing up, I had my supportive family, and in Boston I had Mr. Whitney and a husband who had made me the center of his life. Everyone who worked for me had protected me from the need to manage the day-to-day details of my life. Indeed, to manage *me*. I needed people who cared for me; that was my security.

Now I had to face the consequences of what I had done. What could possibly be more awful for the conscientious artist I had always tried to be than to arrive at a Met rehearsal in such a state? Only if it had been a performance could it have been worse! I vowed such a thing would never happen again. Nor did it!

Mr. Bing was extremely kind to me. I had sung my "Figaro" as scheduled the following day, but a few days later he asked me to stop by his office to see him. Very gently he told me about some of his own personal problems, and then pointed out that I couldn't afford to let mine spill over into my public life any more than he could. He said that my appearance at the "Figaro" rehearsal could reflect very seriously on my reputation as an artist. He was understanding and sympathetic, but very firm in suggesting that I do something to straighten out my life.

My friends at the Met understood that I had been under a strain for a considerable period of time and that this had been a highly unusual occurrence; but there were others who magnified the story, so that there were numerous times as the years went on when, if I was particularly gay or a little boisterous, people would claim I had been drinking, whether I had been or not. If my drinking occasionally gave me private cause for concern, except for this once I don't believe it ever interfered with my work.

It had been a bad scene, no doubt about it, but I had to forget it and get on with my job. This was another one of those times when I was really almost ready to walk away from the whole career, but I wanted to live it down, so I *had* to go on.

I made a vow in my diary: "I must make a constructive plan for the next 10 years of my career. There are so many things which I would love to do *just for myself* — for Eleanor — but I must remain true to the people who expect so much from me and who have supported me so faithfully all this time. So I must try to go on.

"If I were to give it up now, people would blame it on my drinking, or say that my career was all too much for me. How can anyone understand what lies in my heart? Somehow I must manage to continue without the love I long for, without the home I dream of. I must persevere in my career, and build upon the success I have already achieved with this talent which controls my life. Perhaps in another 10 years — who knows?

"And yet, *I want to sing*. Singing is my job, my responsibility, my cherished task. To give it up would be to give me up; I can never do it. The fact is, I am never so happy as when I am singing. So I must continue for myself, even through times which often seem unendurable, to win the high satisfactions of concerts and opera performances well done, plus the transient comfort of public admiration, and the cold satisfaction of facing down cynics and ill-wishers. Will it be worth it? Could I ever live without it? We will see."

I didn't want for work. Once securely ensconced within the ordered and comfortable haven Diana Ross provided for me, I waded into a 30-day period during which I sang a performance of some sort every day, about equally divided between operas and concerts. I sang something more than 20 performances with the Met alone that season, including a handful on tour. I worked Firestone broadcasts into the schedule, performed with a couple of other opera companies, and with Dimitri made a recording of "Les Nuits d'Été," which, after I heard it, I decided was even better than our performances the previous year.

This was one of the few recordings I made that I liked at once. Usually I hated them all because when they were played back, I would hear things in them which no one else did. (We had no such things as tapes and splicing in those days. You did it over and over until you got it right!) I've always had a tendency for my overtones to ride a little sharp — it's in the timbre of my voice and could seldom be heard in a hall — but my ear would pick it up and I would cringe; or I would hear a turn or a phrase that didn't come off the way I wanted. But on the few occasions when I listen to any of them today, the Berlioz, the Mozart with Walter, the Verdi Heroines, "Knoxville," and my operas, "Butterfly," "Così," "Faust" and "Vanessa," I am astonished. I listen and think, "My God, is that me?"

I was polishing up Donna Anna for the inauguration of the new "Calling Card Opera" which eventually became the "new" Chicago Lyric

Opera Company managed by Carol Fox and Larry Kelly. They gave me my first chance at my dream role, and once again an opportunity to work out a role before I sang it at the Metropolitan.

Since this was the first opera of their first season, it was all terribly hectic. During the frantic dress rehearsal when the stage hands were having difficulty with the scene change routine, I volunteered to save time by running through "Non mi dir" in front of the curtain while they were working on the set. Occasionally sipping black coffee from a plastic container, I sang through the aria unaware that the superb British actor and comedian, Reginald Gardener, was sitting in the empty theater. Afterwards he was heard to say to one of the producers, "And they say the stars have no understanding of management's problems!"

Another big event was my first *staged* performance of "Tosca" with La Scala of Philadelphia. Although I had learned the part for my earlier concert performances with Mitropoulos, I restudied the part with Renato Bellini and worked out the misè en scène with Maestro Agnini.

Convinced that Tosca would eventually become one of my best roles—although Mr. Bing did not think mine a Puccini voice—I invested in my own costumes. They were perfectly magnificent, but they cost a damn sight more than my fee for the performance, and I could only trust that the future would justify the expense.

Back in New York, and firmly back in artistic partnership with my adored Dimitri, I sang the "Missa Solemnis" at Carnegie Hall, and then, with Maestro Pietro Cimara, worked enthusiastically on yet another new role, which I would sing with Dimitri in May in a wholly new setting.

After a disastrous start, 1954 began to look as if it might turn out to be okay—and so it did, musically at least.

Carola and Minnie

The previous summer as I boarded the train out of Bayreuth, my European manager asked, "What would you think of singing Puccini's 'Girl of the Golden West' with Mitropoulos next summer at the Maggio Musicale in Florence?"

Half way up the steps, I turned and shouted, "Anything with Mitropoulos. Yes!"

So when I finished that tough 1953–54 season, I gathered up Pat Young and headed for Europe. Paul Strauss, who was planning to link up with Mitropoulos in Italy before taking off for engagements of his own elsewhere in Europe, flew over with us. We arrived in Milan exhausted, but caught a second breath and whisked ourselves over to La Scala in time for the "provo generale" of "Elektra" and "Harlequin," which Dimitri was conducting. To add spice to my arrival, I was greeted by my Otello, Ramon Vinay, Giulietta Simionata, Cesare Valletti, and other old friends. It almost made me forget the chilling brush-off off I had received from La Scala's Director Ghirenghelli when I had auditioned for him two years earlier.

Pat and I parted from Dimitri and Paul and flew down to Florence where, after some confusion, we were settled comfortably at the Albergo Anglo-Americano, right next to the opera house. My lovely room overlooked a gracious courtyard, and Florence seemed to be everything I had dreamed it would be. I was as excited as a young kid.

I had prepared Minnie with scrupulous care and thought I had her down cold—and I guess I did, but I still sweated it out that first afternoon trying, with my operatic Italian, to catch the stream of instructions which rattled at me like machine gun fire. I wasn't quite sure just how well I was doing; but then I also had something more than music on my mind.

After rehearsal I headed straight for the Ippica, the local riding stable, to find a horse to ride in the third act. The stories of disasters-on-horseback suffered by a variety of Minnies over the years are uncountable, and new ones are created each time someone mounts the opera. I had ridden horses since I was a kid, however, and I was determined to avoid this operatic hazard. To make sure, I planned to choose and train my own horse!

I dickered cautiously in simple Italian with the stable master, explaining why I needed a special horse I could work with on stage. He must have missed the point, however, for he put me on a huge beast I couldn't even get my legs around. I couldn't get that monster to do *anything!* The horse didn't understand me and I didn't understand him. A total mismatch! Some special horse, hah!

Frustrated to the point of tears, I slid off the great beast, threw the reins at the groom and fled the stables. This was the last straw! All my hopes of galloping on stage in a great third act entrance seemed doomed.

The emotional strain of finally separating from my husband and the whirlwind visit to Milan, where I left Paul, added to the anxiety of my first long rehearsal. My disappointment with that damned horse was the last straw. I was now in such low dumps that the prospect of singing Minnie in Florence began to look like the biggest mistake of my life.

Pat Young had gone off on some engagement of her own, so I was at loose ends. On the way back to my hotel I picked up a bottle of Italian brandy, left word at the hotel desk I didn't want to be disturbed, and locked myself in my room. I sipped away at the brandy throughout the evening, all the while writing a long angry letter to someone—I wish I knew who—then slipped into bed and a wonderful long sleep.

The next morning I felt absolutely marvelous and filled with renewed optimism. "Dammit," I thought, "I'm not going to do 'Fanciulla' at all without a horse, so I've got to find a good one somehow! First chance I had, I returned to the Ippica and demanded another mount. This time they gave me a graceful retired cavalry horse named "Carola," just like an American pinto pony. She was just right for Minnie and perfect for me. After riding her happily around the ring for a bit, I tried a few of the high phrases Minnie sings as she gallops in midway in the third act. The horse loved it! Just *loved it!* After that, it hardly mattered to me what happened at rehearsal. The important thing was that I had my horse! I worked with her before rehearsals every day and taught her to stand up on her hind legs.

Soon I started riding her down to "La Cascina," a delightful local park with bridal paths. To get there Carola and I paraded together down the streets of Florence—a matched pair—me in my Central City "Frontier Suit" with black cord pants, white shirt, black vest and white cowboy hat neatly color-coordinated with Carola's white with black markings.

Meanwhile, back at the opera house, after I had struggled through two weeks of disorganized, half-hearted attempts at rehearsal, Dimitri arrived and started to pull the production together on the stage.

The stage director was an elusive fellow named Curzio Malaparte, whose chief professional qualifications seemed to stem from his wartime connection with the Americans in Naples, about whom he had written a book entitled "Le Pele," which means "skin." It was all about the street women of Napoli and the American soldiers who consorted with them. That this had been made into a popular movie did not necessarily make its author a good stage director.

For all practical purposes, the opera was directed by his assistant, Carlo Maestrini, while Malaparte himself stood around looking gorgeous. It all sounds kind of silly today, but at the time I thought it was outrageous. Malaparte's lack of expertise, added to the general confusion of the rehearsals, made my own problems of creating this new role in a strange opera house particularly harrowing. If it hadn't been for Maestro Maestrini, I never would have made it. (Maestrini is still sharing his talents with young American singers in Texas today as I write.) If the last week of rehearsal was a nightmare of frustration and temperament, the dress rehearsal was a soap opera (the third act hadn't even been blocked out) with everyone quitting, much tearing of hair and noisy hysterics.

I had awakened shortly before dawn that day in a good mood and determined to make the best of it. I dressed quickly and rode Carola through the park, put her through her paces and then took her to the opera house and rode her alone onto the empty stage, weaving her in and out of the scenery so she would be familiar with the set. The stable hands were ordered to bring Carola back to the theater for the 6 p.m. rehearsal.

I naturally expected the dress rehearsal to be a straight run-through. No such luck. We made it through Act I well enough, but the second act went straight downhill. Since Malaparte wasn't even concerning himself with Minnie, I had to work out all my own stage business myself without ever having seen the opera.

Fortunately, the second act set worked quite well. It had a fireplace with a barrel chair in front of it and all the standard props for the cabin scene. But when we got under way and I made my entrance, the barrel chair had disappeared. Malaparte hadn't liked the way it looked. Just where he expected me to sit to take off my boots, I'm sure I don't know. Certainly it didn't concern him! So I simply stopped singing, walked down to the footlights and addressed Dimitri. "Maestro," I intoned in my most intimidating prima donna voice, "I will not continue until the barrel chair is replaced. I cannot do this act without it!"

Suddenly everybody was shouting at once with Maestrini and Malaparte and everyone else yelling, "Che cose? Che cose? What does she want? Che? Che?" I stood my ground, and the rehearsal stopped cold until they put my chair back.

Now came the moment when I, as Minnie, get to receive my "first kiss" from a young Mario del Monaco as Dick Johnson. Del Monaco burst through the cabin door on cue, stage snow billowing in with him; we opened our arms and ran toward each other and almost blew right by each other. My kiss landed somewhere in the vicinity of Del Monaco's left ear. I don't know if his landed anywhere. I never felt a thing. "What kind of a 'First Kiss' is that?" I demanded. Between acts Dimitri came and took me aside. "Elinor, be careful about that kissing," he cautioned in a whisper. "Del Monaco"s wife is watching from the wings and she is very jealous. She says she will 'tear out your eyes' and that Mario will not sing if she thinks the kiss is too big!" Oh my God! How could I figure out how much kiss was too big?

Now we come to the third act and the horses. By now it is nearly midnight and my darling little Carola has been waiting off stage since six o'clock. The other horses—for the posse—were police horses, the only horses available in Florence. So they dressed up about a dozen policemen in cowboy outfits, and they galloped on in the third act chasing the "bandit," crossing the stage, circling through the flats backstage and galloping in from the other side, over and over. They looked for all the world like a string of target horses in a shooting gallery.

Finally I made my entrance on Carola. I spurred her forward to the footlights and brought her up on her hind legs just as we had rehearsed. Everyone on stage was terrified, but Carola behaved beautifully. Del Monaco, standing on a stump waiting to be "hung" was simply terrified of horses, and whenever I moved around the stage, he and the cowboys on foot huddled together, shifting this way and that to avoid me and my horse.

When I dismounted, I discovered that my nicely trained grooms from the morning had been replaced by a couple of stage hands who had no idea what to do with my horse until I finally hissed instructions at them myself. When they reached for her, Carola tossed up her head and rolled back her lips, flashing those great yellow teeth, and snorted so violently that the chorus men jumped back in fright, crashing into each other like ten-pins. Absolute pandemonium.

Amid all this racket, I missed a musical cue and cursed. Del Monaco, who was supposed to mount the horse behind me and ride off into the sunset, refused. He finally agreed to lead off the horse, keeping the reins a good six feet ahead of us as I, once more astride Carola, tried to sing Minnie's heart-rending "Addio, California, addio bei monti" as a single in the saddle.

When I returned to the stage after the final curtain had been raised again for production critique, Dimitri had completely lost patience and was in absolute rage. "I will not go on in two days. I cannot accept this as a dress rehearsal. We will repeat it tomorrow!" That would mean pushing all four performances ahead a whole day.

Now it was my turn to blow up; so I blew: "Well, then you'll only have a Minnie for three performances, because *I* will be in Amsterdam the final day!"

Searching frantically for a solution, Maestro then announced, "Then we will have to do the opera without the horses!"

"If you don't have the horses, you don't have Steber," I shouted back. (In a funny, self-conscious way, I knew I was starting to play out a scene, but I couldn't help myself.)

I stalked off the stage in "high dudgeon," charged into my dressing room with tears streaming down my face, and stormed around throwing things in all directions, at the same time shouting my displeasure, loudly and dramatically, in highly graphic American.

Until this moment I had been courteously trying to speak Italian to everyone; but when Martin Taubman came into my dressing room, before he could say a word, I shouted at him: "I am not going to speak one more word in Italian! I have done my best with these people under impossible conditions. They say we are bad about not having enough rehearsals in American opera houses, and tell me that Italian houses are so great, that everything is so well planned with rehearsals conducted in the most orderly fashion! Bayreuth was heaven, but this is unbelievable! I don't care what happens! I don't care if I go home tomorrow! I'm finished!" I worked myself into a full-scale tantrum.

Two of the opera officials tiptoed into my dressing room and tried to soothe me. "Ahhhhh, Signora, Signora. . . ."

"Don't talk to me," I roared. "I don't want to talk to you. Get out of my dressing room! Go away! Go!"

They disappeared and descended on Taubman. With eyes popping, and whispering in case I should still be in earshot, they told him, "Dio mio, we didn't know the American diva was so temperamental. . . what shall we do?"

Needless to say, Dimitri heard all this and he finally came himself to pacify me. Dimitri tried. "Never mind, Elinor, after the audience goes, we will do that last half of the third act again."

I looked at him for a minute, considering; then I wailed, "But what good will that do? They've already sent my horse home. *I* don't need the rehearsal—the horse needs the rehearsal!"

So they brought the horses back and we went through the whole thing again. But just before we started to run through the third act again, while I was sitting on my horse in the wings waiting for my entrance, Dimitri sidled up beside me. At first I didn't see him. When I did, he looked scared to death, whether of the horse or me, I wasn't sure. He reached up and patted my knee, and taking all the blame upon himself, he said, "Elinor, I'm very sorry I made you cry." He was so gentle and so penitent, I had to fight back the tears once again.

As so often happens after a catastrophic dress rehearsal, the four performances were a triumph. The Italians were happy. I regained my sunny disposition and even Del Monaco, nervous to the end, summoned up the courage to mount the horse behind me for our ride into the sunset.

Word about the wild dress rehearsal must have spread amongst the townsfolk (many of whom had been an informal audience at it), so there was a gala crowd opening night which saluted us at the end with bravos, screams, stomping and at least 10 curtain calls.

Gladys Swarthout and Frank Chapman came down from their villa in the hills to attend and Paul flew in from Milan, admonishing me in a note accompanying flowers before the performance to "Lay 'em in the aisles, Minnie!" It was great!

There were the usual messages and telegrams, masses of flowers and glowing notices in the papers, but the memory I cherish most was my daily ride on my beautiful Carola through the streets of Florence. I wish I could have brought her home with me. Instead, I left my white cowboy hat and gloves in the opera museum in Florence.

Anyway, we did it! And Carola did it! And that's why they never forgot me in Florence!

Going to the Dogs

I lifted off from the Rome airport in a triumphant mood and stopped over in Amsterdam for a pair of concerts with Eugene Ormandy and the superlative Concertgebow orchestra. Without any portent of special significance, I sang the two excerpts from Alban Berg's opera "Wozzeck" which Ormandy had asked me to prepare.

When I flew back home from Europe that summer, I was determined to take control of my own life. But the world crashed down around me the moment I landed in New York. I was met by such a cadre of family, friends and managers I should have known something was wrong. And there was. My husband had suffered a complete breakdown and they had joined forces to help me face the shock and after-effects of this tragedy.

Edwin had inexplicably packed our car with all my off-and-on diaries, correspondence, and everything else he had conceived, in his unhappy fantasy, to be possible weapons against me. Then he had irrationally headed west. I can't think of anything significant in that random collection which I have not already recounted here, but it hardly mattered anyway, because Edwin had lost his hold on reality and was almost immediately hospitalized.

In time, thank God, he persevered in his recovery, eventually trained himself in computer finance (which was always his natural bent), established himself in business, remarried and had a daughter. With the healing passage of time, we eventually forgot the bitterness of our parting and remembered the good years until his death in 1981.

But that July I saw my hopes for the freedom of a divorce and a new life disappear. Not knowing what else to do, I sent Martha Smith to reclaim my car and private papers. I was torn between my personal disappointment, my compassion for Ed, and frustration because I believed that divorce was not possible while he remained incapacitated. I saw myself living endlessly in limbo.

Divorce has become so commonplace today that it is difficult to remember what a social trauma it was in 1954. No matter how much of a rebel against social custom I may have been in many ways, divorce, under any circumstances, was antithetical to all my instincts. It would have been easier for me had I been able to conjure up some all-consuming hatred toward the man I wanted to divorce, but I could not. I knew I could no longer live with him, but I could always see the lovableness of the man.

All this was churning about me as I arrived at the Tanglewood Festival on July 10 to sing "The Damnation of Faust" with Charles Munch and the Boston Symphony. The performance was sheer torture of heart and mind, for I sang it with and for people from Boston with whom Edwin and I had grown up musically, and with whom we shared our early hopes and dreams. I remembered the girl and boy we once were, strolling hand-in-hand through the Fenway imagining the life we would lead together. Young love, expectant love filled us both, and I was so certain that such a love could not possibly fail that I had taken a firm stand against my family. Our love, we believed, was strong and beautiful enough to survive all life's vicissitudes. Yet, in the absorbing pursuit of success for me, upon which we both spent all our efforts, we somehow lost that love. I had seen it pass little by little as I began to realize it was no longer love we shared, but my career. I don't think we were ever again as happy as we were when we walked the Fenway together. *That* was our time!

Somehow I got through the Tanglewood performances—superbly, I was told, but they passed as if I were in a dream. I dreaded that some-one from our early days would ask me about Edwin, but no one did.

From Massachusetts I flew to the West Coast for a concert in the Hollywood Bowl with Jan Peerce, and I thanked God for an unusually heavy summer schedule. I scarcely had time to think. Immediately after the Hollywood Bowl, I drove to Santa Barbara to sing a benefit for dear Lotte Lehmann's Academy of the West. Although I yearned for the soothing comfort of a long visit with her, I had to settle for the sight of her face beaming at me from the audience and a quick embrace backstage because I was due immediately in Denver to sing excerpts from Richard Strauss's "Salome" in concert with the Denver Symphony in the breathtakingly beautiful new amphitheater at Red Rocks.

Then it was back to the Bowl in Hollywood again for a gigantic presentation of Handel's "Messiah," a quick flight to New York for a Firestone broadcast, and back up to Tanglewood again, this time for a performance of "Les Nuits d'Été."

Finally I flew west again to Lake Tahoe to vacation with my friend Diana Ross. Hardly had I arrived when my attorneys informed me that it was possible to get my divorce after all if I would establish residence in Nevada immediately. What a welcome respite it turned out to be! I had time to sit in the sun and think of nothing, to enjoy a brisk swim in icy cold water, even to knit or take a turn at a slot machine or two and always, of course, to read. I wanted Paul to join me there but had to agree with him that it was not appropriate. Our letters flew back and forth for almost two years. We passed each other in planes, but seldom had a moment together.

I felt completely renewed when I left, luckily, because I swept into a three-and-a-half month concert tour during which I performed every two or three days and used my days off to learn a wonderful new opera role. Back in early January of 1954 I had enjoyed my most satisfactory contract negotiation with the Metropolitan. Arthur Judson himself had handled it all, and with him beside me, for once I felt properly represented.

Mr. Bing surprised us both by asking me to learn Richard Strauss's "Arabella." I was dumbfounded! I hadn't had a clue, not a whisper that "Arabella" was in the works. To top it all, Mr. Bing finally agreed to let me sing a couple of Donna Annas, my first at the Met, plus "Don Carlo," "Manon" and "Die Fledermaus."

I was so happy about all this and my Arabella assignment I never gave a thought to the usually absorbing question of my performance fee, which, it occurs to me now, might have been the point of the whole proposition. So, it was Arabella I was studying on tour. Then, about midway in the schedule, I made a quick side trip to Nevada to pick up my divorce decree. It seemed as if I should celebrate, but I had no heart for it. Paul was the only one I could have celebrated with anyway, and our schedules still kept us apart.

I kept telling myself that I was "free"—free to do what I wanted, live as I wanted and love whom I pleased! Was I really free? Would I ever be? Is anybody—ever?

Arabella! Ah, that was a role I loved! It is such a charming opera, thoroughly Viennese, with a special intimate mood of its own. And it was like—well, I felt somehow in this opera as if I had been reborn. In it I was freed of the uncertainties which had been hanging over me for such a long time; in Arabella was a new start. For me "Arabella" was not only fresh music and a delightful new role, it was a whole new life.

I felt like Arabella. Here, after fairy tale conflicts and a kind of "Wienerische Masquerade," as the Marschallin would say, was a happy, gemütlich ending. I had been introduced to "Arabella" on my first trip to Vienna where it played in the little Theater an der Wien. I never forgot the magic of the staircase scene in the last act, when Arabella welcomes Mandryka and offers him a cup of pure water as a pledge of betrothal, and as a symbol of her trust. This was what I wanted life to have—a happy ending—and I put my whole heart into that role. Oh, I felt beautiful in that opera!

Louis Biancolli of the *World Telegram & Sun* commended the Met generally for this sumptuous new production with "handsome people and handsome costumes. . . I found much to relish in the singing and looks of Eleanor Steber and Hilde Gueden as the pining sisters in the romantic mixup that ends in double marriage."

The *Philadelphia Bulletin* said I "sang like an angel."

More importantly, however, people remarked that our "Arabella" had caught the same kind of magic they remembered from the "Rosenkavaliers" of the 1940's. I felt much that way myself.

"Arabella" was even more enjoyable for me because I was allowed to use my own golden spotted Dalmatian, Beppo, as Arabella's coach dog. He was perfect for the part. However, after dress rehearsal, stage director Herbert Graf took me aside and warned me that I would upstage myself on my entrance if I brought the dog in, for he would surely steal the scene. I didn't care. I'd share a scene with Beppo any day.

Later on I used my young golden cocker spaniel, Paco, in the first act of "Rosenkavalier" when I was singing the Marschallin. Paco was a born "ham." He made a real "entrance" into the Marschallin's salon, looked over the audience and sniffed around until he caught my scent. Then he dashed for my chair and sat up for me. It was charming—and utterly distracting.

I had used Paco for the first two performances that year and planned to use him in the third, which was the broadcast. Kurt Baum was scheduled to sing The Tenor, the part in which he had made his Met debut but which he hadn't sung in some years.

Two or three days before the broadcast I was surprised by a call from stage director Hans Busch (son of the conductor), who politely asked me not to use Paco for that performance. When I asked why not, he told me he was simply relaying Mr. Bing's instructions. What a deal! "Oh, really, Hans," I said, "don't you think that's going a bit too far? What's that poor little dog done that Mr. Bing wants to keep him off the stage?" After all, when Irene Jessner, one of my Marschallins when I still sang Sophie, sang the part she had always used her own little dachshund, Annina, and I simply couldn't understand why Mr. Bing should make such an arbitrary ruling about Paco without any explanation whatsoever.

A few days later someone told me that Kurt had threatened to walk off the stage during the performance if my little dog had upstaged him by trotting on and wagging his tail beside my chair while Kurt was singing "his aria." By the time I heard this, however, I had mobilized all my dog-loving friends in and around the Met, including Mary Van Kirk with her three big Irish setters, and Sam Barber with his huge Belgian sheep dog with the hair hanging down over his eyes. We decided that since Mr. Bing was acting unfairly to theatrical canines, we would organize a union called DOGMA and picket the Met. What a great stunt that would have been!

In the end we chickened out, but I did send a telegram to "Pip" Bing, our general director's dachshund, which said: "Due to my indisposition and on the advice of my psychiatrist, I have decided not to appear in Saturday afternoon's performance. Signed: Paco Steber."

I received a return telegram immediately which read: "Sorry to hear about your indisposition. I myself gave up the stage long ago. Hope to meet you in the park sometime. Signed: Pip Bing."

Plan "B"

World War II was 10 years past and European sopranos were arriving at the Met constantly to compete for the roles I sang, or hoped to sing, all of them getting higher fees than I was getting after 15 years with the company. It was frustrating and insulting.

I longed to sing Tosca, and more Puccini and Verdi roles, but except for a few "Traviatas," that repertoire remained the exclusive property of a few sopranos, only one of them, Dorothy Kirsten, an American. Then, beginning in 1954–55, Tebaldi arrived to take over Mimi and Desdemona, and to split the Toscas with Milanov. Callas would arrive the following season. So, feeling I had no choice, I refused to sign a contract under those conditions, and took a leave of absence.

I know now that, as disappointed as I was then, if I had not been so driven, I would never have sung many of the unique things I did, or had such extraordinary adventures in fascinating corners of the world. And go to an almost unknown corner of the world is what I decided to do in the spring and summer of 1955. Under the auspices of the American National Theater Academy, arrangements were made for me to be the first American opera singer to venture into the then-unexplored artistic reaches of Yugoslavia.

In those days the "cold war" persisted as a very present danger. Mine would be one of the first efforts to cross the border of that independent Communist country. Before 1955, the only American performers known to the Yugoslavians were violinist Yehudi Menuhin and a touring company of "Porgy and Bess" (poet Maya Angelou was in that cast and describes the country in her third autobiography much as I found it a year later). Of American prima donnas they had no knowledge. But whether they were ready for me or not, I was on my way.

As I sailed out of New York Harbor on the Liberté, I conceived of this trip as something of a journey in search of a new me, setting off as I was for a four-months' trek into Mediterranean Europe completely on my own—no husband, no secretary, no family, not even a lover in my agenda, except that I was planning to visit Paul Strauss in Switzerland on my way.

The bond between us had endured for two years in the face of a great many conflicts. But when I arrived, unannounced, in Zurich, Paul was not pleased. Something had changed.

Apparently, I found it much easier to maintain a feeling of continuity in spite of our frequent separations than did Paul. Love, for me, constantly fed into the emotional content of my singing. This did not seem to be the case for Paul, a musician of a more detached and analytical nature. Nor did he seem able to envision any hope of a future for us together. Not only did the impossibility of sustaining a steadily growing relationship trouble him, he found it impossible, as a struggling young American conductor, to reconcile what he perceived as my more exalted stature as a prima donna with his own, which was just plain silly. I had long tried to convince him that he was already a success. His subsequent success in Europe justified that judgment. Nevertheless, we planned to meet again in Vienna before I went to Yugoslavia.

When we did, it was a bittersweet reunion, and we tried to end it there—the first of several such partings—victims of our divergent careers. I wanted Paul to come with me to the Festival in Dubrovnik later in the summer, where they also wanted him to conduct, but Paul had to visit his ailing father. We made vague plans to meet later in Italy. I began to realize we were drifting apart through sheer inability to be together, for Paul would not accept a relationship that would put either of us in an unacceptable light. We agreed to wait for an uncertain future; to continue as friends, forever holding warm and cherished memories of our time together, feelings which, for me, have endured to this day.

I arrived in Vienna just 24 hours too late to sing Donna Anna in a "Don Giovanni" recording with Cesare Siepi, Fernando Corena and Lisa Della Casa. When the original soprano fell ill, they looked for someone in Vienna to take her place and found Suzanne Danco the day before I arrived. Missing this opportunity almost broke my heart, but I still thought there was a "Don" recording in my future.

To add insult to injury, my European manager knew Herbert von Karajan needed a soprano for the Beethoven 9th late in June and suggested me, since I had sung it with Walter, Ormandy and Mitropoulos. *Von Karajan turned me down!* I was tempted to make an international incident of this insult to an American artist, but thought it might boomerang upon me in some way. Oh, for the brains of Grace Moore! *She'd* never have let this pass!!

I arrived in Zagreb on May 22 and plunged into three weeks of furious activity which included six opera performances and a concert. I sang "Tosca," "Faust," and "Traviata," learned that visiting artists don't receive special rehearsals for standard repertoire (the same old story everywhere), heard some native opera which impressed me tremendously, and discovered audiences in that city to be both discriminating and enthusiastic.

Some operas were vastly different in concept from my previous experience. "Faust," for instance, proved so much more "modern" than ours that it bordered on the Daliesque. Despite the fact that everyone except me sang in Serbo-Croatian, I was given no rehearsal. Before each act someone casually described a few details about the scenery and staging. Sometimes not quite well enough. During the love duet with Faust, I mistook a perfectly designed painted window for the real thing and was downright frustrated when I couldn't open it to the *nuit d'amour.*

Since my sojourn in Yugoslavia was a "first" for an American soprano, both my publicist Edgar Vincent and I had reasonable expectations for at least nationwide, if not worldwide coverage. Once again, however, as with my Pearl Harbor Day broadcast and the "Knoxville" premiere, history short-circuited our hopes when both Bulganin and Kruschev chose that exact moment to make their first trip ever beyond the borders of Russia to visit Yugoslavia.

Edgar couldn't get any news of me at all and finally, in pure desperation, called the *Wheeling Register* in my home town and got them to query the International News Service. "Where is Eleanor Steber?" they demanded. And, so nudged, the international press finally "found" me and we got some news about my performances into the American press.

I was astonished to discover that even in those lean post-war days, there were 12 active opera companies in Yugoslavia, all operating at least 10 months of the year, with their houses utilized for other performing arts during the other two months. Opera was offered in Zagreb every other day and, between operas, Shakespeare, operettas, original works by national playwrights, ballet, concerts and student performers.

All the arts flourished at different levels. National composers were producing fine work and while at the time I thought many of the operatic voices were unrefined, by our standards, you have to remember that Yugoslavia had lost almost a generation of singers and study to the war. Considering what they had to work with as they rebuilt the country, there was a tremendous creative excitement in the air.

That is not to say I did not have problems. Since it had been impractical to take my own costumes, I had to use theirs. I nearly cried when I tried on the "house costumes" for Tosca. (Of course their native prima donnas owned their personal costumes, as we do.) However, adding a few touches of my own, like my white mink stole and some jewelry, I managed to dress her up. I switched hats from a bonnet to a coach hat, which my Cavaradossi knocked off my head and had to replace during our Act I duet.

They weren't kidding when the cannons boomed at the end of the act. They used an honest-to-God small cannon which just about blew the heads, hats, ears and whatnots off everyone on stage. I thought we were being bombed. Talk about realism!

I was picked up in Belgrade by Tess Mravinc, a wonderful woman who was our Cultural Attaché in Yugoslavia, without whom I simply could not have survived. When I stepped into her U.S. Embassy limousine I was exhausted and ill, but a day in bed worked wonders and I was ready to start over.

I was originally scheduled to sing Butterfly, but the costumes were so terrible that I protested and suggested "Traviata" instead. When the State is running an opera house, they can do that sort of thing overnight. They liked the idea because their regular Violetta had tuberculosis—what irony!—and the opera had not been given for some time.

Several times during the tour I was moved to tears, because after some of my performances people simply refused to go home. Once this included a group of Russian artists who had been given special permission to attend, all believing this would be the only chance they would ever have to hear a prima donna from the "great Metropolitan."

My "Tosca" in Novisad was memorable. The theater itself was so small and so old, it was a miracle they could stage anything there, but they certainly lacked nothing in spirit. I was greeted when I arrived not only by a committee of officials, but by the entire chorus, orchestra and all the solo artists. There were roses, kisses, embraces and welcoming handclasps—and the inevitable toast with Slivovic in the Intendant's office.

The set alone provided sufficient difficulties to keep me on my toes, but the company idea of makeup was *something else!* I ran into one of

Baron Scarpia's henchmen backstage in the dark before the performance and he scared me half to death. They all looked as if they had stepped out of Dante's "Inferno." And when my Cavaradossi, whom I had met just a few hours earlier, came to say good evening in my dressing room, I didn't recognize him. Standing 6-foot, 4-inches to start, he had built up his nose, put on a wild wig and a costume, which was a flaming caricature of a "Bohemian artist."

Just before the beginning of Act II, I found there were neither candles nor crucifix, so I had to rig up something. I never even met my Scarpia at all until we were actually in performance (his makeup shook me up, too), and suddenly I found myself literally fighting for my virtue. That great bear of a man did everything but rape me right there in front of the audience; his hands were everywhere, and I half expected him to rip my costume off then and there. I was struggling for my life, and I wasn't "acting"; but even in the heat of battle, I knew it was all making for one helluva performance, and in spite of (or because of) it, I was having the time of my life!

When I collapsed just before "Vissi d'arte," my amorous Scarpia refused to settle anywhere, but prowled around upstage, shoes squeaking grotesquely with every step. I waited so long to begin the "Vissi d'arte" that the conductor gave me a panicky look; so I sang it anyway while Scarpia stalked up and down. When the curtain rang down, I told him off in no uncertain terms—in English, to be sure, but he got the message!

I ended my first sojourn in Yugoslavia with a benefit for crippled children. It's always a shock to realize that the Continental people I'd met didn't seem to understand either "benefits" or the spirit of volunteer work that we know in America. The poverty and, even more, the apathy which I began to see around me, except in the arts, depressed me dreadfully. Communism, which had been simply an "ism" for me at home, was evident in the dehumanizing and lack of independent spirit of the people.

Nevertheless, the people were always wonderful to me and this trip was one of the most intensely moving experiences of my life. *And* I quickly developed a profound gratitude for the facilities, training and discipline of our American opera theaters. I became grateful too for the freedom of artistic expression which I had always taken for granted. I hoped that I had given them a glimpse of a brighter future. I am completely sold on the value of continuing cultural exchanges everywhere. No matter what governments attempt to achieve by fiat, creative artists and audiences will always find a common spiritual unity.

After my first three weeks in Yugoslavia I had to leave for France, a trip which necessitated stopovers in Vienna and Paris. My destination was the annual Pablo Casals Bach Festival in Spain, where I remained for nearly 10 days rehearsing for my appearance with the Bach Aria group, subbing for Eileen Farrell, and listening to the incomparable master himself play Bach's suites for cello and, in my spare time, soaking up what I could of Basque history.

I had already known when I left New York that I was to spend those months in Europe entirely alone, but it didn't really hit me until one night in my Prades hotel as I stood at the window wondering where the hell I was going—and why. Those moments come and go for us all, I suppose, and this was another darkness before dawn, for like so many other artists who have made music at Prades, the experience of singing there simply lifted me out of myself. When it was over, I set off much more cheerfully for Vienna.

During a stopover in Vienna I had met up with a former Auditions of the Air winner, Mary Van Kirk. On my return I sang a couple of concerts with Ormandy and saw a couple of operas. I found Mary at loose ends and talked her into returning with me for the rest of my stay.

I had planned to vacation on the Italian Riviera where I would work on Ilia for Mozart's "Idomeneo," which I was scheduled to sing at the big festival in Greece later in the summer. However, when I learned I couldn't take any money out of Yugoslavia, I decided to spend my vacation at Dubrovnik. When the government offered to send someone to rehearse with me there, I couldn't have been happier.

The man they sent to play for me had actually conducted my Belgrade "Tosca." Bogdan Babic was an excellent musician and a charming man. That he and I were "simpatico," I already sensed; and Tess Mravinc had written me in Vienna that he was already in a "rosy cloud" at the prospect of working with me for an extended period. The plan turned out to be more than agreeable on all counts, and my memory of what I can only call my "Yugoslavian Idyll" remains rhapsodic to this day.

We did an unforgettable concert together in the lovely Castellet in the city of Split. The Castellet was a small monastery which had been restored by the great Yugoslav sculptor, Mestravic. After rehearsing the program in this enchanting setting the afternoon of the concert, Babic and I went our separate ways to dine and rest before the performance.

I dressed in my favorite moonlight blue chiffon bouffant gown, and while I waited to be called for, I strolled out onto the little balcony off my suite. I gazed across Spoleto toward the Diocletian Palace where I would soon sing "Faust," and savored the glorious evening. A full moon shone down from cloudless skies and I watched with pleasurable anticipation.

Suddenly I felt a presence behind me. When I turned, I saw my handsome accompanist, splendid in his white summer tux, looking as if he had stepped out of a movie. "How very beautiful you look," he said. And while I did not say it, I wanted to return the compliment. I almost blushed before his ardent eyes. If we looked half as beautiful to others as we looked to each other, what a pair we must have been! We were bewitched.

I don't think I ever sang as well as I did that night! There wasn't anything I couldn't do. And Bogdan Babic was superb. We performed as one—the whole evening was divine.

During the following weeks in Dubrovnik, we worked on "Idomeneo," brushed up "Faust" and prepared another concert; but we had plenty of time to relax and enjoy ourselves despite the precautions we had to take so he would not be accused of "fraternizing" with a western artist.

One day we enjoyed a long and leisurely swim down the Adriatic coast. We must have swum five miles. We dried off finally on the rocks by the Castellet, then sat and talked for hours mostly in German, because he couldn't speak English and I couldn't speak Serbo-Croatian. It didn't matter. We understood each other very well.

Strangely enough, it was Babic whose gentle insight helped me accept what Paul had been trying to make me understand all along. Babic said that, "As one must always take time for making love, one must also take time to nurture love if it is to last." And there never seemed to be enough time, then or ever. It is hard to know what thoughts and dreams this charismatic man may have held within himself during those days, but I know that he brought loveliness and welcome healing to me in his own special way. He left such an impression in my heart I felt sure that even if he were never able to visit my country, I would take back a bit of him to give my people through my singing, just as I know I left something of myself behind in his country.

Rested and restored in spirit, I gathered up Mary, said goodbye to the Balkans for a while, and set sail on a little Yugoslavian ship which hugged the coastline all the way along the Illyric Islands to Greece. I was following the route of Ulysses, perhaps on an Odyssey of my own!

I spent almost two weeks in Greece, a land of stark, bright beauty and rugged living. Here I was overcome with the pervading sense of great antiquity and agelessness which permeates the whole region.

At the Acropolis, in the ancient Odeon of Herodius Atticus, I portrayed for the only time in my life the role of Ilia, dramatic heroine of "Idomeneo." The Greek reviews were ecstatic: "A miracle that had to be seen and heard to be believed," cried one. "I've never heard anything like her," said another. Other notices proclaimed me "an artist whose singing overflows with emotion, expressiveness and color . . . her entire interpretive powers were a true poem."

On the crest of such resounding acclaim, after concerts in Athens and Salonika, I returned to New York, full of high hopes and expectations for the coming season.

Rebellion

During the Metropolitan's 1955–56 season, I sang 19 performances of six major roles, including my first Puccini "Manon Lescaut." My relations with the Metropolitan management seemed amiable enough because I was just sailing along doing my job as usual, minding my own business.

Renata Tebaldi's star was high at the Met and she was singing roles I had been awaiting impatiently for years. Callas, along with Mr. Bing, had already captured headlines. Rightly or wrongly, I still considered the treatment accorded to the post-war European sopranos highly preferential and there was still that large difference between my performance fees and theirs.

I was the House workhorse, had been for 15 years. I'd stepped in any number of times to substitute for others as Micaela, Marguerite and Donna Elvira; twice I'd done two operas in one day and only once by design—but nothing I did ever seemed to be enough. I cherished my reputation as a hard worker, but recognition was important to me too. Public applause and curtain calls were great, but I wanted and needed the Met management to acknowledge my value by giving me a contract which was at least commensurate with sopranos who worked far less than I. But I still couldn't get more than $800 a performance, while recent imports were started off at $1500.

As negotiation time arrived that year, I found myself and the management at a complete stalemate. Through my personal representative, Bill Judd, I had insisted on at least double my current fee—or better. But Mr. Bing stood pat. What was worse, he offered me only a single role, that of Arabella, at my present fee, for the 1956–57 season.

I had to make a tough decision. If I gave in and signed on such terms,

I'd be stuck for keeps. If I held my ground and refused to sign what I felt to be almost a punitive contract, I would be taking a huge gamble. All this was going through my mind in late December of 1955 because I knew that I must make a decision one way or another shortly after the first of the year.

When the Metropolitan first revived the Johann Strauss "Die Fledermaus" a few years before, the Met had cast the famous Bulgarian soprano Ljuba Welitsch as Rosalinda, over the behind-the-scenes objections of conductor Eugene Ormandy who had insisted that the part should have been given to an American, specifically me.

For whatever reason, the management eventually agreed and I finally made my debut in the part on New Year's Eve of 1953, a fact almost entirely overlooked by the press since it also marked the Metropolitan debut of world-famous prima ballerina, Alicia Markova, as the second act guest artist.

Since then, however, I had been a regular Rosalinda and I was again scheduled for a New Year's Eve performance to close out 1955. My secretary and I arrived in my Met dressing room early, toting a jeroboam of champagne with which to toast the New Year after the performance. I felt particularly excited and happy that night, and was chattering miscellaneous nonsense with a couple of friends as I dressed. Then started a string of visitors. Bob Herman, Mr. Bing's assistant, came to see me first. Then Mr. Bing himself wandered in to say hello, kind of gingerly, I thought. Finally, after the overture had started, Mr. Bing's chief administrator, John Gutman, appeared. With elaborate calm, Gutman said, "I think you should know that tonight's special guest in the ball scene is Renata Tebaldi." Once he had said his little piece, Gutman beat a hasty retreat, leaving me standing white and speechless in the center of the room.

This was simply too much. I was already pretty bitter because Tebaldi, however innocently on her part, was the personification of my rivals, and rightly or wrongly, I was convinced that Tebaldi's presence on the roster made Butterfly, Tosca, Mimi, and Violetta inaccessible to me. She also symbolized what I perceived as management's consistent deference to the new European sopranos. How could I not feel that they were purposely using Tebaldi in this performance of "Fledermaus" to intimidate me? My resentment, of course, was toward management alone and in no way reflected personally on Tebaldi herself, but her appearance in "my" performance this night enraged me.

I vaguely wondered why none of my earlier visitors had mentioned Tebaldi, and why Gutman had waited until just before I was to go on stage to tell me. What did he expect me to do? Did he wait until the last minute so that it would be too late for me to walk out, or was that what they expected me to do? I'll never know.

Before Gutman arrived and destroyed my good mood, I had been kidding around with all kinds of accents. Now, as I headed down the hall toward the stage, I got an idea. I lifted my chin off the floor and straightened myself up to my full 5-foot-6-inches and said to myself, "Okay, if that's the way they want it, I'll show them!" Without telling a soul what I was planning to do, I went out on the stage and delivered every single line of that entire opera in the thickest Southern accent I could muster!

The audience that night was a happy, non-subscription New Year's Eve crowd. My accompanist Ed Biltcliffe was among them. "When you started," he told me later, "I just couldn't believe my ears. There was a long, stunned silence while the audience listened to make sure they were really hearing what they thought they were hearing. Then they collapsed in laughter and couldn't wait for your entrances to see if you would keep it up."

On stage, tenor Charlie Kullman and baritone John Brownlee bit their lips to keep from cracking up and my broad comic improvisation played havoc with their concentration. Only my Adele, a high-spirited, quick-thinking Patrice Munsel, slipped into the mood of my performance so completely that at one point she responded to one of Rosalinda's lines with an explosive, "Yassum!"

Behind the frivolity, however, my loyal friends of the chorus and ballet were furious when they heard about the management's move, which seemed so obviously calculated to steal the thunder from an American colleague. Several of them sympathized with me off stage, voicing their chagrin. As they walked away, I heard one of them say, "What a helluva thing to do to Steber!"

Under all the bravado, I was hurting. Before going on stage for Act II, I unburdened myself to those in my dressing room: "My God, what a deal! Now I have to go out and bust a gut singing the damned 'Czardas' and Tebaldi will walk out and deliver a couple of Italian numbers and take down the house!"

But I was by no means completely resigned to that fate! As Rosalinda (now disguised as a Countess sporting a "Su'thun Hungarian" accent) I sang a resounding "Czardas" and retired, elaborately feigning imminent collapse, to a chair placed down stage left, close to the footlights. "Gasping" for breath, I held out one hand for liquid refreshment and clutched my breast dramatically with the other. Just your basic overblown melodramatics!

When Tebaldi came on stage to sing, I briefly cooled the histrionics; but when she finished, I rose quickly during the applause, walked directly to her and impulsively kissed her on the cheek. Tebaldi walked off the stage somewhat dazed, with no encore, and I took back my show.

The opera became hilarious! Everybody on stage and off got into the spirit of the thing as it got funnier and funnier. Everyone (including me) was wondering what I was going to do next. I was told later that two members of top echelon management were pacing out front during the entire opera, repeating over and over, "She's spoiling our opera! She's spoiling our opera!" At the same time, they were spreading the fiction that I had started to celebrate the New Year before the curtain went up. Not a bit of it! I was just being myself. That was pure, clear Eleanor Steber!

That was the most fun I ever had at the Met. It was really something! And I'm sure that I was just too much . . . too much to handle, so I guess I have no one but myself to blame for what happened.

Mr. Bing wrote me first thing the next day and chewed me out for my su'thun Rosalinda: "We can't have this sort of thing at the Metropolitan," he wrote. "I expect you to sing 'Fledermaus' as it is written and not in some outlandish dialect!"

Whatever perverse fun I had during the performance vanished when it was over. I was still so angry that I asked to be released from the remainder of the performances; but Mr. Bing refused and said he would expect me to stand by my contract.

"Well," I answered, "then I hope you'll have the courtesy not to ring in any more of my competitors on my performances." He replied icily that he wouldn't. But it was ridiculous, really, since the only time there were special guests in the second act was on New Year's Eve, so the dispute was now academic. Why had he chosen my chief rival for this performance? I will always wonder.

The dreadful aspect of the whole episode was that both of us hardened our positions when we met to negotiate my contract. I refused to budge on the fee question, and so did he. As a result, that "Fledermaus" flap cost me the entire 1956–57 season at the opera house I loved. Maybe that was the point of the whole maneuver.

But life is funny, because in spite of all I lost because of it, I had an experience the following year which, for good or ill, changed the rest of my life.

Chicago

Now that I had successfully managed to talk my way right out of the next Met opera season, I had to *DO something*, not merely to fill the vacuum, but to enhance my professional position for my next confrontation with Mr. Bing.

During my earlier travels in the Balkans I had been intrigued by the possibility of a more extensive tour to the Far East. So I told Bill Judd to accept the U.S. State Department's open invitation. While he set to work on my itinerary, I knuckled down to complete the Metropolitan spring tour and my own concerts.

That summer was neither restful or peaceful. I had a constant houseful of visitors, including two friends who stayed all summer together with five dogs. Not surprisingly, then, I was already tired and under a strain when I left for my American concert tour in late September as a prelude to appearances with the Chicago Lyric Opera where I was to sing "Andrea Chenier," an opera entirely new to me, and "Girl of the Golden West."

My last concert before reporting to Chicago was in Atlanta. I had been living on nerve, and my throat had felt a little rough from time to time during my tour. Whether it was the result of my tumultuous summer, or that I had irritated my vocal chords during the gala but noisy and smoky reception after the concert, I will never be sure. But as I headed for Chicago, I knew I was in vocal trouble.

By the time I arrived, I was obviously hoarse. Consequently, although I normally sang all rehearsals in full voice, I elected to sing my part an octave down and save myself wherever I could. Since the first opera was "Fanciulla," I personally had no worries about the part; but this was a new production for Chicago, and my presence during rehearsals was important to the rest of the company, so I kept going. The next day I couldn't make a sound. *Nothing!*

For someone who had always considered herself damn near indestructible, it was frightening. Bill Judd had flown in from New York to discuss my next Met season, so he took me to a doctor who diagnosed a hemorrhagic chord. He told me in no uncertain terms that if I did not maintain total silence for at least a week, I would not be able to sing Minnie, and that he wouldn't give two cents for the rest of my career.

A number of people urged me to cancel—not the Chicago people, of course, because they had nobody to cover for me. Bill Judd tried to talk me out of singing, but he couldn't—nobody could. I was absolutely nuts to do it, but that's me!

For six days I walked through stage rehearsals for "Girl of the Golden West" without making a sound. If I had a question, I scribbled it in a little notebook. Someone sang my music from the wings while I mimed the part of Minnie. Finally, the day before the performance when everybody had gone, I carefully tried a couple of measures to make sure the voice was still there. Minnie is a voice-buster under the best of circumstances. It needs a healthy voice and a rock-solid technique. I was sure of my technique, and my voice, as I tested it, felt fresh after its rest.

The Chicago doctor had also told me not to ride the horse on stage assuming, I suppose, that this would be an added strain I did not need. He had it all backwards. He might as well have tried to stop Niagara Falls than to try to keep me off my horse! I sang the opera, complete with horse. I galloped onto the stage in the third act like gangbusters and pulled up, rearing my horse on his hind legs so close to the footlights that the prompter fled, and Dimitri Mitropoulos looked so terrified I think he expected both me and the horse to land on his head.

Poor Dimitri. The sight of me thundering toward him on horseback left him terror-stricken. One of the papers published a whimsical cartoon of me on a rearing horse with two blazing six guns aimed at a protesting Maestro Mitropoulos in the pit.

It turned out to be a remarkably fine performance. We had a splendid cast and company. Carlo Maestrini from Florence was now our stage director, and Mario Del Monaco was an old hand at working in the frantic atmosphere which almost invariably accompanied productions of "Fanciulla." By now I was also good friends with both Mario and his wife and, along with Tito Gobbi, we had a beautiful working accord among us during this "Girl" and Chicago's new "Andrea Chenier."

My throat improved daily and we rehearsed my first "Andrea Chenier" with a minimum of difficulty. I must say, though, I was extremely careful of how I used my voice and concentrated on trying to remember everything Mr. Whitney would have said to me.

The first performance of "Chenier" was a little rocky, but the second one really took off. This opera is set in the French revolution, and I will forever remember the second scene of the last act as we, Chenier and Maddelena, rode off in the tumbril to the guillotine singing that extraordinary dramatic duet. For both of us it was simply transcendent, an experience which Mrs. Del Monaco rapturously confirmed. Then, when that lady who once thought she wanted to "tear out my eyes" said, "You are a wonderful person." I was very proud. Mario's death in October 1982 at only 67 touched me deeply.

Retracing Some Steps

When I left on the first leg of my State Department tour, I more than half believed I would never return. One night shortly before I left I even jotted down the names of musicians I knew who had died—usually flying—overseas. The fine Italian conductor Guido Cantelli had recently gone down in a crash just outside of Paris. Grace Moore's life had ended on the tarmac at Copenhagen; and there was also William Kapell, and several others. Even Lillian Nordica had fallen ill and died, alone, on a Pacific island thousands of miles from her New England home.

I took off from New York the day before Christmas in 1956 and was in London Christmas night talking with John Coast, who had made the arrangements for my trip. Originally I had planned to fly from New York over the North Pole to Finland where I would meet with the aged but still active composer Jan Sibelius. Then I was scheduled to fly into Russia to sing "Tosca" in both Leningrad and Moscow, which would have made me the first American soprano to sing there. I was tremendously excited about it.

But once again, history intervened. With the outbreak of the Hungarian Revolution, our State Department sternly insisted that I cancel my Russian dates. John Coast arranged for me to sing instead in Vienna.

Some years later in New York I met the Soviet official who had negotiated those performances I didn't sing. He stared at me icily. "The operas you canceled were completely sold out, Madame Steber, and we will *never* forgive you. Because you broke your promises to us, you will never again be invited to sing in our country." What made it worse was that Van Cliburn, then a young pianist who had astonished everyone by winning the Russian Tschaikowsky competition and was terribly popular there, had told them that I was the "greatest Tosca," so that they had booked me on his recommendation. Obviously, I couldn't tell anyone the truth about why I had canceled, so I just stood there tongue-tied and took my lumps. It was a damn shame, really.

Instead, I flew off to Vienna where I was supposed to make my debut in the reconstructed Staatsoper as Donna Anna in "Don Giovanni." What a thrill it was to see the snow-whitened fields of the Austrian landscape as I touched down at Schuilpoll Airport! There were so many sights familiar to me from my earlier trips: the same buildings, the same green uniforms of the officials, the same faces looking out from their little cubbyholes asking for papers and passports.

I stepped into bitter cold winds and skittering snowflakes, searching the passing crowds for a friendly face. I wanted to shout, "Vienna, love, I'm back! What have you waiting for me this time?" Then my old friend Angelo Eagon, our Embassy's liaison for the Arts in Vienna, came to meet me and we drove together into the city chattering excitedly. He deposited me at the Sacher Hotel, where I enjoyed a sentimental homecoming and settled into the same dear old cozy suite which held such sweet memories from 1953.

Ed Biltcliffe and our photographer Halley Erskine arrived from New York in time to celebrate the New Year with me to the ringing of church bells. We watched fireworks light up the sky around the Schönbrunn Palace; but this celebration, indeed all of life in Vienna at that moment, was dimmed by the thousands of Hungarian refugees streaming across the border.

Vienna was filled with tales of both horror and heroism, and I felt painfully guilt-ridden thinking of the freedoms I took so easily for granted as an American. What did it matter, I wondered, that I was to sing an opera when Hungarians were fighting in the streets, weaponless, for the most elementary rights, for life itself?

Nevertheless, I reported promptly to the Staatsoper. No one had informed the management that I sang Donna Anna only in Italian. Casts were called together and the opera was changed from "Don Giovanni" to "Tosca," back to the "Don" and finally again to "Tosca" which, because of the small cast would be more easily adaptable to a dual language performance. This suited me fine, for I felt more secure with the principals and the simpler staging.

I was upset, however, when I discovered I was to sing a "closed performance." Performances were often given for special groups and tickets for them were not sold to the general public, so it looked as if none of my friends could come. After considerable politicking on my part, the problem was finally resolved, and my Viennese opera debut turned out to be as rewarding as I had hoped. There was such a crush of people at the stage door afterward that I got separated from my friends. I was pressed into a doorway, cornered, and verging on panic when someone rescued me.

The European edition of the *Herald Tribune* reported that not only was I cheered and called back more than a dozen times, but that "in appearance and voice timbre she awakened in many . . . memories of Maria Jeritza . . ." a beloved Viennese favorite.

Three nights later I presented my first solo recital in Vienna at the Mozartsaal. It was a long concert—almost three hours—and the audience received each of my songs as if mesmerized . . . certainly I was. It was as if I had pulled all my loves together, my private memories and my love of singing and my affection for Vienna and offered it all in this concert.

The next day I was suddenly alone. Not a single one of those I loved was there to share it with me. "What do ovations matter now that I am by myself?" I pondered. "My only consolation is that I know I was able to give once more that which the Lord has given me to share and I know I gave my best; but is there nothing left for "me"?

That night my little "troupe" left Vienna by Balkan Express, a very tired but gay company. We four—Biltcliffe, Halley Erskine and my road manager, Keene Curtis—boarded our train for Yugoslavia with *23 pieces of luggage, 200 pounds* overweight! (Keene Curtis later became a superb character actor, appearing in countless television shows and movies.)

We arrived in a cold, murky, redolent Zagreb shortly after dawn. The poverty in the city was so much more forcibly evident that early winter morning than during my previous summer visit. To watch women in the streets swinging picks to chop up the ice, and hundreds of peasants and workmen, poorly clothed and apparently pitiful, yet so full of life, warmed me with kindred feeling and revived my own zest. I was glad to be back in Yugoslavia, glad even for the musty smell of the city which one can never forget and must eventually come to love.

I had a performance of "Traviata" the following day, so I stayed in bed until afternoon, had some lunch and got my hair done. Then, back at the hotel, I had a glass of the ubiquitous Slivovic, some hearty soup with dark bread, and left for the theater, where I received a marvelously spontaneous welcome from the cast. They told me I had become something of a legend in Yugoslavia, and now I began to believe it. We sang in a lovely little opera house full of history now already enriched by the vigor of its new endeavors. They seemed to me a people who, while still poor in material things, were wonderfully rich in spirit. It may have been true that theirs were not the most elegant opera performances in my experience, but they gave to it all they had, which meant unlimited time and loving effort. I thought there was much we could learn from them, and I was proud to be singing with them.

It was colder than blue blazes when we left for Belgrade a couple of days later. People were on their way to work as we left: peasants with big baskets on their heads, others carrying live chickens and yet others balancing shoulder yokes holding baskets of produce, and office workers, dressed in a fantastic jumble of styles and colors, all teeming with life and vitality. I began to anticipate my return to Belgrade with such excitement that my heart began to pound like that of a girl in love.

Friends at the station, flowers, shouted greetings, the hotel and then to the opera that night to hear Bogdan Babic conduct "Lucia." A fine performance...charming sets...and Bogdan much improved as a conductor. But perhaps I will be pardoned if I say that what I remember most was entering the theater, for when they recognized me, the audience stood and sang a greeting to me.

A few nights later, I sang for them—the people of Belgrade. If I thought Vienna was a triumph, Belgrade was unbelievable! I gave them just about everything I knew, and the Yugoslavian audience went wild; there is no other way to put it. They cheered and clapped and crowded down around the stage, refusing to let me go. Finally, as I had done in Vienna, I returned to the stage for my last bow already wearing my fur coat and strewing my flowers among the people.

At last I found myself alone in my hotel room, exhausted but still perched on the pinnacle, and wondering what the rest of the long tour ahead of me could offer which could even begin to approach the exaltation of this evening.

Constanza, *Seraglio*

Arabella

Steber's Four Metropolitan Premiere Roles

Vanessa (also World Premiere)

Marie, *Wozzeck*

Countess, *Marriage of Figaro*

Sophie, *Rosenkavalier* (debut role)

Micaela, *Carmen*

Fiordiligi, *Così fan Tutte*

Donna Elvira, *Don Giovanni*

The Marchallin, *Rosenkavalier*
(G. Maillard Kesslere, B.P.)

Manon—*Manon*
(Sedge LeBlang)

Donna Anna—*Don Giovanni*
(Sedge LeBlang)

Elsa—*Lohengrin* (Sedge LeBlang)

Desdemona—*Otello* (Sedge LeBlang)

Tosca (Sedge LeBlang)

Finally got her man. Major and Mrs. Gordon Andrews after wedding ceremony.

Composer Samuel Barber consults with quick-study Steber during *Vanessa* rehearsals.

In concert singing from Menotti's *The Telephone*.

Steber greets fans after a 1961 *Tosca*.

After a concert at Cleveland Institute of Music with a young James Levine, conductor.

Made a West Virginia Hall of Famer in 1976, Steber signs autographs.

Madame Ambassador

What can I say about my tour into the East? It was tougher, more exciting and more demanding than I could possibly have imagined, but somehow I fulfilled all and more than was asked of me. I had flowers thrown at me, pressed into my arms and hung around my neck. I held more press conferences and met more people in those few months than I had during my entire life. I was gloriously welcomed everywhere and never had a single problem in my person-to-person relationships in any country I visited. We were given red carpet treatment everywhere. Local and U.S. officials greeted us with open arms, and when we had done our "turn," sent us off with assurances that as ambassadors we achieved more with our music and ourselves in a few hours or days than politicians had in years.

After 17 years of concert experience in America and Europe, I thought I knew everything there was to know about barnstorming, but my previous tours were child's play in comparison to what lay ahead of me now.

Ed Biltcliffe and I had completed our musical preparations before we left New York, carefully working out four different programs including a special one for audiences in Jakarta and Singapore where German and Dutch were familiar, and a French program for the Middle East, where French had long served as the diplomatic language. As it turned out, we did variations of all four programs, along with operatic arias and English and American music. I had more than 100 songs and arias ready to sing at any given moment.

Before we were done, I had sung some 33 formal concerts in 17 countries, and traveled in excess of 50,000 miles. This converted into an average of two concerts per week, which didn't impress me as too strenuous when I first received the tour schedule, and vocally it was not. But then I had to find the time to fulfill the other purpose of the trip — to share cultural experiences with the nationals in each country.

By hook or crook, I had to find the time to meet foreign musicians, absorb their music, and find and learn Eastern music which I might take home to incorporate into future programs to be shared with audiences in America. All this called for tremendous stamina, constant travel (including the repeated red tape of customs), the frequent changes in time zones, climates and foods, plus the endless packing and unpacking, all took their toll. We seldom rested for more than an hour or two. In some places my concerts started late in the evening, as they do in Spain. What was worse, three times running we had to board commercial flights at 5:00 a.m., so going to bed at all on such nights was pointless. I did most of my sleeping in the air. My performances, however, always revived my spirits, but what consistently turned me on were the *people*!

We began the tour in Istanbul, on to Ankara, Beirut and Karachi. By the time I arrived in Iraq, I was sick with a dandy case of flu and literally drenched with perspiration as I got off the plane. I was met by a group from the Women's Club of Baghdad. These were women of tremendous courage who had broken away from many of the restrictive traditions which had kept women subservient for centuries. Only four years before I arrived, they had daringly discarded their filmy burkas (veils) and chosen to dress Western style in dark conservative suits. Now they had undertaken, all by themselves, to sponsor my concert as a benefit for their many charities.

I went straight from the airport to my hotel and took my fever to bed. (While an Asian Flu epidemic swept the U.S., I enjoyed my Asian Flu at its source.) I couldn't consider canceling this concert under any conditions. I was not only the first American soprano, but probably the first Western woman to sing in that city, and these determined women had risked everything by inviting me to come. They had even had to import a piano all the way from Ankara just for this concert.

The local press opposed them, making dire predictions that no one would come to hear me or if they did, would walk out after my first song; but these remarkable women persisted. They were ultimately rewarded by a sell-out crowd of 1500 with an extra 300 standing.

The only available hall was a movie theater, and before my concert at 10:30 p.m. they showed Judy Garland's "A Star is Born." There was no dressing room, not even a closet. But there was a boiler room in which those darling Baghdad ladies had improvised a dressing room for me with an ingenious tent of sheets which gave me both a modicum of privacy and protection from the heat. They insisted on helping me dress and proved so solicitous and hovered about so anxiously, I half expected them to follow me on stage.

There was just room enough for the piano and me on the stage, but no stairs to get me there. So the club contrived a makeshift set of steps just for me. I teetered my way onto the stage in a billowing gown surrounded by my ladies with half a dozen pairs of hands reaching up to catch me if I stumbled.

Toward the end of the concert, with the audience completely won over by my songs, I was midway into a little piece about a bird when a kitten came out of nowhere and strolled across the stage. I didn't bat an eye, but when I finished, I laughed and told the audience, "I think that cat is hunting for my bird."

I had such a fever during that concert, I wonder that I got through it so well. The audience demanded encores until I was completely exhausted. The next day one of the papers which had forecast my downfall did a complete turnabout, proclaiming: "The Sun of the West has risen upon our Eastern land."

I soon recovered from *my* bout with the bug, but everyone in my little company suffered intermittent stomach upsets throughout the tour except Biltcliffe and me, although we ate all the native foods. Neither Ed nor I drank anything but bottled water, and were so well supplied with the finest of "spirits," those intestinal bugs never had another chance with us; we simply drowned 'em!

When I was a very young girl I had once briefly dreamed of traveling to the Orient as a missionary, and now I realized with some amazement that in rather a different way that's exactly what I had become. As the first American singer to make such a tour in modern times, I was breaking entirely new cultural ground.

That many of those in my many huge audiences had come to see me chiefly as a curiosity didn't bother me. Most of them had seldom, if ever, heard a voice like mine, but they stayed to listen with great attention. It demonstrated profoundly that music is truly a universal language and that my audiences in the Far East didn't have to be "educated" in our so-called "Western idiom" any more than I had to comprehend the Oriental mystique to enjoy their music.

When I discovered, quite early in the tour, that my audiences were composed chiefly of special guests invited by the embassies and consulates, I demanded an opportunity to sing extra concerts for the general public. I also insisted on meeting each country's most revered musicians. These artists and I invariably established instantaneous rapport. I made tapes of our conversations and of their music. Everywhere I went I tried to learn one or two of their songs and something about their local instruments, once in a while managing to accompany myself in one of their short songs.

I soon learned to send someone on ahead of us to arrange visits to universities and women's groups. Because the public auditoriums were small and local businessmen underwrote some of my appearances, tickets were priced so high students could not afford them; so I made impromptu visits to Beirut's Women's College, the University of Madras, and the Dacca School of Fine Arts.

"Reaching an audience" is an overworked expression, and yet I cannot find a better phrase for it. To be able to sing for Indian students a Bach aria, "My Heart Ever Faithful" as a sample of our classical musical literature; or to demonstrate through the opening measures of Lakmé's "Bell Song" or parts of Lucia's "Mad Scene" that our music possesses, in a different way, the technique of vocal embellishment which forms the basis of the Indian ragas, and to show them by singing the "Sempre Libera" from "Traviata" how a composer like Verdi used such vocal embellishments purely for dramatic purposes — these were far more exciting than the official appearances, even with all their ovations and flowers.

I heard unpublished songs in Dacca, for example, which had been passed directly from person to person for uncounted generations. In Bombay I saw a fabulous play performed in a courtyard by superb Indian actors. I met the most famous singer in southern India, Srimanthi Vasanthakamari, and we talked together about the difference between Eastern and Western singing techniques. She explained to me that in India voices are never trained into the higher registers, but that *all* study is concentrated in developing the low voice for volume, timbre and purity of tone. It is largely because of this emphasis that the Indian has difficulty understanding the Western soprano voice. It is hard for them to "hear." *I*, on the other hand, was amazed to find that their music is hard for a Western soprano to sing. I tried some of their "ragas" and found my voice sticking somewhere around middle C. It was like trying to sing bravura passages by Bellini or Donizetti an octave or two lower than usual.

The physical conditions under which we performed in Asia were challenging. I sang in everything from large reception rooms to hotel ballrooms, classrooms, out-of-doors, and in auditoriums heavily rugged and hung with heavy drapes or tapestries which made me feel muffled in cotton wool. In airless halls I sang under huge ceiling fans which blew hot, muggy air in my face. Concert tours in the United States were a snap compared to this.

I knew, at last, that my predestination of death, which had haunted me back in the States, was upon me the day our KLM plane prepared for a landing at Bangkok, Thailand. After making several passes over the field, the plane began to circle round and round while we watched fire engines and ambulances line up along the runway. Our little Thai stewardess looked terrified and I clung, white-knuckled, to Ed Biltcliffe's hand while he chattered nonsensically on, trying to distract me.

When the pilot finally touched down—very tentatively it seemed to me—we learned that the nose wheel had never locked. I sat frozen in my seat, thinking of Grace Moore. Biltcliffe tried to make some sort of cheerful quip, but all that came out was a dry croak.

As our caravan persevered through the musically uncharted countries of the Far East, I could not help becoming aware of the political unrest. An atmosphere of incipient rebellion simmered just below the boiling point. I often thought of us like the Children of Israel, dashing through the parting seas of red tape and political turmoil just before they closed behind us. Sometimes we barely made it, for there had been riots in Jakarta (where Lillian Nordica died) just before we landed, and all kinds of disturbances in other countries, ranging from assassinations to hurricanes as soon as we left.

The international press, in numbers I had never seen before, met me at every stop, jumping on every word I uttered. I had to keep my wits about me because I never knew what they were going to ask. Once a Soviet reporter challenged me about the "immorality" of American popular music, and another time I had to defend our Cultural Exchange Program against an attack by one of our own Congressmen. My Japanese encounter with the press was the only one which completely defeated me. Surrounded by 50 reporters with absolutely no interest in music, I was called to account for the atomic bomb and the destruction of Hiroshima and Nagasaki. What could I say?

During these three months I met peasants and students, premiers and geishas. I visited shrines and national monuments and talked with professional musicians and actors. I met heads of state and their wives. But perhaps one of my most cherished meetings was that with Han Suyin, author of the best-selling "A Many-Splendored Thing." She was not only a world-famous writer but a working physician, devoting herself to the poor and disadvantaged throughout the Indian peninsula and Malaysia. She had the extraordinary simple and unforgettable beauty of total selflessness.

I explored the markets of every country, picking up materials, jewelry and native costumes. From Ceylon eastward I was "sari-happy" and crammed dozens of the diaphanous creations into my luggage.

Our tour, which had started way back in Lebanon, had taken us through Turkey, East and West Pakistan, India, Ceylon, Singapore, Indonesia and Thailand, and now I was scheduled for a stop in Vietnam before finishing up with visits to the Philippines, Formosa, Hong Kong and Japan.

It was in Saigon, between concerts and visits to schools and the unending schedule of public appearances, that I attended a party at the La Relais Club thrown by movie director Joseph Mankiewitz for the cast of "The Silent American," which had been partly filmed there. Audie Murphy was the star, and Claude Dauphin and Michael Redgrave (later Sir Michael) were also present.

It was an especially gay party, and I remember mugging for photographers with Michael Redgrave as we did a duet of Noel Coward's "I'll See You Again." Somewhere in the midst of the of the noise and confusion, Mankiewitz walked over to my table accompanied by a perfectly gorgeous man with the most incredible blue eyes I have ever seen. "Gordon," he said to this dark-haired officer, "I want you to meet Eleanor Steber, the original Prima-tive Donna!"

When our eyes met, the world stopped. We danced and we talked, and for the rest of my stay in Saigon I was oblivious to everyone except Gordon Andrews, a Military Assistance Group captain. It was the same for him. We lived in a dream, and those around us left us almost entirely alone as we lived within our own radiant aura of light.

When my inexorable schedule tore me away from Saigon a few short days later, the Pacific Airlines were inundated by our frantic correspondence. Sometimes Gordon's letters wandered from island to island, often arriving late or at the wrong address. He cabled flowers to me everywhere I went, although they often arrived the day after a concert because of the confusing time zones. Every night, no matter how late, I sat down at my typewriter, and filled hours when I should have been resting by writing long, impassioned letters.

The grand finale was set for Japan, our longest stay in any one country. My itinerary swept me up and down the islands with such speed that I often lost track and had to ask where I was. I sang major concerts in Kyoto, Osaka and Tokyo. I sang in the gigantic Takarazuka theater which rivaled Radio City Music Hall in size although it was then miles from nowhere in a town called Nara. I visited a fishing village and watched girls dive for pearls on Mikamoto's Island. I was entertained at a tea house, watched a performance of the spring Geisha Apple Blossom Festival, and somehow even found time to investigate the provocative mysteries of the Japanese public baths.

Some 80 million people saw me sing "Butterfly" on TV. That's an audience of stunning size. I was terribly self-conscious about my height in that world of shorter people.

I learned to sign my name in Japanese characters, to handle chopsticks with skill and, as I had done everywhere, I learned a song and a few remarks in their language, a small extra effort which invariably took down the house whenever I did it. In public I was constantly surrounded by hordes of people openly staring in fascination and frequently reaching out to touch me.

Although we were now almost terminally exhausted, we never lost our sense of humor. After one particularly tough day, all of us somewhat slap-happy with fatigue, we returned to our hotel for a lifesaving drink and a bushel of fresh oysters. Thus refreshed, we ducked out to play a fast and funny game of miniature golf. Then Ed Biltcliffe and I played a mad game of ping-pong until dinner. There were too few such carefree moments!

Despite the hectic schedule, I had loved almost every second of my trip. In a letter to Gordon I wrote that I would really love to repeat the whole thing. "Only the next time," I said, "I want to visit China and more out-of-the-way places like Kuala Lampur, Lahore, Teheran and so many others. Dreaming, dreaming, I am always dreaming," I admitted, "but I am mad about this part of the world, and I don't know how I shall be able to accept that old life back in New York. After a year I know I shall be wanting to be off to new horizons again."

My heart was torn now between East and West, because against my better judgment, I was beginning to build dream castles around the compelling Army captain who was obsessing my thoughts. I tried desperately to relegate my encounter with Gordon Andrews into the category of an "adventure," but could not. When Gordon wrote that he was determined to come to New York to marry me, I was ecstatic. Yet I replied quickly that his first loyalty was to his present wife and family and any decision he made must be his alone; that I must not be used as the râison d'être for breaking up a family. I made a determined effort to confine my dreams within reasonable bounds. I had long since documented (for my own enlightenment) a pattern of "seeking," so urgent in its intensity that it carried seeds of destruction. My life search for the one I called "The Beloved" was obsessive and now, I believed I had found him. I laid open all my feelings in a long letter to Gordon.

"Through many years I have felt you coming toward me," I wrote. "I saw you in many people and sought you in many ways. You were a boy who read poetry to me . . . you were a boy who loved children and worked with them. Then you were a great athlete, knowing the cheers of the crowd; then again, a brilliant musician. I have looked for you long and found you in many places. You are the essence of all my dreams.

"You cannot possibly know the years of seeking, thinking that 'this is the one,' or, 'that is the one'; of allowing myself to be deluded by a semblance of the 'Beloved One' only to discover that I was wrong. How can you know the pain that has seared all the falseness and absurdities from me, when what I believed to be true proved yet merely another trap to trip me up.

"And yet I will go on. I must! Everyone must go on living. To die is to lose hope; but nothing will ever be the same again. I shall be unable to find solace even in the need of others for me. What I was once able to accept, I can accept no longer. Without love, I am all at sea!"

I was beguiled. The boundaries between dream and reality crumbled. Theatrical as though they might seem, such internal dramas often embodied the only reality which belonged to me alone. As I headed toward home, the "idea" of this new man gripped my imagination, but I rested the future in the hands of that fate which had guided me, and half hoped that the miles between us would protect me from having to make any decision at all. Perhaps this, too, would fade with time and distance.

By now I was totally exhausted. I had hoped to rest for a while in Hawaii, but my people in New York already had another big schedule set up for me. So once more I battled in sleep my terror of flight and, after waking in a sweat as usual after the same old nightmares, I pulled myself together and boarded the plane for home.

Return from Paradise

I flew directly from Hawaii to tell the story of my Far Eastern tour on Steve Allen's late night TV show. I was particularly anxious to report on the dangerous political conflicts I had observed in Pakistan, Indonesia and Vietnam. I told the story in more detail the following day at a press conference Edgar Vincent had arranged for me.

But whatever success I had achieved personally as a cultural ambassador in the countries I visited, I had little, if any, at home. They listened to what I had to say, but nobody took seriously warnings of potential international eruptions from a mere opera singer. It was no comfort at all to see all my prognostications gradually coming true, all climaxing with the Vietnam tragedy.

This was temporarily driven from my mind by the news that Ezio Pinza had died just as I arrived home. I had been away so long, I hadn't known he was ill. So many memories! It seemed unbelievable now that scarcely three years out of conservatory I sang my first Marguerite with the great Ezio Pinza! Then the "Figaros," "Magic Flutes" and "Don Giovannis." He was such a vivid, dynamic person to work with, thoroughly professional in his application to his work, but so exciting as a performer that the very air was alive when he sang. And, to answer the unasked question: No, I didn't, but I sometimes wished I had!

Before I had fully comprehended the fact that he was gone, I received a call from Edgar Vincent, who was assisting Mrs. Pinza with the funeral arrangements. He asked me if I would sing at the services scheduled to be held at the Cathedral of St. John the Divine.

I was honored and touched, but puzzled, for although I had always loved and admired Pinza as a colleague, I'd never been what you could call a personal friend. "Why me?" I asked.

"Well, honestly, Eleanor," Edgar replied, "I think you're the only one who could get through it."

Licia Albanese, Pinza's compatriot, thought she would break down, and several others who had been close to Ezio felt the same. As I returned to New York, Edgar suggested to Mrs. Pinza that I might be able to handle it.

So I found myself that day standing in the pulpit high over the packed congregation singing the "Ave Maria" from "Otello," unable even by lifting my head to avoid the presence of the casket below me. I'm pretty tough, but I barely made it through. There will never be another like him. I had little time to mourn the passing of this charismatic man and superlative artist. Within hours I was back in California on concert tour; then, at long last, home for four precious weeks at Melodie Hill to rest, and then to review the five roles I was scheduled to sing in Chicago and at the Met the following month.

While I had been on the other side of the world, the Metropolitan had been preparing the world premiere of a new opera by Samuel Barber, with a libretto by his friend Gian-Carlo Menotti. I had heard all kinds of rumors about this new work of Sam's, and because everyone kept saying that the title role of "Vanessa" was perfect for me, I could not understand why I had not been asked to do it. Pride kept me from asking.

Earlier, during a flight to Puerto Rico to sing three operas, I shared the plane with my good friend Rosalind Elias, who was immersed in a large manuscript of "Vanessa" in which she was to sing Erika. I pretended not to notice, but it hurt to realize that I had not been asked to sing Vanessa.

Echoes of my Far Eastern trip and the uneasiness of my return to a complacent America disquieted me during the weeks that followed. The French had already left Saigon, and I could not believe that the Americans would not have the wisdom to follow. I had written home that "America seems unaware; the French are already bankrupt, and the Vietnamese children are playing with live ammunition." And it was still only 1957!

I felt such a bond with the people I had met that it filled my letters. In one such letter I wrote Gordon: "In my dreams I am often still back in those exotic lands. While I was away, all my American heart and soul reached out toward home. Now that I am home, I find myself almost an alien, compelled to remember over and over my unique experiences in those Eastern lands.

"I must find a way to tell 'my story'. Somehow this 'American prima donna' must slice through the impenetrable wall of headlines so obsessed with Italy's 'La Superba' and the Greek 'La Divina'.

"How frustrated I am with what press and public alike seem to demand from artists who, *only* by the Grace of God, have the opportunity to express through their voices the music written for them by the really great ones—the composers—the true creators.

"I am weary of interviews and the constant chatter," I wrote. "I am tired of endless repetitions of the stories I must tell because I cannot possibly display for public consumption the deeper experiences of these past four months, the untranslatable gifts to my soul, my most secret self. I wish only to walk in my own secret garden, but must go on acting the great extrovert that my career demands of me. Someday the walls around my secret garden will crumble from the sheer persistence of those who constantly seek to invade it.

"And so I have come back to what I had before and try to live within the bounds of my nature. I am enchanted once more in trying to catch the 'will o' the wisp', knowing that I will continue to be enticed by dreams I cannot catch or hold. But dreams are not enough. I have lived one for the past four months. I lived others in the past. It is reality which escapes me.

"What do all my achievements matter when I must inevitably come home to an empty apartment from a world where I am daily confronted with misunderstandings and frustrations. I spend my energies to satisfy, if only for a moment, all those who each expect something different from me; to filling the coffers of agents who, no matter how sympathetic they are, still enjoy their 15 or 20 percent from my labors; and, worse, on friends who propose with giving hands, but consciously or not, seem to expect repayment of my very self.

"I should be thankful for so much that life has given me, but I would give it all up for someone who would not demand of me what the rest of the world seems to expect, but only that I should be myself.

"While I was in Vietnam, I had a moment that impressed itself so vividly on my mind, it symbolizes the 'weltschmertz' which momentarily overwhelms me: I watched a family in a sampan, the woman standing in the stern, guiding its course while her man throws out his nets to catch their food. Inside the little craft were perhaps two young children, and inside the woman's belly she undoubtedly carried another. How beautiful it was! How wonderfully simple!

"A man laboring for his family and a woman content to work hard for her man, with no desire for riches beyond those which could be fulfilled through him and the children who will continue the pattern. If this scene is all I brought back with me from the tour, it is enough. I sometimes think I would exchange all I have just to be that woman on the sampan!"

But a singer, like a ball player or a dancer, must inevitably be defeated by a schedule. A career is committed so far in advance that a day when I could awake and ask myself, "What shall I do today?" was unique. No matter how often I thought I longed to have done with my whole career, there was always one more commitment and, before I realized it, I was swept into the whirlwind once more.

My great anticipation for the 1957–58 season was the Met's major production of "Don Giovanni," which was to be directed by Karl Böhm. I had, you remember, opened the new Chicago Calling Card Opera (which became the Lyric) as Donna Anna in 1954, and had sung two performances at the Met in 1955 with Max Rudolf, but this was different. This was an entirely new production.

Rehearsals started early in October and we were all excited by the presence of Maestro Böhm. Eugene Berman had designed fresh new sets and costumes for our cast, which included the handsome Cesare Siepi in the title role, Lisa Della Casa as Donna Elvira, Roberta Peters as Zerlina, Giorgio Tozzi as Leporello, Cesare Valletti as Don Ottavio, plus Fernando Corena and Theodore Uppman.

I will always regret that Mr. Whitney never lived to hear me sing the role he always claimed was meant for me. He had died in December of 1949, but he was much in my thoughts the night I sang Donna Anna in the first performance of this production. I could almost see him nodding his head and smoothing his mustache with his right forefinger and saying, "That was pretty good, Steber." Between my teacher and Mozart, I couldn't miss.

It was a glorious fulfillment of my dream to be singing this role which I always felt was destined for me. That Donna Anna was truly my part was heartily confirmed by the critics who hailed the entire new production. *Time* magazine declared that I "presented a rich, blazing, gusty-voiced Donna Anna..." Even the sometimes cynical *New Yorker* magazine wrote, "As Donna Anna, Eleanor Steber was an altogether stunning theatrical figure, providing the sort of fire that is seldom encountered in this part..." and Winthrop Sargent (*Saturday Review*) put the icing on my cake, writing: "First honors go to Eleanor Steber for a Donna Anna rarely equalled. Spectacularly, she commands the power for 'Or sai che l'honore,' the finesse for the ensembles and the florid flexibility of 'Non mi dir,' which mark her as a Mozart singer in a hundred." This was delicious food for my soul.

I had a few performances scheduled on and off in Chicago with Lyric, and *almost* made a trip there during rehearsals to substitute as Desdemona in "Otello" when Renata Tebaldi became ill. Unfortunately, Mr. Bing made it quite clear that if I took off for the Chicago performance I would jeopardize his new "Don Giovanni," and I would suffer the consequences. I stayed in New York.

After the second performance of the "Don," however, I headed for Chicago to sing the Countess in a couple of "Figaros." I received a message at my hotel: "The Oriental stinker is back in New York!" Gordon Andrews was back. I hardly knew what to think or feel. He had seldom been off my mind since that brief sojourn in Saigon, and I kept every letter he had written me. I longed to see him, but on the other hand, knowing he was married, I had tried to put the whole incident behind me as a kind of "brief encounter."

Two nights later, after a performance of "Don Giovanni" back at the Metropolitan, suddenly he was standing before me, resplendent in Army dress uniform, boasting that he had kept his promise to return to me. I was rhapsodic!

Still bound to my schedule, I was no longer cautious, and when I returned to Chicago Gordon went with me. I sang "Tosca," then sped on to Detroit where I sang "Traviata" in my one and only appearance for the New York City Opera Company. Then another "Tosca" in Chicago and more "Don Giovannis" in New York. No one had to reassure me that those performances were brilliant. They had to be, because I was incandescent with happiness. And even if I had known all the pain which would eventually follow, I would never, never have given up a minute of it.

Following the Met broadcast performance of "Don Giovanni" there was an Opera Guild reception, I think, because I know it was the first time Gordon formally escorted me to a public event. He was already urging me to marry him, and that night we visited his mother in Darien, Connecticut. On our way back we ate dinner and returned to my apartment, talking non-stop all the way. It was very late that same evening when the phone rang. It was Edgar Vincent.

"Max Rudolf wants to see you first thing Monday," Edgar announced, "because the Met is about to cancel the entire production of 'Vanessa' and Max agrees that you are the only one who can possibly learn the role in time."

I was mute for a moment, wondering what to say. I was still hurting because I had never even been approached about the part. I knew that Maria Callas had turned it down because she felt Erika was a stronger role, and that Sena Jurinac had agreed to do it and had been working with both Mitropoulos and Sam Barber when she suddenly canceled her entire New York season. A great deal of effort and expense had already been put into Sam's new opera, and canceling it would not only mean a terrible loss, it would mean rescheduling much of the season. I really don't know whether Mr. Bing wanted me to do the part or not, but I was obviously his last chance.

All this flew through my mind while Edgar waited on the other end of the phone. "All right, Edgar," I said, "I'll see Rudolf first thing Monday."

The Fire Horse

When I walked into his office, Max greeted me with a big smile. "I told them all along that you were the one for this part!" Then he escorted me in to see Mr. Bing, who asked me if I thought I could learn the role in time for the premiere, a bare six weeks away—could or would?

I said, "Give me the score for a few hours. I'll let you know."

From the Met I cabbed directly to Sam Barber's apartment where he played for me as I sang through Vanessa's music. I knew at once that Vanessa was for me. I had to do it. In the same way that "Knoxville, Summer of 1915" was right for me, so was Vanessa. From that moment on Vanessa possessed almost every working moment, and I poured all my energy into it. Well, not *quite* all; because hardly had I agreed to learn the part when I also said "yes" to Gordon. The "Vanessa" premiere was scheduled for January 15 and we set December 29 for our wedding. There was consternation in all quarters. Everyone in and out of the Met urged me to postpone the wedding until after the premiere. Sam Barber, understandably apprehensive because he was sure it would distract me from concentrating on his new opera, had been heard to mutter, "That's all I need, Steber off on a mental honeymoon just before the premiere of my new opera!" He begged me to put it off. Finally I laid it out for him in simple terms. "Honey, unless I marry Gordon now, I won't be able to concentrate on your opera at all."

I was well aware that both friends and family were strongly against my marriage, believing that I was unduly hasty and was, perhaps, urged unnecessarily toward a quick wedding, particularly since my lifestyle would have permitted a more informal arrangement. But I was raised to the whole idea of marriage, and it's what I thought I wanted. Not only that, but Gordon was pressing me to marry him quickly. So, in my own headstrong way, I persisted. There were moments, however, when even I wondered about the wisdom of it all. But I have always had this defiant streak which has sometimes caused me to commit myself to actions I might not otherwise have taken had I had the freedom to think things through. I have paid dearly for this, particularly in this case. But at that moment I wasn't going to let anyone stop me from what I believed was my only real chance for happiness. I really felt I had met "my guy" at last.

Between December 17 when I made the decision to do Vanessa and my Firestone Christmas broadcast on the 23rd, Gordon flew to Mexico and got his divorce (for which *I* paid, incidentally, although for the life of me I can't remember why). When he returned, I had to pick him up at the airport, when I should have been working on Vanessa. I feel so stupid about it all now, that I hate to talk about it. Even that very day, before I left for the airport, I ducked into St. Thomas Church on Fifth Avenue and prayed that the whole thing would work out all right. I didn't know that 10 years later I'd enter a little church in Mexico and ask God to forgive me for the suffering my haste and willfulness had brought about.

We worked intensely on "Vanessa." And, although I loved the part and sensed that it fit perfectly into my life at that moment, I found it difficult to get into the voice, memorize words and music, and take it onto the stage in such a pressure-cooker atmosphere. I just worked straight ahead, like a horse with blinders, and did what I was told.

Two weeks before the premiere, however, I kept to my resolve and was married in the U.S.Army Chapel at Fort Slocum on Governor's Island, New York. Our guests ferried over to the Island in varied degrees of anticipation, a lot of them dubious. Sam and Gian-Carlo commiserated together, I am told, their conversation boiling down to, "Why now? Why now?"

I was excited, but not particularly anxious. I sent mother and my secretary, Jean Westbrook, off together in the chauffeured limousine Gordon thought I should use, and I drove my father in my own car. Wouldn't you know, I lost my way. I almost didn't get there at all and they had to hold the ferry for me. I thought to myself, "My God, Eleanor, what a Freudian thing to do!"

It all happened so fast! But despite my vague misgivings, married I was, with all the color and fanfare of a full military wedding and deliriously happy to be with Gordon at last. End of scene; curtain down and back to real life.

The "Vanessa" premiere was upon us. To the end I was still working with a score propped up somewhere in the set and people were feeding me actions, pushing me first one way and then pulling me somewhere else. And somehow we made it!

Our world premiere of "Vanessa" was a popular success and "Vanessa" came into its own as a great new opera, achieving an acceptance that perhaps no other American opera has ever had. Even Sam, who'd had his doubts about me throughout, was quoted by the *New York Times* as saying, "I cannot adequately extol her gallantry in undertaking this difficult role in so short a time." And to someone else, "She sang it wonderfully," and then as a kind of irrelevant afterthought, he exclaimed, "Oh, I tell you, this opera world is quite something!"

While nearly all the critics acknowledged my achievement in learning the part under such extraordinary circumstances, I think my performance stood on its merits. *Newsweek* summed up: "To her enormous credit, Miss Steber sang and played Vanessa as if it had been written for her."

None of us knew at that moment how closely my life was beginning to duplicate Vanessa's.

Strangely enough, I don't think I really enjoyed "Vanessa" with my usual relish that season. I had learned it so fast that I was never quite as sure of it that first year as I was of my other roles. I was always conscious of small mistakes, and that bothered me. The recording, on the other hand, is musically perfect.

Nevertheless, I loved the opera. I don't think I could have done what I did if I hadn't adored the work itself. It not only *seemed* to have been written for me. It *was me!* I was totally involved in it, except that I didn't know it. I didn't understand at that time that I had just married my own Anatol.

Anyone who was backstage during the first and subsequent performances of "Vanessa" knows that I came off the stage after that big first act so near to collapse that the story got around that I had fainted. I know that several times I was helped to my dressing room. The emotional tension of the first act was so intense that I came off stage with terrible headaches that started in the back of my neck and shot up into my head. Sometimes it was so bad I thought I was having a stroke. Vanessa took absolutely everything out of me. Until then, I'd always been able to keep something in reserve. I had always been able to do my roles and have a little bit left over. But as Vanessa, I spent everything.

If you had asked me, however, I would have told you that I was blissfully happy about both my marriage and the success of "Vanessa." Mr. Bing was especially gracious, and shortly after the premiere he wrote me: "Now that the smoke has cleared away a little, let me say once again how immensely grateful we all are for your courageous and helpful action in taking over Vanessa. You proved once more that a great artist need not worry about false dignities, but that such an extraordinary feat and wonderful performance justify everything. Indeed, it was a triumph for you."

I didn't get a real honeymoon. The best I could do, by canceling and shifting a few dates, was to snatch a week or so after the first "Vanessa" performances so Gordon and I could share a few quiet days together at Sam Barber's estate in Katonah, New York.

Later that season I finally got to sing my first Met "Tosca," one of two originally scheduled for me. An earlier performance had been sacrificed, as were a number of concerts and other dates, so I could spend all my time on "Vanessa."

The whole season turned out to be really tremendous for me because, counting the tour, I sang nearly 30 performances with the Met, enough by itself, but during the annual Company tour I had to use my free days to make up my canceled concerts and operas, among them singing "Knoxville" in Knoxville, "Manon" with the New Orleans Opera and, of all things, a single performance of "Faust," which I hadn't done in the U.S.A. since 1951, in Houston.

Opera singers are just about the only performing artists I can think of who must continually keep 20 to 30 or more roles memorized and fresh enough in their minds to sing competently when called upon. In my day, if I were lucky, I had a rehearsal or two; more often it was a quick brush-up with the régisseur while I was putting on my make-up. If I was smart, I found time to stroll around the darkened stage so I wouldn't walk into walls or try to open painted windows, check my props—little things like that.

The same demands on the memory exist on the concert stage, of course, except that there you are your own boss and can be a little more flexible. In those days of nationwide concert networks we did many more concerts on each tour than is customary today.

We took "Vanessa" to the 1958 Salzburg Festival in Austria as an official Metropolitan production, a package deal arranged long before the New York premiere. The Festival directors originally wanted us to sing the opera in German. Whatever the rest of the cast felt, I knew I could not face a crash restudy in German after all the sweat of learning the opera in six weeks. There was also a principle involved here, because it had always been a Salzburg tradition to present operas in their original languages. Why should our American "Vanessa" be singled out for exception? In the end, it was not. We sang three "Vanessas" to what you might call "mixed" reviews which, I suspect, had something to do with the opera being American, plus our singing in English. One of them, if I recall correctly, found my performance indeed overwhelming. But far more meaningful to me was the visit of Elizabeth Schwarzkopf, who came backstage to compliment my performance.

Gordon, on leave from the Army, had accompanied us. When he had to fly home, my family and I spent a few days at Zermaat, Switzerland, where I used most of my time to work on a concert program for the Brussels World Fair where I was planning to preview a new concert for Carnegie Hall in October.

My arrival in Brussels was a humdinger! Loaded with a handbag in one hand, a suitcase in the other and with a camera slung over my shoulder, I started down the long escalator to the street. Concerned for my parents' safety, I glanced behind me up the escalator. Before I knew it, I was backside down on the floor, completely entangled in my paraphernalia watching, panic-stricken, as a seemingly endless column of people descended toward me down the escalator. It flashed through my mind that I might be trampled to death and not live to sing my Brussels concert. Another typical Steber three-point landing!

The interior of the American Theater at the Brussels World's Fair was hung with gold and scarlet. The audience was largely French-speaking, and very elegant; their enthusiasm for my new program was all I could have desired. But I was singularly intent on my fall performance of this program, and although I wasn't consciously thinking about my 1950 Town Hall recital with Dimitri, deep down, I suppose, the memory still rankled. But I had sung so much music in so many places during the eight years since Town Hall, it didn't really matter to me any more. I knew what I could do, and if there was a little bit of "I'll show 'em" in my attitude, well—I guess that was true enough.

I planned the most spectacular program I could conceive. I warmed up on the "Alleluia" from Mozart's "Exsultate, Jubilate," "Zeffiretti, Lusinghieri" from "Idomeneo" and the dazzling "Martern aller Arten" from "Abduction from the Seraglio." I sang both the "Knoxville, Summer of 1915," and "Les Nuits d'Été." I added the Mad Scene from Bellini's "I

Puritani" and the Kaiserin's two big arias from Strauss's "Frau Ohne Schatten." For sentimental reasons I added "Ernanì, involami" with which I had won the Auditions 18 years before. I did four encores, including Ed Biltcliffe's setting of Christina Rosetti's "Poem," "Depuis le jour," "Vissi d'arte," and "Un bel di." *Newsweek's* Emily Coleman wrote that I had chosen a program which had to be perfectly sung; the only alternative being total disaster. But my favorite critique was the one which read: "To put it relatively mildly, Miss Steber committed herself to sing one of the most foolhardy recital programs of modern times. And, being Eleanor Steber, she planted her feet on the stage and sang it!"

It was sheer bravado, of course, but I knew I could do it. I just brought together everything I could sing to a fare-thee-well, as if to say, "Look, folks, maybe you didn't notice, but I've been singing these things for you all along. Here it is—all I can do, the best I can do. Now somebody top it!"

The truth was that I loved singing tours-de-force, and I enjoyed every minute of that concert. I'd have to or I wouldn't be a singer. No one would. It's too dangerous, because all of you is out there on the edge every time. But you see, there's something that happens when you sing—and I don't know if people who don't sing can imagine it—but there is an exaltation to the point of pure ecstasy, when singing takes you out of yourself, and the music takes you over. And for me, in the act of singing—for that brief time, I transcend my mortal self.

There were times now, however, when it seemed that the triumph— and it was a triumph—of my Carnegie Hall concert had come a year too late, as a matter of pure business. My contract negotiations with the Metropolitan in 1958 once again left me uneasy. Instead of being offered more after my big "Vanessa" year, I had fewer performances, although my fee finally reached $1000 for each performance.

Bill Judd argued that my eagerness for more work played against me in some ways. He has said, "I don't think Steber was ever sufficiently acclaimed by the press because she was always too available, always too willing to undertake anything under any circumstances. She'd break her neck to learn a new role, or rework an old one, even for a performance or two."

Over the years I had filled in at concerts and operas many times for Licia Albanese, Nadine Conner, Leontyne Price, Nelson Eddy, Lisa Della Casa, and many I've forgotten. About this Bill said, "That automatic reflex to step in at a moment's notice—it's the 'old Fire Horse syndrome'.

Somebody would ring the 'save the show' bell and, just like the old fire horse who automatically backs into the shafts at the first alarm, there would be Eleanor, ready to go. But that's Steber. Whatever else she may be or do, the big ring of truth is in the voice! More than any other singer I have ever known, she loves to sing. It is as essential to her as breathing!"

Chips Fall Everywhere

My original fate for the 1958–59 season had been sealed way back in November of 1957 before all the excitement of "Don Giovanni," "Vanessa," and my wedding. While I was singing the Countess in Chicago, Bill Judd made a special trip out to tell me in person that, except for a handful of Donna Annas, the only role the Metropolitan was prepared to offer me for that next year's season was that of Marie in the Met's premiere of Alban Berg's "Wozzeck."

I listened in bitter silence, my bel canto soul crying out, "Why?" If I had had a bad season the year before, I might have understood; but everything was going great guns. No! I told Bill I wouldn't do it. He pretended he hadn't heard me. "Wozzeck is a great drama, Eleanor," he said, "and it's going to be an important premiere. I really believe that musically you can prove something with it. If you refuse, I'll understand, but why not try it?"

In the end, I took his advice because I respected him, and because I had begun to realize that the occasional musical detours I had taken through the years had, in the long run, been good for me. And he certainly was right about "Wozzeck" being a challenge.

I agreed to do "Wozzeck" also because I suspected Mr. Bing was looking for a way to ease me out of the repertoire. I wonder now if the terrible headaches I suffered in the winter of 1958 weren't largely because underneath I was slightly hysterical about my future at the Met. I knew I was losing "Rosenkavalier," which saddened me. I don't suppose Mr. Bing had any idea how deeply this opera was imbedded in my psyche. I had grown up as both a singer and as a person, from Sophie to the Marschallin. I probably should consider myself fortunate to have had as many performances as I did, because Mr. Bing always insisted the Marschallin was not a role for me. He apparently thought it unsuitable for an American girl to sing so essentially a European role. Yet, barring the 17-year-old lover, everything the Marschallin sang and felt was part of me.

If there is some of the Marschallin in me, there were also aspects of Marie which fascinated me and stirred up forgotten memories. I may have had my doubts about Marie as a part for me until I got into it, but I certainly was going to give it my best shot.

I had seen "Wozzeck" in Vienna in 1953, and as I suspected, it proved to be a highly-controversial work. Alban Berg's music was still very avant garde in 1958. (Berg, of course, was a pupil of Arnold Schönberg and took his own tonalities even further afield that those of his master, adding, however, a strong lyric quality of his own.)

Briefly the plot revolves around a frightened young soldier and a prostitute trapped in a hopelessly poverty-stricken environment, which they escape only when Wozzeck kills Marie and then himself. Not at all the kind of make-believe I prefer. The music called for *sprechstimme*, a technique of half-speaking, half-singing. Since my background was completely bel canto, I really worried about what *sprechstimme* might do to my voice. But I was attracted by the music and worked very hard on it. That I succeeded is in a large part thanks to Ignace Strasfogel, the wonderful coach and conductor who helped me learn it.

The only passage in the entire opera which might be called a song is Marie's Lullaby, "Maiden, What Song Shall You Sing?" For all the rest, I simply had to think the pitch of each note in relation to what had come before. I have a keen sense of relative pitch, but I would have given my high C for honest-to-goodness "absolute pitch" at this time. Each of us in the cast clung to every musical anchor we could find.

Dramatically, Marie left her mark on me. It was a role I couldn't leave behind. Normally I could sing any part and come off happy as a lark, but not with Marie. I couldn't pull out of it, and I would feel down in deep dumps for two or three days after each performance.

When we got it onto the stage, I played it in bare feet. In rehearsal, while I was sitting on the stage reading the Bible with my foot on my knee, I unconsciously pretended to dig the dirt from between my toes as I read; instinctive perhaps, but I kept it in. I pondered Marie and her so-called "degradation" as a prostitute, her love for her child, and her hopeless spiritual striving toward something better. And then I thought of Marguerite in "Faust," who has everything and loses her virtue by choice, then kills her own child. Which of them was truly redeemable?

Working on Marie reminded me vividly of things I had seen in West Virginia as a child. I had never been poor myself, but I used to go with my mother to collect bills owed at my grandfather's grocery store. We'd go into the hills to the shacks of miners or dirt farmers, and even before we started up the hill there was a particular "smell of poverty" which drifted down. I never forgot the barefoot, ill-clad children, the houses and clothes unwashed because people simply could not afford soap, and the smell of cats being boiled for food. I unconsciously drew on these and other experiences for Marie.

While I strove chiefly to get on top of the music the first year, gradually I got the role from underneath, both musically and dramatically.

There were no curtain calls until the end of the opera. Then there was a 20-minute ovation, and "Wozzeck" played to sold-out houses for the remainder of the season. Once again the fate that guides my life had brought me a success which, left to myself, I might have refused. Paul Lange wrote of me in the *Herald Tribune*: "She sang the cruel role with impressive security, never hesitating to let her voice soar. Her acting was very good, and at times, as when she read the Bible, gripping." Howard Taubman in the *Times* said, ". . . her Marie is earthy . . . moving in her humility."

What about my initial fears of developing a "vocal hernia" over that business of *sprechstimme?* Obviously, I didn't, and I think Erich Leinsdorf put his finger on it when he said that I managed it well because I approached the *sprechstimme* from the singing side rather than the theatrical. Had I subjugated my singing to the drama, then the *sprechstimme* would have worked *against* my voice. Instead, I made my voice work with it, fully supported by my breath, as I would have sung any other music. Marie never hurt *my* voice, but I have heard that other sopranos who let the drama control their delivery of it, suffered for it.

When Bill Judd was rearranging my schedule to accommodate the Met's rehearsal schedule for "Vanessa," he had asked Mr. Bing for the 1959 broadcast performance of "Tosca" to replace the one I had given up to have more time for "Vanessa." Mr. Bing had agreed readily, but when we got to the 1958–59 season he asked me to relinquish the broadcast performance in return for another date.

In my whole career I sang only six "Toscas" at the Met (dozens elsewhere), so I didn't think it was fair to ask this of me. I had waited too long. I think that after "Vanessa" was safely on the boards, Mr. Bing may have convinced himself that Bill had pressured him into giving me the "Tosca" broadcast, but he hadn't. To have pressured Mr. Bing would have inferred a threat that if I did not get the "Tosca," I would not sing Vanessa, and *that* simply was not true. I *wanted* Vanessa!

I told Mr. Bing I appreciated his problem. I knew he had a stable full of Toscas, each of whom felt she had a right to the broadcast. But so did I. I had earned it. I held him to our contract. (Actually I don't believe any of my colleagues ever sang more than one "Tosca" broadcast.)

I sang two Toscas before our broadcast performance on April 11, and after one of them my husband mentioned that my leap off the parapet at the end wasn't visible to the audience. "If you are going to risk breaking your neck," he quipped, "why don't you do it out where everyone can see you?"

We experimented before the broadcast, setting the mattress so I could leap dramatically but safely to my death. When Tosca plunged from the Sant' Angelo *that* afternoon, it was only a two-point landing. I gave the jump all I had—which was too much—and tumbled off the far side of the mattress. My head hit the floor with a terrible crack; I chipped a tooth and cut my lip.

Stage manager Patrick Tavernia ran toward me, yelling: "Oh, my God, we've killed her!" I staggered to my feet with his help, unaware I was bleeding; then pushed him aside and gasped, "Out of my way, Pat, gotta take my curtain calls!" First things first, after all!

During that evening's performance of "Cavalleria Rusticana," Pat was chatting in the wings with Zinka Milanov (one of the Met's great Toscas) and asked, "Did you hear what happened to Steber this afternoon?"

"Naw," replied Milanov. "Vat happent?"

"Well, when she jumped from the parapet she overshot the mattress, cracked her head and cut her lip."

Milanov arched an eyebrow. "Vell, I always told Eleanor the part was to heavy for her!"

I made my debut in the ballet that season. Not, I hasten to add, *as* a dancer, but *assisting* the dancers. The centerpiece of a full evening's program was Anthony Tudor's "Hail and Farewell" which was set to the "Four Last Songs" of Richard Strauss. That's where I came in. I sang the songs. They draped me in miles of filmy stuff shaded from mauve to purple to black, all conceived in the imagination of designer Lucian

Prideau. I felt like Medea. The dancers performed around me as I stood in the middle, high on a pedestal. There's nothing like being put up on a pedestal, I always say!

The last performance of "Hail and Farewell" was part of a Metropolitan Gala benefit the week before my Tosca tumble. In addition to the ballet, the program included scenes from three operas. I understood I was to sing the second act of "Tosca." When I arrived at the opera house, however, I discovered that Licia Albanese was listed as Tosca. No one had said a word to me, and I was dumbfounded.

I have completely forgotten the sequence of events of the uproar that followed. I know I lost my temper, and although I cannot remember what I said, I am sure it was loud and to the point. After the performance, I learned that my husband and Bob Herman, Mr. Bing's assistant, had continued the argument through to the front of the house where it was overheard by too many people. There had apparently been some shoving, if not actual fisticuffs.

The degree of violence hardly matters. I will never know how seriously the battle between Gordon and Bob Herman affected my future; but it seriously damaged, and maybe destroyed, the remaining good will between the management and myself. Fortunately we left on the spring tour almost immediately. I had more than enough to think about with Donna Anna, Vanessa and Tosca to sing. What with singing every third night, traveling and worrying about the altercation, I was sick in more ways than one by the end of the tour.

After a week's rest at home, I was feeling almost normal when I joined conductor Newell Jenkins for a benefit he had arranged to save the Phoenix Theater. This was the first of his Clarion Concerts. I sang the Mozart concert aria, "Bella mia fiamma" for the first time in New York. I had done it once before at the Salzburg Mozarteum between performances of "Vanessa" in 1958. This particular concert was especially important to me because it planted in my mind a seed which was to bear fruit within the year.

What I was zeroed in on that summer of 1959, however, were some performances of "The Girl of the Golden West" (which I had to restudy in English) at the stunning Red Rocks Amphitheater outside of Denver.

Although I have always enjoyed Minnie because there's a lot of Minnie in me, I seemed never to get it on stage without some sort of "Hairbreadth Harry" melodrama. And there was a jinx over this "Girl of the Golden West" from the beginning. Gordon and I, with two of his children, drove all night to reach Denver on time, even driving through a rainstorm so violent that our car was caked with mud.

I arrived in Denver to find rehearsals a shambles, with everyone milling aimlessly around, wondering what to do. There was no conductor to be seen, and the rehearsal coach didn't even know the opera. Brian Sullivan was worried because he hadn't quite finished learning the role of Dick Johnson, and John Coleman, the Sheriff, had never done the part before and desperately needed to work on it.

Dear Herbert Graf, one of the truly great international stage directors at the Met for many years, was trying to block the opera, but was stymied because neither principals or chorus were musically prepared.

I really couldn't comprehend such a cavalier approach to the production of any opera, and immediately got myself in Dutch because I recklessly sounded off to a *Denver Post* reporter. The paper instantly raked me over the coals—in print—and we came near to having a big public brouhaha. Already I wanted to go home.

Instead, I found a piano and started to work with Brian and Bill Coleman. I pounded out notes for hours and the three of us worked out our ensemble together.

My special interest with "The Girl of the Golden West" was, as ever and always, my horse, but I had to get myself in shape for it; so Gordon and the kids and I rode out on the trail every morning from our lovely mountain house in Evergreen, up above Red Rocks. When they got horses on stage for rehearsal there was another disaster, because the floor was so slick that the first horse and rider went down and the other mounts slipped and slid around perilously. I began to get the willies about riding for the first time. Someone, however, came up with the brilliant idea of putting rubber caps over the horses' shoes—and *that*, thank goodness, worked!

The conductor, when he finally showed up, was somewhat "under the weather" and remained so throughout. Midway in the dress rehearsal he left the pit and disappeared for some minutes, leaving the entire company stranded. I can still hear Dr. Graf calling after him, "Where are you going? Who takes a break in the middle of dress rehearsal?"

I was so disgusted that when I went back to our little house, I called Bill Judd back in New York and begged him, "Get me out of this!" But he sweet-talked and soothed me, as Bill always could, and I stayed, because no matter what I threatened, I'd never yet walked out on a commitment, however bad the conditions. (I must admit that once when a piano collapsed as I walked on the stage for a concert I was somewhat perplexed about how to go on.)

After the stormy rehearsals, we should have been well prepared for the performance, because smack in the middle of the first act, a vicious rain-squall blew down from the mountains, whipping props, hats and what-not all over the place. I was clinging to the scenery and struggling along with the crew to keep it from blowing away. The performance came to a dead halt and the conductor happily closed the louvered hood over himself and the orchestra and vanished. Brian's hat sailed out into the audience, never to be seen again. Our Sheriff apparently thought the jig was up and escaped to his dressing room (or to parts unknown, to judge from the time it took to find him). It looked as if Minnie wouldn't get her first kiss or anything that day.

Nothing, however, shook that Red Rocks audience, certainly no mountain squall. They stayed put and pretty soon they began to clap and stomp for the performance to go on. Eventually the conductor emerged from his hutch like an abashed rabbit and fumbled around trying to find an appropriate place to start over, while the cast, wet and windblown, waited on stage to pick up the pieces.

The opera continued with only minor disasters, as voluminous dark grey clouds billowed around the amphitheater, often brushing the scenery. When Minnie and Dick Johnson prepared to ride off in the finale, the swirling clouds so enveloped the stage that all the audience could see of us as we rode off was my white cowboy hat bobbing up and down through the clouds.

Beating the Odds

I had not been feeling really well since the end of the spring tour, suffering once more from asthma, a general edema and swelling of my joints.

Immediately after my marriage to Gordon I had sought medical help to reverse the natural course of events so that I might have a child. All that summer of 1959 while I worked on new roles and concerts, my knees and elbows were so swollen and painful I could barely pull myself up the stairs at Melodie Hill—and Melodie Hill is all stairs. My regular doctor pumped me full of antibiotics and cortisone so I could keep performing; at the same time I was taking drugs supposed to help me conceive a child. I sought help from a famous obstetrician and told him what I had done.

He sat me down that summer and said, "I think you are very foolish to tamper with nature. God has given you the gift of a great voice; you were created to use it. Stop trying to interfere with nature." I took his advice. Eventually I realized that however much I thought I wanted it at that moment, the life of a traditional wife and mother was not for me, nor, I suspect, would it have been a good thing for any children I might have had.

I had been scheduled to sing the Dyer's Wife in "Frau Ohne Schatten" in San Francisco and had a California concert tour set for fall, but late in August and early September, I was immobilized by what was finally diagnosed as a toxemia from all the hormones and steroids I had been given. I was forced to cancel the entire trip.

I probably should have gone into seclusion for a couple of years, but we were living very expensively by now and it was financially necessary for me to keep working. When the drugs were stopped, I began to improve, but it was months before I felt myself again.

Although I was still far from the peak of my form, I started working on my second Carnegie Hall recital for October. I felt some vocal unease while I rehearsed with Biltcliffe, but I was certain that once I got on stage I would be able to deliver. I had to because it was the sort of program one either sang well or didn't sing at all: the Bach cantata for soprano and trumpet, "Jauchzet Gott," "Casta Diva" from "Norma," Debussy's "Cinque Poèmes de Baudelaire," and the "Seven Early Songs" of Alban Berg. I was right and I was lucky. The Carnegie Hall audience roared its approval that night, and the critics confirmed my decision to chance it.

The season proved tougher than I had anticipated. I performed the entire Berlioz "Les Troyens" with Sir Thomas Beecham. This is a tremendously long opera in its original form, so we performed it as two separate works. I sang Cassandra in "La Prise de Troie" and "Les Troyens à Carthage," with performances in both New York and Washington. I was still suffering from painful joints on the Washington trip, and had to endure the indignity of using a wheelchair to move from the train to a taxi.

During the 1960 half of the season, I sang six Donna Annas and my last Marschallin at the Met; not much of a season.

Since Mr. Bing had repeatedly expressed a preference for dealing directly with his artists rather than their personal representatives, Bill Judd advised me to handle my own negotiations for the following 1960–61 season. So, even before this curtailed 1959–60 season had even begun, I knew that the best Mr. Bing would offer me was eight performances: four each of Donna Anna and Marie. I signed, but I was tormented by his apparent determination to downgrade my status at the Metropolitan. More important than status, I simply wanted to *sing!*

After storming about the house for a few days, I decided to do the only thing I could do. "By God," I declared, "if he won't give me anything at the Met, I'll go out and do something on my own!" What I had decided to do was hire my own orchestra and do an all-Mozart concert at Carnegie Hall in the spring. You might say I was 'flapping my wings,' trying the only way I knew how to stay in the picture."

I realized that I had to get out and make my own career and by golly, I did it. I had arranged *and paid for* all my past Carnegie Hall concerts. The Mozart concert was no exception, and cost me a considerable investment before I even got on stage. Concert bureaus in those days never underwrote concerts even for their own artists, and outside sponsors were as-yet unheard of. Thanks to Firestone and my out-of-town concerts and operas (Chicago always paid me half-again as much as the Met), I had achieved a state of financial security which let me feel I could afford to risk creating a program to please myself.

My Carnegie Hall Mozart Concert was set for April 13, 1960. Robert Lawrence was to conduct the Symphony of the Air for me. Being prohibited from recording in Carnegie Hall itself, we recorded our dress rehearsal in a studio.

The night before the concert I was nearly destroyed. I had sung my last Met performance two weeks before, so I had to read it in the paper: Rudolf Bing announced he was going to open the 1961–62 season with a new production of "The Girl of the Golden West" for Leontyne Price and Richard Tucker. So much for all his protestations to me that he would never put on "Fanciulla" because he hated it so much. I could not believe what he had done. I was beside myself. I didn't know what to do or where to turn. The only means I had ever found to keep myself from exploding was to write—longhand. If I couldn't write something out of my own head, I'd copy inspirational writings by others, trying to calm my nerves and clear my thinking. I'd write letters, then tear them up.

I was so furious with Mr. Bing that I stayed awake almost the entire night before that big Mozart concert writing a long letter to him. Oh, how I wish I'd kept that letter. To get even an hour or two of sleep that night, I had to reach down for the last ounce of reserve within me. I tried to empty everything but Mozart from my mind, and I prayed hard for simply enough rest to get me through the next day.

The next night I waited nervously off stage in Carnegie Hall, feeling that it would take my final ounce of strength just to make my entrance; but when I took that first step onto the stage, I was lifted by a wall of applause. It was the audience! I cannot possibly describe the incredible shock of support it gave me, and I was suddenly filled with a sublime faith that I could do it.

With gusto I sang the entire "Exsultate, Jubilate," seven operatic arias and two long concert arias, "Bella mia Fiamma, Addio" and "A Questa Seno, deh vieni, Idolo mio." It would be indulgent to describe the reaction of my audience, and gratuitous to quote the reviews. They were tremendous and I felt vindicated.

In all the excitement surrounding that concert, there's one private moment I will never forget. I threw a party at my house after the concert, and Lawrence Tibbett, who had almost totally withdrawn from public life, came to my concert and to my party as well. He pulled me aside during a quiet moment and said, "I've known you for years, kid, but I've never heard you sing like you did tonight!"

Can you imagine how I felt, receiving such an accolade from that giant of opera whom I had first known as a radio and movie star and whose "Glory Road" I had so brashly appropriated as a teenager?

Milestones

Until I began my treks to Europe and the Far East, I had returned each summer to Wheeling for homecoming concerts. After a lapse of several years, my old friends, led by photographer George Kossuth, arranged a 20th anniversary celebration complete with parade and concert.

Before I reached Wheeling, I sang at the University of West Virginia, where I was also awarded an honorary doctorate; a few days later, the same thing occurred at Bethany College. In the years that followed, I was awarded 11 honorary Doctorates in Music, Arts and Humanities. I began to feel very academic—and very comfortable back in the university atmosphere.

After my home town celebration, I returned to New York to sing a concert version of "Il Trovatore" at Lewisohn Stadium. I had, of course, sung many performances at the Stadium through the years, but the "Trovatore" was a first. Alfred Wallenstein conducted and Kurt Baum was Manrico, Robert Merrill, Count di Luna, and Nell Rankin, Azucena. Sound systems were not so sophisticated then as they are today, and we singers rated only two microphones set up on opposite sides of the stage; one ostensibly for Rankin and Merrill and one for Baum and me.

Kurt was a large man and certainly I was no sylph. When it came time for our duet, I found that Kurt had planted himself firmly in front of "our" mike, and by no maneuver could I get my share of singing room; so I did a quick pivot and hiked across the stage to the other mike. We sang our passionate duet some 20 feet apart.

After I sang the Beethoven 9th and Berlioz "Damnation of Faust" at Tanglewood, Gordon—now retired from the Army—and I gave ourselves a long vacation, traveling up into New England by car with trailer attached. We had a marvelous time, but I was still fighting a continuing laryngeal and bronchial infection even after we arrived home. (I did not know it then but I already had the beginnings of emphysema in 1959.)

The whole business flared up seriously as I left for Shreveport, Louisiana in late October to sing another new role, Amelia, in "Un Ballo in Maschera" conducted by Peter Paul Fuchs. This was the only time my sister-in-law Sally, brother Bill's wife, ever traveled with me, and she cried for me because I was still sick. Amelia is a beautiful part, and ordinarily it would have been a splendid role for me, but my partial laryngitis persisted. Instead of canceling I insisted on singing the performance.

I always refused to announce any vocal indisposition, believing that if I did, people would look for the worst. Oftentimes it turned out that when I could hardly speak off stage, I could sing perfectly well once I got on it. This time, however, it didn't work so well and Walter Herbert, then conductor of the New Orleans Symphony, came back to see me afterwards. "Eleanor," he scolded, "you really should let people know if you are ill, because you did not sing well."

Years later, after a concert I sang in San Diego when I had just turned 60, Maestro Herbert remembered the incident and remarked, "I'm so happy that you are still singing so wonderfully, for if you had asked me after that Louisiana performance, I would have sworn that your career was finished."

The fascinating denouement of the whole painful episode was the press reaction. The critic from the *Shreveport Journal* wrote: "The internationally famous Steber voice undoubtedly was the highlight of the evening. . ."; and another critic, "Eleanor Steber was superb as Amelia. . . her entire performance, both dramatic and vocal, was consistently that of a genuine artist: and the crowd recognized the fact." So, you pays your money and you takes your choice; but *I* knew what *I* knew!

In 1948 a group of enthusiastic young people had established the Eleanor Steber Music Club which grew and prospered impressively. If I had merely acquiesced in its formation and activities at the start, I had long since learned that its membership comprised many of my most faithful and generous friends. I saw members frequently all over the country and sometimes even in Europe. I had hosted a few "conventions" over the years and had often entertained local members at Melodie Hill.

When they asked for a special celebration of the 20th Anniversary of my debut at the Met, I held an open house at Melodie Hill for all who could make the trip, after which we banqueted at the Whaler's Inn in Port Jefferson.

They presented me with a silver loving cup and earrings and an album of testimonial letters from friends and colleagues, including notes from Erich Leinsdorf, Mildred Miller, Risë Stevens, Lucine Amara, Roberta Peters, George London and others, topped by a friendly sentiment from Rudolf Bing himself.

I was deeply moved by all of this and, perhaps for the first time in my life, I indulged in a bit of public introspection, trying to tell them what had happened to me as an artist during the years they had known me. Since my comments were taped, I can quote some of it verbatim:

"Even with 44 roles already under my musical belt, I feel like I have just begun, but I must admit that strange things happen to an artist as she progresses in her career. In the beginning, you are merely nervous, hoping only that you can accomplish the sheer musical mechanics of each performance. Since you have little experience, you are very brave, you don't know what you're stepping into. You find yourself doing things you hardly believe possible – you don't know how; maybe it's just youth and the newness of it all. Then, before you know it, you are 20 years in the business, having sung all these roles, and now you know what was really good, and what you were not too proud of – no matter what anyone else says, because only the artist knows whether he has done his best or not. This is when you begin to discover what 'nerves' really are!

"You go on singing your roles which are by now deeply ingrained within you. Yet, knowing you have sung so many performances that people remember, now each time you go out on the stage you wonder, 'Can I still do it as I did before? Can I find something new to give to this piece of music?' It is so different from when I began, when it was pure technique and the joyous physicality of singing. Now, when I do a part or a song, I know it has grown and magnified within me, but somehow I must find something more to give it."

At the Met alone I had already sung 32 roles – and how many more to come? Nellie Melba spent a lifetime of singing a repertoire of less than a dozen roles; Lily Pons, not much more. I had already sung enough for two lifetimes.

A letter written to me on this occasion by Risë Stevens more nearly reflected my attitude toward my career than any of the others. "The time has come when the Metropolitan Opera will present you with a silver clock," she wrote. "Looking at it, you will have tears in your eyes just as

I did last year. My life has been made richer for having sung with you so many times and I still remember your debut with me vividly. It was a glorious event and I also remember being so happy you were not a mezzo-soprano!

"We are living our professional lives hand in hand. Perhaps we will sit some day on a bench in front of the new Metropolitan Opera, 'knocking' all the young singers, and saying that they are not as good as we were. You and I know that this will not be before the year 2000. May God bless you and keep you singing forever."

As long as I had been at the Metropolitan, artists who attained their 20th Anniversary would be briefly honored on stage after a performance and presented with that silver clock by Mrs. Vera Gibbs of the Opera Guild, or some Met Board official who would say: "In celebration of your 20th year with us, we'd like to present you with this silver clock as a memento." For reasons I cannot fathom to this day, the Metropolitan sent my clock to me at home. I sent the clock right back and I spoke to someone — probably Francis Robinson, long on the Met staff — and said I refused to accept my clock in this impersonal way. If they didn't see fit to present it to me on the stage, I said, at the very least an official of the Metropolitan should present it to me in the opera house. That is what eventually happened — not on the stage in the company of my peers, but privately, in my dressing room.

I suppose seasoned artists should not admit to sentiment, or to be hurt by the lack of it, but I was. I felt more and more unwanted — and I was right. All Mr. Bing offered me for the season a year hence was a single "Traviata" and the responsibility of "covering" all my regular roles for the 1961–62 season. I reluctantly and painfully refused.

During these abortive negotiations there had been a direct reference to my weight as a factor in the Met's refusal to offer me a respectable season. This left me sputtering with rage, since I could easily have named others who sang at the Met at similar or greater weights through entire careers. I have battled scales — no pun intended — as long as I can remember, using the skills of my friend Diana Ross, diets too numerous to mention, sojourns at "health spas" and uncounted self-help regimes, but it seemed I had only to look at a plate of food, a cocktail, or even an innocent canapé, and I would instantly put on two or three pounds. It has been a lifetime battle, and although I occasionally won a brief skirmish or two, inevitably I lost the war. At the Met my weight was only an excuse, and I knew it.

I found myself once again without a Met contract. I hated it, but I felt that a year's clean separation was far less destructive to my career than to have remained under a contract which undermined my own self-respect and my artistic stature. Artists have often been faced with this dilemma, both before and since, but the advantage is always with management.

Nevertheless, I have never had any reason to believe Mr. Bing acted out of any personal animosity toward me. Goodness knows, he had shown much kindness and concern for me in the past, and had seemed very appreciative of the half-dozen or so occasions when I had pulled his operatic chestnuts out of the fire. And I have to acknowledge, as I review those years, that from Mr. Bing's point of view, I may often have caused him considerable consternation by my unpredictability, my impulsiveness, and the Steber sense of humor.

I have been told by a friend who knew us both that in his own strange way, Mr. Bing loved me. Whether he did or not, and despite the fact that he was never overtly unkind to me, Mr. Bing's ultimatum, in this case, left me in despair.

It was an uncertain time, and I was reminded even more poignantly how life had changed when I was invited to sing in a Memorial Concert at Carnegie Hall for my dear Dimitri Mitropoulos, who had died of a heart attack the previous year. I had known of Dimitri's difficulties with his health for many years. He had already had one heart attack before 1953 when we met in Bayreuth, and he was forced to stop smoking which was agony for him. I can still see him walking down the street fingering prayer beads to keep his hands busy. He had always driven himself, and by now he was beset by anxiety and so haunted by a terrible fear of death that he could not sleep. His friends eventually arranged that someone would always stay with him so he could sleep.

My musical comradeship with Dimitri was unique, and the imprint he made on my music and my spirit is still vividly etched within me. Sometimes I dream of him. Often I have dreamed that he has returned, and I throw my arms around him crying, "Oh, Maestro, you're not dead. You're real! You're alive! It was just my bad dream that you had died!" And in my dream, as I embrace him, I can feel his thinness, and when I look at him, he appears ethereal, almost transparent. I have always been grateful for these dreams, for they bring him so radiantly back into my mind. So many of the most exalted moments of music making sprang from the spiritual miracle that bound us together.

To stand still in my business is to give up and I had no intention then, or ever, of giving up. I stayed busy that winter singing everything that came along because I needed to perform as I need to breathe.

I added to my Mozart and Strauss repertoire in 1961. I made a brief return to television in the CBS Camera 3 production of Mozart's "The Impresario." Except for scattered variety and talk show appearances, campaigns to "Save the Met," opera broadcast intermissions, or to promote various charities, I had not really performed on television since the Firestone Hour went off the air in 1954. The timing of TV appearances was not advantageous for me since TV techniques were still primitive and color was still a few years off. If I were starting out as a youngster today with the powerful media saturation and recording techniques which have become commonplace, I would have had a whole different career.

But my career was mine, and I still wouldn't change it today. I might, for instance, have missed the chance to sing my first Ariadne in Strauss's "Ariadne Auf Naxos" with the Cincinnati Zoo Opera that June. This was my sixth Strauss role in my fifth Strauss opera.

Actually, I hesitated to accept Ariadne because it lay in an awkward part of my voice, as had the Dyer's Wife in "Frau Ohne Schatten." Thanks to conductor Karl Kritz, however, I not only enjoyed the part, I learned something from it. Although I had to sing it in that part of my voice which was most affected by my asthma, Maestro Kritz cautioned me not to try to force my voice *through* the orchestra, but to let it roll naturally. He assured me I had more than enough volume for the part if I remembered not to be intimidated by the lush Strauss orchestration. Max Rudolf had told me the same thing at the Met in 1954 when I did my first two Donna Annas. I remember trying to sing the drama into Donna Anna's first aria, "Or sai chi l'onore," and it didn't seem to be working as I thought it should until Max told me to lighten up. "Eleanor, sing it as you would sing 'Mi tradi'. Sing it as if you were Donna Elvira."

They were both correct, of course, and that's what I tell my students today: if the voice is properly focussed and supported, it will cut through almost everything. But singing is subjective; it's internal, and one needs always to have wise "ears" listening for you to remind you of what you already know.

"Ariadne" also gave me a chance to get my dog on stage again. As the Prima Donna in the first act, I brought in my little golden cocker spaniel, Paco, perky as could be. He trotted right up to the footlights and gazed around, looking for all the world as if he were counting the house, afraid of nothing.

I finished off the year by singing a pair of concerts before some 44,000 people in Grant Park, Chicago followed by a trio of major recitals at the Syracuse University Festival and a memorial concert of John Alden Carpenter's Music at Ipswich, Mass., where I met Adlai Stevenson. Then I flew to Hawaii for concerts, including one in the Waikiki Shell, and enjoyed my long-postponed island vacation.

Overshadowing all of this, however, was the call from my alma mater, the New England Conservatory of Music, which conferred upon me an honorary Doctorate of Music. Everything had come, as it often seems to do, "round robin" as I accepted this ultimate academic accolade in the place of my beginnings. Mr. Whitney was gone, of course, but his wife, Leta, was now head of the Music Education program and a number of my classmates were now members of the faculty. Even one or two of my original teachers were still active.

I never really left the New England Conservatory. I returned to Boston often with the Met, and did many concerts there; but I also managed to get there each year for the finals of the scholarship I had established there in my name. And until Mr. Whitney's death, I also provided another scholarship for a student to study specifically with him.

Rosalind Elias, who was a student there during the first decade of my career, told me once: "Eleanor, the whole place just fell apart with excitement when you came for the Finals. When you walked in, the Conservatory turned upside down."

What neither Roz, nor anyone else, knew was that no matter how high I rose in my career, no matter that I have returned for years to teach master classes there, when I walk through the door of the New England Conservatory of Music, to this day there is a part of me which reverts and remains forever "student."

If You Can't Beat 'Em...

During those first few years of my second marriage, I thought I could live a different kind of life. I was terribly in love and I believed I had found someone who would take care of me, providing a home and security. I intended to carry on my professional responsibilities, of course, since my rather expensive lifestyle had already been shaped by my career. But I thought—hoped, at least—that I might be able to cut back the continuous expenditure of money to hire people to do everything.

When I married Gordon, the idea of "being taken care of" meant not needing to work to support the retinue. I was tired of the merry-go-round and longed for a simpler existence. I wouldn't stop singing of course; I just wanted relief from having to make so much money to pay for everything and everybody.

At first Gordon and I worked happily together on many projects at Melodie Hill. Gordon was fascinated with tropical fish, so we had tanks and tanks of them. We enlarged the gardens and continued the expansion of the house with a new underground garage, an extra room, and broad front terraces and steps. Gordon seemed to be my dream come true. He was a sturdy, dark and dynamic man with, as I mentioned, astonishingly blue eyes. He had been born in Orange, New Jersey, attended Columbia University, and started work with Marshall Field as a merchandise designer in the New York office. He entered the Army as an infantry officer in the Ninth Division, serving in the campaigns in Africa, Sicily and Italy during World War II. He stayed in the Army and became a public relations man, chiefly in the New York area, except for that one assignment in Saigon where I met him.

He could do anything! We got a Gravely tractor and he cut down trees and extended the lawns. He anticipated my every need. He could not only repair the car, he could do my hair and fix my gown. He had physical strength, sex appeal and irresistible charm, when it suited him. He seemed to be everything any woman would want.

If things had gone on that way, who knows? But the "trappings" I was ready to drop may have been what he really desired; and it may also be that Gordon never truly understood the nature of my career. What's more, he certainly over-estimated my financial position.

Those first four years I took my happiness in each day's living as I could, but the days became peppered by the caprices of this man who grew increasingly erratic and extravagant. Yet this was a man I adored— absolutely! So I rationalized and let things pass.

Even before he retired from the Army in January 1961, Gordon tried to take over complete management of my career. Since I had gone this route with Edwin, I resisted as best I could. He claimed that I showed a lack of trust in him when I refused to put everything I owned into both our names; but, as with Edwin, I kept hoping he would forge his own career when he left the Army, and we would live happily ever after.

Before we had been married two years, however, I found myself involved with him in a new project of immense scope—one which inevitably destroyed my carefully planned financial security and the course of my professional life as well.

My career as a recording artist never received the emphasis I felt it deserved, chiefly because of the sudden profusion of new, inexpensively made European recordings in the 1950s and '60s featuring voices enhanced and magnified by new electronic techniques. From a repertoire of 56 roles, I recorded only half a dozen complete operas and, by 1958, very little of my vast concert repertoire. I had done some oratorio and songs for RCA and considerably more for Columbia, starting with operetta records with Nelson Eddy. For Columbia I recorded my Verdi Heroines with Fausto Cleva, Mozart Arias with Bruno Walter, and the complete "Butterfly," "Faust" and the fabulous recording of "Così fan Tutte." The Met's original cast recording of "Vanessa" was done by RCA, as was "Fidelio" with Toscanini and the Brahms Requiem. My Bayreuth "Lohengrin" was released by London Records. Both my Berlioz "Les Nuits d'Été" and "Knoxville, Summer of 1915" for Columbia are now Legendary Performance releases on Odyssey. In 1979 our gorgeous "La Fanciulla del West," recorded at the Florence performances of 1954 with Mitropoulos and Del Monaco, was released by Cetra. But there remain major omissions such as "Don Giovanni," "Der Rosenkavalier," "Figaro" and "Arabella."

The "project" started in 1958 when the Magnacord Company asked me to try out one of its new tape recorders with a view to endorsing it if I liked it. Gordon experimented with the new outfit at my first Carnegie Hall concert that October. When the excitement after the concert had died down and we finally found a free moment to play our "amateur" tape, we were astonished at the quality and sense of immediacy about the performance. We played it for friends, and when the friends started asking for copies, we decided to do something about it. With sublime assurance that our tape was something special, Gordon took it to each of the companies I had previously recorded for. They all turned it down. We were both angry and frustrated. Finally Gordon said, "Never mind, we'll produce it ourselves." Which we did.

With the assistance of some wonderful technicians, we got our recording pressed for us by RCA Victor (what an ironic development!). A pair of innocents, Gordon and I transformed ourselves into a record company, turning my New York apartment upside down. We designed an expensive and not-too-practical record jacket and planned to sell "Eleanor Steber at Carnegie Hall" at my second recital in October of 1959. Just a few days before the concert, my apartment was inundated with stacks of records and their jackets demanding to be united. I came home each day completely bushed after rehearsing my program and started stuffing records into jackets with Gordon, like a pair of stockroom clerks.

The record sold fantastically at the concert, and several major New York book shops and music stores took the album and gave it window displays. It was reviewed by all the critics, and we felt marvelously vindicated when the *New York Herald Tribune* named it "The Best Vocal Recording of the Year."

We created a company name and trademark combined, drawn from both our names—Steber/Andrews—so that we ended up with ST/AND Records. Completely dazzled by our success, we decided at once that we would use our company to record deserving artists and repertoire which other companies found too esoteric or commercially limited to produce.

I recorded a new album of sacred songs which were especially meaningful to me. Through my husband's association with Christian Science, I recorded two albums of Mary Baker Eddy hymns, one of which I repeated in French and German translations. These were never sold publicly, but are still available through the Church of Christ, Scientist.

Not so with my own repertoire, however. During the next two years we issued a fresh presentation of "Knoxville" with the Trenton (NJ) Symphony, several albums of familiar "Songs at Eventide," one of American composers, and several programs of my own in which I recorded most of the previously-mentioned works plus Rameau's "Le Berger Fidèle," Beethoven's "An die Ferne Geliebte" cycle, and my entire Mozart Concert with Robert Lawrence.

We also made quite a few albums featuring young instrumentalists and singers, all accenting unusual repertoire. We had an honest-to-goodness record company going, and for the first year or so, it was delightful. I sat at home hour after hour listening and watching while Gordon, who had an instinct for it that was little short of genius, edited the tapes. It was tremendously exciting and really fun. I think we'd have done very well with it if we'd continued to run a limited operation. But Gordon had grandiose ideas of competing with the giants, and we had neither the know-how nor the finances. When we went after large-scale distribution and put salesmen of our own out on the road, it all turned sour and the finances hit rocky shores.

While I can be generous enough with my home, myself and my hospitality, I was a child of the depression and I had been taught to keep a careful eye on business expenditure and to protect my future security—a direct inheritance from my parents: from Mother with her eagle-eye for the main chance and my banker-father's scrupulous sense of accountability.

The fortunes of the record company were at their rosiest in the spring of 1960 when I did my all-Mozart concert and recording, but for the next two years, beginning when Gordon tried to expand nationwide, we slipped into financial quicksand and began to lose money—my money. Gordon's Army pension went into a stipend for his children—and cigarettes.

Mi Tradi

Perhaps I should have been happy when I signed to sing five Donnas in December of 1962 after a season's absence, but I felt these were token appearances, and I was unsure of just which way the chill winds of Mr. Bing's artistic whimsy would blow next. Once again I chose the big "tour de force" and decided on not just one, but three major lieder concerts, the first of which would go into the record books as the first vocal recital in the new Philharmonic Hall in Lincoln Center (now Avery Fisher Hall).

I worked for several months learning my programs with Ed Biltcliffe. Then I asked conductor/coach Thomas Meyer to help us polish it. Maestro Meyer, who had been at the Met for all-too-short a time, later became head of the Cincinnati Conservatory of Music. His inspired sessions with me proved invaluable for my concerts, and sustained my spirits.

I remember especially the day we were working on Brahms' Magelone Lieder when he crystallized for me a musical concept which I had instinctively known but had never consciously formed into words. He reminded me how often a singer can be uncomfortable with a song because it has started a little too fast or too slow. Each song has its own built-in tempo, and there is a specific place in each song where this true tempo is established. Since it is seldom at the beginning, you may not discover it until the middle, or even the end of the song; but this "heart," once located, makes the entire piece fall into place and you become entirely at ease in it.

It was fortunate I had this wonderful music to work on and these two excellent musicians to stimulate my mind, because ST/AND Records was in deep trouble. My own instincts, when I persevered, were usually

quite sound. In the matter of ST/AND, that instinct had been to oper-
ate conservatively; but I was not sure enough of my ground to fight for
it against Gordon's persuasiveness. So often in my life I have taken the
easy way, allowing other people to take over, and I let it happen now.

At Gordon's urging, I agreed to go on all-night talk shows to promote
our records, and got involved with a character called "Big Joe" who
broadcast every night on ABC. I appeared on this show whenever Gordon
could arrange it. I also let myself get talked into doing an unworthy bit
of hokum over at the Brooklyn Academy.

All this time I'd sing my performances or rehearse my programs and
come back to my apartment on any given day, only to find strange
women there. My most recent secretary, Jean Westbrook, who worked
in the apartment, finally resigned, explaining little except to say, "I'm sorry,
but I just can't stay with you any longer, Diva. I just can't take it."

I closed my eyes to what went on around me, and I continued to
permit Gordon to use me as a pitch man, touting our records in a last
ditch effort to save something. The turning point came when I let myself get talked into appearing in a show for "Big Joe's Night People" down
at the Manhattan Center. Everything had a bitter taste, but I kept trying
to believe in Gordon and in our company.

My parents and the Kossuths came from Wheeling that night to see
an audience of the strangest weirdos and crackpots you could imagine.
When I came out on the stage to sing and took a good look around me,
I was overcome with shame, and I realized that the things I was doing
at Gordon's urging were destroying my professional integrity.

If I couldn't bring myself to put it into words, my parents certainly
could. "Eleanor, what have you come to?" they demanded. "What are you
doing?" How could I tell them? I didn't know myself.

Then I found it had all been for nothing. The house of cards collapsed. I was faced with a mountain of bills and found myself paying
them – out of savings accumulated from 25 years of hard work. By then
I had poured nearly $100,000 into the company and it was a total loss.
In the end I was not even able to win a tax claim for some $35,000
in equipment losses. It was disallowed because ST/AND was a "family
corporation," composed of husband and wife. If we had been unmarried
roommates I could at least have realized something on the equipment. The
company was bankrupt.

They even tried to attach my home, my car and my fur coat, things
I had bought for myself with money I had earned by my own sweat. If

I had put my possessions in both our names, as Gordon had originally wanted me to do, I'd have lost it all .

All of this climaxed in court on the morning of my first Philharmonic Hall concert, which was also the day before my first "Don Giovanni" rehearsal at the Met. However, in my stubborn, single-minded way, I blocked it from my mind, and made New York musical history with the first of my three recitals the night of October 18, 1962.

I planned the concerts as a set to demonstrate the development of lieder through the years. The reviews were excellent, both comprehensive and perceptive, and they presented ample evidence that I was at the top of my form.

I had worked particularly hard on this first recital and, without a chance to catch my breath, had to report to the Metropolitan the next morning for a stage rehearsal of "Don Giovanni." Donna Anna, of course, was an old friend. Under normal circumstances this rehearsal should have been a piece of cake.

I was undoubtedly tired and perhaps a little tense at returning to the Met after a year's absence, but I was also faced with a brand new young conductor, Lorin Maazel, who was preparing his first "Don Giovanni." Midway into the rehearsal, as I started on the "Non mi dir," Maazel stopped me and began to instruct me on how to sing the aria, and, indeed, even how to sing the recitative which precedes it.

God knows that most of my life I have accepted suggestions and directions without hesitation, but I had learned this role with Mr. Whitney, developed it with Wilfred Pelletier, Max Rudolf and Bruno Walter, expanded it in Chicago with Nicola Rescigno, and polished it with Karl Böhm, and now this novice was telling me how to sing it.

I just looked at him, and then matter-of-factly told him, "Mr. Maazel, I have sung this role for more than 25 years with the greatest conductors of our time and I'm not about to change it now. I will perform it as I have just sung it."

From that moment on he was openly antagonistic. I tried to ignore it and worked with him as hard as I could. I felt unusually apprehensive, although my vocal security had never failed me, and I put my trust in that.

I did a brilliant dress rehearsal, singing at full voice because it was an open rehearsal for an Opera Guild audience. I had mentioned to Mr. Bing earlier that I had a bit of a bad throat, which could have been from fatigue or nervousness, I didn't know. He suggested that if I didn't feel right, I shouldn't do the rehearsal, but I had been away for a year and needed to work on the stage; then there was this new conductor—no, I had to sing the rehearsal. When it was over, I felt very good about it.

Two nights later at the first performance, however, when Maazel got to the "Non mi dir," he slowed the tempo down dreadfully—not what we had rehearsed at all. It was laborious, leaden and deadly—and it pulled the heart right out of me. I panicked. I knew I was headed for trouble. It is essential in a florid aria like this one that the orchestra maintain the fundamental rhythm underneath, particularly through the melisma, which can be tricky. That support was non-existent.

I have heard other sopranos come a-cropper on "Non mi dir," but I had grown up on it; it was special to me, and I had been proud that I always handled it with ease. But I could not manage it at such a funereal tempo. My voice simply dried up and collapsed. I completely flubbed the roulades. To have it go—like that!! I recovered, finished the aria and made my exit from the Metropolitan stage with my back straight and my head up, but a part of me had died.

If Edward Johnson had still been General Manager of the Metropolitan, he would have been right there off stage to comfort me, just as he was for Dick Tucker one night early in his career when he miffed the high C at the end of "Salut d'amour." Mr. Johnson would have taken my hand and given me back my confidence. No one, except another singer, can possibly imagine how you feel when something like that happens. Mr. Johnson was a singer and he understood. Mr. Bing was not, so perhaps he just didn't understand. In any case, that was not Mr. Bing's way, and I understood that. I finished the opera, of course, and in the duet with the tenor, which follows "Non mi dir," I polished off all the high B's I had not been able to sing in the aria.

The whole incident was agonizing, not only to me, but to everyone who cared for me and understood what might be the consequences of this momentary fall from musical grace. I had always made it such a point of pride to be an accurate and sound musician...it meant everything to me! There was an instinct about the whole thing: that "music-making" that is at the core of me, that "singing," which is my true essence. When this "essence," which I trusted, absolutely, suddenly deserted me in the midst of the aria, I was, for the moment, lost.

If anything could possibly have made things worse than they were, there were 300 independent out-of-town concert bookers in the audience as guests of Columbia Concerts. I didn't discover this until some days later, but it could not have been more unfortunate.

Backstage after the performance, I tried to smile and greet visitors as usual, supporting myself by keeping a death grip on Ellen Martin's wrist the entire time. She, among others, truly understood. That night she wrote me a note I have treasured: ". . . somehow in the face of misfortune – in spite of it – you presented a picture which I shall never forget; one of courage, poise, pride, fortitude and, yes, of radiance – the kind which emerges from one who faces and accepts the worst and will not be defeated – a shining inspiration. You must know your friends are, and always will be, with you!"

I was to find out more quickly than I cared to.

Most of the critics had left the theater before the debacle so that only one was present when it occurred. Winthrop Sargent of the *New Yorker*, who probably left early, nevertheless made particular mention of the inexperienced conductor's uneven and unorthodox tempi; and during the broadcast performance some days later, George London flung epithets of his own at Maazel from the wings about those tempi.

But the *New York Times* critic *had* been present, and wrote me off completely with the terse judgment that I could "no longer handle the role."

I could and did handle the role for four more performances. At the second, however, while I was singing "Non mi dir," I felt again that lick of panic and, on the spur of the moment, I interpolated a simple little variation instead of the melisma. After the performance, instead of speaking to me, Maazel complained to Mr. Bing. So Mr. Bing wrote me a scolding letter, stating in part, ". . . this sort of mutilation of Mozart simply is unacceptable for the Metropolitan Opera. Maestro Maazel," he continued, "who was apparently completely unprepared for your changes (who wasn't?) was naturally upset and feels. . . that he will be held responsible for this distortion.

"Consequently," Mr. Bing concluded, "Maazel informed me that he could not accept variations at a Metropolitan performance and the question therefore arises whether you would feel comfortable doing the aria on Monday as written, or whether you would like to cut it, which we are perfectly willing to do."

"No, Mr. Bing" I replied at once, "I do not intend to take the aria out. If you insist upon it, you can take me out of the opera."

Maazel, I am sure, wanted me out and he almost managed it because if Mr. Bing had insisted on removing the aria, I think I would have had the guts to refuse to sing. I did, however, volunteer to sing the aria a tone down as a compromise. This apparently enraged Maazel even further.

Actually there is no reason why this or any aria should not be sung a tone down or up. Such adjustments have been made many times in the past in many operas. Many sopranos have had "Ah! fors' é lui" and "Sempre libera" put down in "Traviata" because it was better for them. There is a routine transposition in the first act of "Bohème." In earlier years, if a prima donna didn't feel quite up to par, she would request a lowering of key in certain places. There are always splendid musicians in the Met orchestra, and it is nothing for them to transpose in either direction.

"Purists" don't like transpositions (if they are aware of them) or new variations, and most of the time I am a purist myself. Harold C. Schonberg commented on transpositions not too long ago in the *New York Times*, concluding that, "Transposition has been a way of life in the opera house from the earliest days." True as that is, I would rather not have done it, but we did.

Not, however, before one last display of open rudeness indulged in by Mr. Maazel at the final performance in plain view of the audience. When we arrived at "Non mi dir," he leaned back against the railing around the podium on one elbow, and half-heartedly waved an anemic baton in my general direction while I sang. Too crude for comment!

My last "Don Giovanni" was on Christmas eve. When I went on stage that night, I felt my whole world had fallen in on me. The Metropolitan Opera Company *as I had known it* was gone. We were at the end of 1962 and I had no idea where I was going. When I went out to take my final bows that night, the thought came clearly to my mind: "This is the last time you will ever stand on this stage."

Almost!

Da Capo

In a da capo aria, a singer sings part "A," progresses to part "B" and returns to begin again at "A" until the designated end. In my life, I had finished "B," and before I returned to "A" I would have to create some new variations if I was to make it to whatever end fate had designated for me.

My name remained on the Metropolitan roster for another three years, although I despaired of ever singing there again. I knew I had to plan my future as if I had no hope of returning to the Met, although I consciously refused to admit this even to myself. I tried to make a cool, calculated plan for my career, but such calculations often seemed to misfire. My so-called "tough" decisions, whether personal or professional, always cost me too much, emotionally. Still, when I had to, I could always gather up my strength, forget what had hurt or disappointed me, and get on with my singing.

Shortly after the first of the year, the head of the Aspen, Colorado Summer Music Festival, Jim Caine, called to say that his vocal artist-in-residence, Jennie Tourel, wanted a leave of absence and invited me to replace her. Teaching was an idea whose time had come, and I eagerly accepted. I had never consciously planned for it, but I always knew as, I guess, did anyone who really knew me, that teaching was an inevitability. I had even taught a young soprano, Virgina Huie, early in my career, until my schedule made it impossible, but the instinct simmered on the back burners of my mind.

Hardly had I agreed to go to Aspen when the great pianist Victor Babin, then director of the Cleveland Institute of Music, heard about it. He needed someone to head the vocal department at CIM and flew to New York to see me. I knew at once I would enjoy working with this wonderful man, whose offer included generous provision for me to continue with my performing career. I stopped briefly in Cleveland on the way to Aspen to look over the facilities and, now confident of an optimistic future, I moved quickly on to spend the summer at Aspen.

Aspen was the best possible experience for me at that moment. Far from the pressures of New York City, my simpler existence there was a balm to my spirit. Gordon and I found a little house which I cared for myself, with the help of a student who came in for an hour each day. We did our laundry at a laundromat and hung the clothes out in our side yard to freshen in the mountain air, reminding me of how my grandmother's white laundry had billowed in the breezes outside the big house down in Wheeling.

What a rich experience it became, giving to young students all that I had learned in the past 30 years. And once again I was rewarded by a quickened sense of Mr. Whitney's presence as I taught. All he had taught me was reconfirmed with each new student.

While in Aspen I sang in four major concerts, one of them as soloist in "The Idyll of Theocritis," that gigantic modern musical complexity by Roger Sessions. I sang a series of melodic Moravian duets with contralto Florence Kopleff and, in recital, I performed the Schumann "Frauenliebe und Leben," Berg's "Seven Early Songs" and, once again, the controversial "Ballad of the Railroads" by Ernst Krenek, which had so upset the musical digestion of the New York critics. In the rarified atmosphere of the Aspen Festival, crowded as it was with eager students and dedicated musicians, the Krenek work had a far more receptive audience.

That summer I enjoyed a kind of relaxation with music and other musicians I had not known since conservatory days. There were frequent outings such as the day we picnicked at Maroon Lake with Dr. Elmer Nagy, pianist Grant Johannesen, (who would one day himself direct the Cleveland Institute), accompanist Brooks Smith, cellist Zara Nelsova, and Chinese basso Yi Kwei Sze. When we had eaten, we sat around singing all the songs I had learned in my youth like Campbell-Tipton's "Spirit Flower," Ronald's "Cycle of Life," and "The Waters of the Minnetonka," all songs that evoked happy memories for me. Afterward, the Sze's, Gordon and I stayed and tried to do some fishing with no luck whatsoever. I did get a swim, in icy water to be sure, but marvelous. We returned to dine at the home of French composer Darius Milhaud, who was also an artist-in-residence at Aspen.

It was a thoroughly refreshing experience and perfect preparation for what became a happy nine-year professional association with the Cleveland Institute of Music. I loved teaching there and enjoyed a marvelous rapport with Victor Babin and his wife, Vidja Vronsky. While there, I added steadily to my concert repertoire and was greatly blessed that Victor Babin played numerous recitals with me. He was so utterly devoted to the music we performed!

One particular day we were working on the Richard Strauss group which I called "Lebenslieder." Victor was intent on his playing and I was absorbed in my songs. As we finished with a flourish, Victor burst out, "Ah, Eleanor! It's not so important, the performance! In the rehearsals—*this* is where we really make music!" Victor was such a devoted artist, a fact forever etched in my memory by one typical incident. Strauss's song "Morgen" concludes with delicate, slow arpeggios ending on a high D natural. As we finished a performance of this song, we were joined deeply together in the music and held the audience in motionless silence as Victor shaped that final arpeggio, ending with a high D of such a tone, like a silver bell that floated away into the distance. I'll never forget it because I had heard him practice that single passage for a whole hour until he felt that the final note was exactly right. Victor Babin was a master who would go to any length to achieve perfection. His early death was a tragedy for us all.

To teach at the Cleveland Institute, I became a musical commuter. If I thought I had traveled a lot before, it was nothing like this. I spent three days a week in my Cleveland apartment, looked in at my New York apartment, and dropped anchor weekends at Melodie Hill. When Gordon became executive director of the Greater Trenton Symphony, I shuttled among all four places. The logistics of getting anywhere on time were unbelievably complicated, the mere remembrance of which exhausts me.

Contentedly back in the Conservatory atmosphere, I was very "gung-ho" about my teaching and I was singing all the concerts I could handle. However, in the winter of 1964, through Victor, I was invited to sing three concerts at Wigmore Hall in London similar to those I had done in New York. I flew to London with Gordon and my student-secretary Jackie Faith, in time to rest and prepare with the renowned Gerald Moore, who had played for me in Edinburgh years before, for my first concert.

Critics in the United States had known me for so long they had gradually begun to refer to my "longevity" and to compare my current work with that of many years before, which was silly, because by now I was giving something entirely different from that girl who came to the Met in 1940. But London audiences and critics didn't know me at all, except through my records, and they heard my three recitals with fresh ears and open expectations. The reviews were exciting.

As you might expect, my programs were blockbusters; the first featuring major arias and songs from "Idomeneo," "Così," Barber's "Hermit Songs," Schubert's "Blümenlieder" and a Handel cantata for soprano. The reviews were great.

They intensified a week later after the second program which included Lieder by Beethoven, Berg and "my own" Strauss cycle.

The *Guardian* declared that ". . . if in the last few decades America has produced a grand lady of singing, it is Eleanor Steber who came sailing in, be-sequinned in crimson, a commanding and imperious figure, but tremendously engaging. It is a marvelous voice, much bigger in volume than I ever expected from records, and it projects beautifully on the half-voice with an individual, sweet tone. In the interpretations, there is great command and more than one former diva was observed warmly applauding the breadth of her artistry."

My final concert included the "Geistliches Lieder," "Cinque Poèmes de Baudelaire" and "Winter Words," a cycle of songs by Benjamin Britten. A few lines in the *Times,* from among all the lengthy reviews, capture the total critical reaction of the London papers. "The even scale of her voice and her breath control must be the envy of many singers. . . Miss Steber's versatility and musical taste have given London some evenings to remember. The magnificent range and variety of her programs have been in striking contrast to the stereotyped pattern of many recitals. . . her singing was like her choice of songs. . . grand, generous, catholic. . . she has an operatic sense of long phrases and a warm, direct way of communicating the musical line. . . she attacks a song in bold, confident brush strokes which conceal more delicacy than one is immediately conscious of. A vigorous musical understanding pervades everything she does."

I hope I will be forgiven for quoting these reviews at length, but they are especially important to me because they seem to have understood and appreciated the essence of my life's work more than any others I can remember.

The whole London experience became a resounding confirmation that tensions at the Metropolitan and at home had contributed significantly to my difficulty with the first Donna Anna and the devastating loss of nerve which accompanied it.

During a brief discussion with him some days after my last performance in 1962, Mr. Bing had said, "You don't have to worry about the Metropolitan. You're going to have a great concert career now. Look at the recitals you have given—great reviews! Don't worry, dahling," he concluded, "you will be fine." The London venture confirmed his prediction, whether or not I agreed with his rationale.

Ironically, just before the first of the London recitals, I suddenly became very attractive to the Met once more. Teresa Stitch Randall, who was currently singing Marie in "Wozzeck," had broken her toe and a desperate Bob Herman called me in London to urge me to fly back to New York and do the "Wozzeck" performances.

"Are you crazy?" I asked. "I'm making my London concert debut."

"You can postpone it," Herman reasoned. "Come and do 'Wozzeck' and then go back and do your concerts."

Probably this seemed perfectly logical to him, but I had confidence now in the path I had taken and not in the momentary exigencies which inspired the Met's call for help. Perhaps if I had actually been in New York, I would have considered it. No, I'll be honest. Knowing me, I would have jumped at it.

The Last to Know

I should have known. Certainly everyone who knew me had tried to warn me not to marry the dashing Army Captain whom I scarcely knew when he swept me off my feet on his return to New York in 1957. But I was in love, and nothing so practical as caution could have stopped me. I was like a train rushing downhill without brakes. No one could tell me anything.

Later, of course, I was appalled, because I knew I was taking the man not only from his wife, but a boy of seven and two little girls three and five. I never should have married the man, no matter how charming. He was wrong, too, but that was on his conscience. I was wrong, and *that* was on mine.

From almost the first month we were married, Gordon did things which worried me. Shortly after we were married, we dined at La Scala Restaurant one night with Bill Judd and Edgar Vincent, both of whom had always done their loyal best for me. I had been out of the room and was returning when I overheard him state, "I have news for you two; I hate being 'Mr. Prima Donna', and I'm going to outsmart you all. You don't need to teach *me* what a prima donna is all about. I know what she wants and needs. I'll see the end of all of you." I sat down, frozen. I told myself I hadn't heard it right, that he was joking, yet I squirmed inside because I knew he wasn't kidding.

It's hard to see clearly, even now, exactly what happened to my career because of Gordon. Whatever happened to a lifetime of good relationships with the people in the music business, and at the Met itself because of things he said to Mr. Bing, and his attack on Bob Herman in the winter of 1959, I will never know. But my career tailed off in many ways after I married Gordon.

But, you see, in those first two years, I was so emotionally happy that I couldn't see where it was all leading. I thought, when I thought at all, that the conflicts between my husband and my management and friends were an occupational hazard, similar — although more destructive — to what had happened during my first marriage.

While I still kept my blinders on, we also had many good times because I still adored the man and thought he was the be-all and end-all of my world. So, despite the embarrassments and disputes, I kept trying to believe it would work out, even when I began to suspect he was enjoying certain little "adventures" while I was out of town. I tried to dismiss it by telling myself, "After all, you are away so much . . ."

I felt so guilty about his family the first full year we were married that I invited all three children and his wife to Melodie Hill for Christmas so they could be together as a family. We usually took one or more of his children with us on trips and had them stay at Melodie Hill with us frequently during the summer. We even visited them at their home in Flint, Michigan, the year we drove to Aspen. I loved the children! His eldest girl eventually became my scholarship student out in Cleveland. A charming girl, Marcia Andrews went on to sing at Spoleto, and kept in touch with me for many years.

I see it all now as a kind of drama that went on off-stage when I wasn't singing. It must have upset me more than I knew, however, because when I look at my performance schedule for those years, I can hardly believe I did it all while everything was blowing up behind the scenes.

With Gordon, money disappeared like magic. While we had our record company, he had power-of-attorney and signed most of the checks, so I have no idea where most of it went. Except for an untouchable annuity, my home, and the other properties I had insisted on keeping in my own name, everything vanished. Gordon's initial threats about replacing my managers came true. I was so torn between my loyalty to my husband and to them that somehow I stood passively by while Gordon literally assaulted one of these men and insulted the other. Because of his high-handed attitude and my blind support of everything he did and said, I began to make enemies at the Met and elsewhere in the music business, *not,* I am told, because of what *I* did, but because of what he did without my knowledge, and what I permitted him to do without objection. Down at the Columbia Concerts office, I discovered, they didn't speak of "Col. Andrews" by name; they referred to him as "The Chocolate Soldier."

Here was a man married to a woman who simply worshipped him beyond reason, yet from the beginning, he "dug his own hole." A close friend once overheard Gordon on the phone shortly after we were married as he boasted to an acquaintance, "I'm riding high and I'm loving it!"

Gordon, who insisted on using his rank long after his retirement, was a chameleon, charming in company and capricious, if not violent, in private. He kept my mind in a turmoil, and certainly life with him was anything but dull. His growing reputation as a "Don Juan" during my absences from Port Jefferson was an open scandal, of which I knew nothing until the end, yet he was viciously jealous of any display of affection between me and my old friends.

Mother has reminded me that I told her during the first year of my marriage that it might have been a mistake, yet I was trying to be sophisticated about it. Perhaps if I had not been so stubborn or if I had not been so dramatically inclined, I might have handled it better. If I had just stuck to my guns and fought my career battles out in New York, and had not taken a teaching position that kept me out of town half the week, things might have been different, but I doubt it. What went on at Melodie Hill in my absence, I could only guess. I kept hoping it would go away.

It all came apart in 1965. I had just learned that my husband was seriously involved with another woman. From my Cleveland apartment I called the Constable who watches over the Belle Terre section of Port Jefferson. I instructed him to drape the piano scarf over the Vanessa portrait on the balcony and to turn out all the lights except the spotlight on the portrait, all of which dramatically recreated the focus of the beginning and end of the opera. I hoped it would scare the hell out of Gordon because he wouldn't know how I had done it.

It's morbid, I know, but I felt that my life was duplicating the plot of "Vanessa." In my overwrought state, I wrote out the parallels in a little notebook. "The horrible thing is that now I am really Vanessa. Anatol has come, taken everything, and thinks he can stay. How many people know and understand the evil which is occurring in *my* house. In a way, this is the death of Melodie Hill for me. Yet it has survived before, and if God wills it, it will survive even this.

"But Vanessa is again waiting, all alone in this little cell, with no one beside her, watching the passing hours. It has not been 20 years, although that is what I thought I had waited. This Vanessa went off with the young Anatol with many questions in her heart. Now she will wait forever in that empty house, and Anatol will be gone from her life for good. Let him have his Erika; she will be left waiting too."

Very melodramatic, to be sure, but it seemed to me that I had lost all chance for personal happiness. Gordon and I fought and reconciled often, and I applied myself seriously to Christian Science (in which Gordon claimed to believe), looking for solutions. In November, 1965, following a party and a mad rush to the station, I boarded the train for my weekly Cleveland trip, which I took with increasing reluctance, suffering dreadfully each time I had to leave Gordon alone at home. As the train approached Poughkeepsie, I couldn't go on. I asked the porter to let me off at Albany where I caught a milk train back to New York.

Barely two weeks later, after a terrible confrontation at Melodie Hill, I reached the end of my rope. When I am pressed beyond my limits, I can give as well, or better, than I get and the encounter sent Gordon scurrying home to his mother, and forced me to cancel my Cleveland trip once more. Sometime around noon on that terrible, very chilly day I ran from my house, and slipped and slid my way down the great sandy cliff across the road. I nearly froze to death as I walked blindly along the harbor beach, trying to figure out what to do.

Even now, I would not give up. Since many of our battles seemed to occur when we were drinking, I decided that while I was looking for answers, we both needed clear heads and calm emotions. That meant no alcohol whatsoever, not even the smallest social drink or the merest glass of wine for dinner. I put myself under strict discipline.

Suddenly Christmas was upon me. To all intents and purposes, Gordon and I were already separated. If I had gone home for Christmas without him, I would have had to tell my parents what had happened. Since I didn't want to burden them with it, I went to Boston and spent Christmas with Mrs. Whitney. I knew my father wasn't well, but I had no idea it would be his last Christmas. Nevertheless, I couldn't have hidden my pain from him, so I believe I did the right thing.

I was back in New York by December 29, our wedding anniversary. Gordon sent me the usual "silver roses," but he took someone else to the ballet that night. I had been distracted briefly from all this before Christmas because with Newell Jenkins I had performed in a long-lost operatic spoof entitled "Arcifanfano, King of Fools," or "It's too Late to Learn," written by Karl Ditters von Dittersdorf in the mid-1700s to a libretto by Carlo Goldoni. This libretto had been tossed from one composer to another until von Dittersdorf came up with the final version in 1777. Joseph

Haydn, no less, was its original conductor. The score of "Arcifanfano" had been missing for years and only turned up after World War II when Newell discovered it in the Szechenyi Library in Budapest, and brought it back for W.H. Auden and Chester Kallman to translate into English. Somehow they managed to retain the broadly comic rhymes used by Goldoni in this farce.

We had done excerpts from the opera in May 1965 at the Italian Embassy, but it was during that awful upheaval at Melodie Hill in November when we presented the entire work in concert form at Town Hall. We added considerable comic by-play among ourselves. This performance brought me back into the delightful company of my old friend, Anna Russell, the singing comedienne so famous for her side-splitting analysis of "The Ring of the Nibelung" and other sacred musical cows.

I had entertained Anna Russell during the 1950s when her one-woman shows were at the height of their popularity, and we turned out to be a natural team. Everyone who knows me is familiar with my irrepressible antics, to say the least, at private parties; and I had enjoyed indulging my flare for comedy to some degree as Rosalinda and the Countess, as well as such concert offerings as Menotti's "The Telephone," a change of pace which never failed to reduce my audiences to helpless laughter.

With "Arcifanfano" we had a ball—just plain rollicking good fun between ourselves and our audience. As two of the six "lunatics," Anna Russell as Folly, and I as Vanity, uninhibitedly indulged our delight in the hilarious. "Arcifanfano" was my only holiday fun that year and I loved it. Now, more than ever, I could not afford to linger over the delights of such a performance, however. I had a plane to catch and students to teach. A perfectly routine, if busy, January lay ahead—or so I thought.

The House that Roared

My life was, and is, crammed with people, basically by choice because I like having people around. But no one can live constantly in company without some time alone to refresh the spirit. Books had been a favorite retreat for me since childhood. I can lose myself in TV "soaps," "Kojak" reruns and old movies. I'm the world's greatest audience.

I also found privacy and relaxation in trains, planes and the beauty parlor. On Saturday, January 15, 1966, I was comfortably settled in my favorite beauty parlor having a facial. I was tired from my weekly commuting to Cleveland, and deeply exhausted by my battle to save my marriage. I had continued on a proscribed regime, eating carefully, and refusing any wines or spirits whatsoever, so that physically I felt fine and looked quite slim.

Anyway, I was sitting with my chin in a sling when someone called from my apartment to tell me the Metropolitan was trying to get in touch with me—after three years of silence. I called Mr. Bing from the beauty parlor—such a mundane exchange of words for such a dramatic undertaking.

"Eleanor," he said, "I understand you know Minnie in 'The Girl of the Golden West'?"

Know it? Hadn't it broken my heart when he gave it to someone else? "Yes, Mr. Bing."

"Do you think you could do it at the Metropolitan on Monday night?"

"Yes, Mr. Bing, I can do it." That was it.

Joy and terror swept over me simultaneously. I had done it again! I had committed myself to do the impossible. I hadn't sung the opera in almost 10 years—and in English at that—but it never occurred to me to refuse. All I cared about was that finally I had my Metropolitan Minnie, as well as the great leap back about which I had never stopped dreaming.

Almost as an afterthought, Mr. Bing had mumbled, "I don't know what we should pay you. . ."

That's where I made a big mistake. I should have said, "Never mind paying me; just bring me back into the company and give me some roles." But I was bursting with excitement and full of bravado, so I replied, "Don't worry about it. Just pay me what you paid me for my last performance." That was a ridiculous $1200, the most the Met ever paid me.

The second I hung up the phone, I dialed Melodie Hill and asked to have my costumes brought to New York. These presented a problem since they had been made for a much larger Steber. I had worried myself down to a size 14. Designer-couturier Max von Waldeck, who lived in my apartment building, came to my rescue and remade them while I got on with Minnie.

The Metropolitan's problem with "Fanciulla" began when their current Minnie, Dorothy Kirsten, reported that she was so ill she could not possibly recover in time for the Monday night performance. Her regular "cover," Beverly Bower, was in the hospital.

Once again, as with "Vanessa," it was my faithful friend and former publicist, Edgar Vincent, who had dropped the word that I was in town and the only one who could possibly do the part to prevent the uproar and expense of cancellation. Hence the call from Mr. Bing.

After one first wild surge of conflicting emotions when I said "Yes" to Mr. Bing, I was not at all appalled at what I had agreed to do. But I was ecstatic because I was going to do *my job* again. I've always had to climb mountains to do my best. I simply knew I could do it. My mind was caught up in a place all its own; I was sheer concentration, everything drawn together for one great effort. When it was over, I knew that if it had taken even one more day to prepare, I could not have done it.

Before the Saturday broadcast ended that same day, I was already deep into a musical rehearsal with conductor Jan Behr. While I rehearsed, the news of the switch was broadcast during the intermission when Milton Cross, the Met's "Voice of the Opera," announced to the entire country the circumstances under which I would sing my first Minnie that Monday night.

The Metroplitan Box Office was immediately swamped with calls and wires about tickets for Monday night. There was a line at the box office

before the matinee was over which remained until the office closed that
night. Monday was a Subscription performance and not too many tickets
were available, so many of my friends came in from out of town and
waited all day Monday for standing room.

I knew nothing of this at the time. I was conscious only of Minnie
for the next 48 hours. I drilled music for six hours on Saturday and started
on the misè en scène early Sunday morning with stage director Henry
Butler, who crammed stage business into my head for two solid hours.

Fortunately, the sets were a loan from the Chicago Opera Company—the same ones I knew from 20 years before. The first stage
rehearsal, which took place in my apartment, was followed by three more
hours of musical run-through. But it wasn't reclaiming the music which
gave me trouble, it was leap-frogging from the Red Rocks performance
in English and getting the original Italian back into my head. The two
languages fought for mastery of my tongue, and I often stumbled.

Stage director Henry Butler described our hectic 48 hours together
as he remembered it for *Harper's Magazine.* "In case you have not met
Miss Steber," he wrote, "she is a tall, handsome lady with champagne hair
and a smile as breathtaking as Texas Guinan's. . . Her energy is boundless,
and she violates every tenet of careful singing by rehearsing always at full
voice, and by talking steadily and with great animation in between. She
charged into . . . this new production like a starving gourmand approaching
a banquet table . . .

"Up on the chill, bleak roof-stage," he wrote, "Steber ran through the
whole opera in a little over two hours. Carrying a notebook in one hand
and sometimes her score in the other, she muttered to herself, improvised
elusive words and patiently repeated musical passages. She strode,
stumbled and fell her way through the West. Her courage was awesome,
but the going was tough."

Anselmo Colsani (Sheriff Jack Rance), and tenor Franco Corelli who
came down to rehearse with me on that cold roof-stage despite an upper
respiratory infection, patiently walked through the opening scene with
me. I understand that there was some talk later that Corelli did not want
to sing the performance with me. I find it hard to believe because he was
consistently thoughtful, gentlemanly and completely cooperative, in spite
of the fact that he quite clearly did not feel well during rehearsal.

Henry and his assistants stood in for missing characters, and Henry
pruned and simplified stage business everywhere he could. We worked
out a system of cue sheets which were stuck to furniture and props, so

that while I was free-wheeling my way around the stage, I could pick up a few clues wherever I landed. One sheet was pasted in Minnie's Bible and one was on the bar itself, and I've made a big thing about never spending so much time behind a bar in my life; but in truth, I seldom even glanced at a cue sheet. It was sufficiently reassuring to know they were there.

By six o'clock Sunday evening, I was verging on tears of fatigue, so I stopped briefly to eat. Then I pulled myself together and continued with three more hours of coaching.

I did manage to sleep a bit that night, but the way my adrenalin was flowing by then, it wouldn't have troubled me much if I hadn't. I had sung numerous performances without sleep, and I knew that once I got on the stage the stimulus of singing would carry me through.

I met Henry Butler at the Opera House exceptionally early that Monday night. I had to meet my horse, of course, an experienced old hand named "Jordan." I didn't worry about not having a chance to try him out, because he had done every performance of "Fanciulla" since 1961; I simply trusted that he, like everyone else, would do his job.

With all I had to handle, Gordon had the nerve to show up. He hovered around trying to get into the act by telling me, with great authority, how to fire my pistol. I wondered how he thought I managed without him in Florence, Chicago and Red Rocks. Anyway, the die was cast and I went to my dressing room to get ready.

Oh, God, it was great to walk into that ancient little room with its tall, filigreed iron radiators, the blacked-out window and all the familiar, cramped clutter of it all—and our darling dresser, Jennie Cervini, still there, waiting to help me.

Out front the whole Opera House was buzzing. I had been away three full seasons, and nobody really understood why. I knew there had to be a few in the audience who were simply curious to see whether I could get through it at all; but most of them were there because they believed in me. I didn't intend to let them down.

When I finally went down the steps to the stage before the opening curtain, I was "jaunty as a hostess," according to Henry Butler, who accompanied me. The men of the chorus were waiting for me, and when I walked on, they gave me an ovation. What a greeting! George Cehanovsky, who was in the cast, didn't even know I was singing and came running to see what the backstage applause was all about. He was astonished to see me. Finally, it was time to slip back into the wings for the long wait until my entrance.

The first scene of "Fanciulla" is very busy, with the miners coming in after their day's work, arguing and playing cards and busying themselves with chores and gossip. If you are Minnie, waiting to make a too-long-delayed dramatic entrance, the scene seems endless. Finally, the miners broke into a noisy scuffle and started knocking each other about. The door on the landing burst opened and I charged out with my pistol blazing!

It was only a split second before I heard the roar of the crowd. I remained frozen, gun in hand, watching and listening as the whole audience stood up and hollered. Through all the clapping and shouting, I heard one thing cutting through, loud and clear—my name— "STEBER!!!" The whole Opera House went up in smoke. The orchestra had to stop, and there was absolute pandemonium! It was great, and I felt fantastic, absolutely fantastic!

Somehow or other they got the performance going again and, as I started down the short steps from the balcony to the stage, the "boys" came up from under the tables where they are supposed to duck when Minnie starts shooting. But these "boys" didn't sing what was written. They were cheering and shouting and clapping with the audience—"Welcome home, Minnie! Welcome home, Steber!" It wasn't just "Hello, Minnie," it was "Hello, Steber! Welcome back, Steber!"

As I threaded my way through the "boys" toward the footlights, I just opened up my arms to tell everyone, both on stage and out front, "Here I am, my wonderful friends, back where I belong. I'm all yours!"

It was the greatest single moment of my life!

Thanks to a fabulous bunch of people on the stage with me, we got through the first act successfully. Paul Franke, who was singing the Bartender, Nick, helped me every step of the way, as did Andrea Velis and Cliff Harvuot. Mezzo-soprano Mignon Dunn was there for me in the second act when I needed her. So many wonderful people helped me now, as others had helped me through all the years!

Nor will I forget prompter William Weibel, who had rehearsed me all through that weekend. I never hugged the prompter's box so much before in my life. And I made it, by golly, I made it!

The first act was a triumph, but we were not out of the woods yet. The jinx that seems to haunt this opera so often was still in force that night. Franco Corelli, who had tried so hard to do the performance, became too ill to continue. He simply could not draw a full breath, and his doctor ordered him off the stage.

After a few moments of panic, someone discovered that a new tenor named Gaetano Bardini, who hadn't yet made his debut, was in the audience and knew the part. He reluctantly agreed to replace Corelli and they fixed him up with some sort of costume (he was a head or two shorter than Corelli), and brought him to meet me so we would not have to play our love scene before we'd been introduced. It was a nervous business, but he got the job done, settling for bare bones in the acting department and concentrating on his music. It was a brave job.

When we got to the third act, the horse and I were on our own. I got Jordan as far as the little bridge which leads down to the stage when he, a placid beast at best, simply stopped. Jordan didn't want to budge; but no horse was going to cost me my big moment. I kicked the dear old thing in the ribs as hard as I could and got him going. The horse handlers stood on stage waiting to grasp his reins, but I shouted, "Get out of my way. I'm riding this horse to the footlights!" Which is exactly what I did. The explosion from the audience as I pulled him up on his hind legs nearly blew the cherubs off the ceiling.

What can I say? The curtain calls continued endlessly. Bardini and I, who had never set eyes on each other before the performance, were hugging each other in joyous abandon in front of nearly 4,000 people who were, themselves, off the floor with excitement. It continued so long that the set was almost completely struck before I left the stage. I was so happy, I didn't believe anything could spoil that moment.

However, the final blow to my Metropolitan career was struck after the curtains closed behind me that night. I started toward my dressing room, glowing from all those curtain calls, when Mr. Bing, who was already leaving the Opera House for the night, passed by. He glanced up at me rather obliquely and murmured coolly, "Good show, Steber." That was all—not a "thank you"— not anything!

Next day, Mildred Shagall, who became my manager when I parted with Columbia Concerts, tried to follow up my rescue of "Fanciulla" with Mr. Bing. Nothing doing. I realized that the performance had only been a fluke, and I had to accept the fact that the Metropolitan and I were quits.

But the experience had proved something to my public and had been absolutely fantastic for me. And nobody—but NOBODY can ever take that away from me!

Addio, Senza Rancor

My return to the Met was so triumphant, despite Mr. Bing's disinterest, that I thought nothing could ever hurt me again. I was wrong.

Gordon insisted on staying at the apartment with me that night, which might have been bearable had not the phone rung at 2 a.m. I answered it. It was the woman with whom Gordon was openly involved. After breezily complimenting my big success, she asked to speak to Gordon. I snapped a quick "Absolutely not," slammed down the phone and turned on Gordon. I can, when need be, out-shout anyone, and this arrogant betrayal was beyond endurance. Within moments I had Gordon cowering in a corner, begging me to stop.

I took to my bed for two whole days before I calmed down enough to pick up my life again. So much for the glamorous private life of a prima donna.

About six weeks after my big night at the Met, I lost my darling father following a recurrence of the intestinal cancer he had fought for many years. I had flown to Wheeling during my mid-term vacation from Cleveland to take him to a Boston hospital where doctors would once more attempt to postpone the inevitable.

The night before we left, I came downstairs and found him at his desk, carefully putting his affairs in order. This scrupulous man of impeccable honor, from whom I certainly inherited my own painful conscience, stayed up almost that whole night making sure nothing would be left undone when he departed. He was hoping for another miracle, but I think he knew, deep within himself, that this time it was not possible.

My brother Bill met us in Boston, and we went together to the hospital where Daddy was operated on at once. The doctors said they had done everything possible. I stayed with Mrs. Whitney in Boston and spent as much time as I could with him, and it seemed to me that as I watched, a refining process had already begun, because he seemed to become more beautiful and more translucent with each passing hour.

I read Christian Science diligently while I was there, and I read to Daddy when I took him home on the plane. It seemed to bring him peace. He had his last fine hour when he walked off the plane into mother's arms—into the love and shelter of our family. He was taken straight to my sister's house and never returned to our Warwood home. He declined rapidly and finally drifted off into a 10-day coma. I have always felt that those 10 days gave us all a chance to prepare for his death.

Throughout this time I was strangely calm—almost as if I was in a different world. For a long time after he died, I could feel my father's presence. He has always been with me; in the last few years, maybe not so much, but every once in a while he comes to me clearly, and I can't help feeling that somewhere along the line, I'll see him again.

When I returned to New York, however, it all caught up with me, although during those weeks, I sang two "Toscas" in Milwaukee, a concert, judged regional Met Auditions in Pittsburgh and Boston, and commuted back and forth to Cleveland as well. When March arrived I had nothing very much to sing and I was overwhelmed by all that had happened. My darling father was gone. I had to accept the fact that I had finally lost the Metropolitan. And, although I kept hoping I could salvage my marriage, I guess I knew it was only a matter of time.

Gordon must have believed that my separation from the Met was the source of all our troubles, because on April 1st, in spite of his earlier fight with Bob Herman, he went to see him. Gordon had once told me that he had pulled some strings to keep Herman out of the Army, and now (if that was true) he apparently thought he could call in this debt, get me back to the Met, and, in one sweeping move restore our life as he had grown accustomed to it. I think he even went so far as to apologize to Herman for the 1959 shoving match, but it was all to no avail.

The Metropolitan was now preparing to leave the dirty yellow brick barn on 40th Street and Broadway, so that even the stage and the House I had sung in for nearly 25 years would soon cease to exist. I felt as if my life was being torn down with the building.

How I longed for the things I once complained about: the crowded dressing rooms, the stingy hallway outside them which was barely wide enough for a hoop skirt, much less for the hordes of people who jammed into it after a performance. I can still feel how exhilarating it was to stand there, soaking from my efforts on stage, amidst the crush of bodies in the dressing room, kissing friends and shaking the nervous hands of admiring strangers.

Conditions which were once objects of scorn, I now remembered with passionate affection: the shallow, dirty wings offstage; the narrow, dark and dusty crossover behind the stage along the 8th Avenue side; rehearsals at the small piano up in the tenor dressing room; and the stairs on the men's side, rutted and worn through the years by the footsteps of countless great artists. Even thoughts of the vast and drafty roof stage, where I had learned so much stage craft, stirred pangs of homesickness.

A Gala Farewell to the Old House was scheduled for Saturday night, April 16 and, naturally, I was among those invited to sing. It was a comprehensive program which attempted in one short evening to present as many samples of the Metropolitan's repertoire as possible between its opening in 1884 and its closing in 1966.

They called a dress rehearsal for the performing artists. I was scheduled to sing near the end of the program in the Farewell Quintet from "Vanessa," but I almost didn't make the rehearsal at all. I escaped with some difficulty from my apartment after a violent altercation with Gordon, and I was still shaking when I entered the Met.

The quartet had started without me. Mignon Dunn, Blanche Thebom, John Alexander and old friend Cliff Harvuot were there, and tall, blonde Beverly Bower was standing in for me. She and I had not met until that day. I arrived, breathless, and Beverly tried to retire from the ensemble, but I needed her there. I gave her a big smile, grabbed her arm and hung on. We stood there, arm-in-arm, while I sang Vanessa, who, in the opera is about to leave her home, as we were about to leave ours. I think we both choked up a bit as I sang: "Who knows when I shall see this house again? To leave, to break, to find, to keep, to stay, to wait, to hope, to dream, to weep and remember."

Of all the artists who appeared on stage at the Gala Performance, the only artists from the year of my debut still with the company were Thelma Votipka, our much-loved "Tippy," who sang her first Marianne in "Rosenkavalier" the night of my debut; Erich Leinsdorf, who conducted that debut; and George Cehanovsky, whose gentle hand had guided me so often on the stage. George, then in his seventies, was easing into retirement when the last season in the Old House was announced. He had gone to Mr. Bing (having already sung more seasons and more performances than any other singer of any voice in the history of that House) and asked if he could do some parts that last year so he could end his career in the Old House, which is exactly what happened. As I write, he's still working for the Met, but he has never sung a note in the new house.

Many other great artists with whom I had the privilege of singing were among those introduced that night: my beloved Marschallin, Lotte Lehmann, and our matchless Octavians, Risë Stevens and Jarmila Novotna; bright Irra Petina, stately Rose Bampton, lovely Nadine Conner, and the piquant Bidù Sayao. There was my dear friend John Brownlee and tenor Charles Kullman, with whom I had sung so many "first" performances; Eugene Conley, whom I had met and sung with while still in the Conservatory, and lastly, that great gentleman tenor, Richard Crooks, whose early recommendation probably secured the biggest plum of my radio career, Firestone.

The message of the evening was inescapable. It was the end of an era, not only for the Metropolitan, but for me as well. After 82 years on 40th Street, the Met would begin anew in Lincoln Center. And I, after 25 years on the roster, was nearly 53 and, although feeling no diminution of my powers, was faced with the need to find a new way to go.

It was Jean Dalrymple, an old friend and long a major force at the City Center on 55th Street (the original home of both the New York City Opera and Ballet companies), who had come along a few weeks before to set that new direction. She offered me a chance to make people laugh in a production of the musical, "Where's Charley?" starring Darryl Hickman.

The strenuous upheavals of the past few months, plus a successful diet, had brought my weight down to a new low. For once, my figure was perfectly proportioned to my height. My costumes as "Charley's Aunt" were gorgeous, and I looked marvelous in them. Offstage, however, I did not look so well. When I look at pictures of the show, I look drawn, my eyes lifeless and sunk deep into my head. I had a happy time on stage in "Where's Charley?" but offstage there was constant bitter conflict with Gordon. One night, as I was dressing for the theater, he threw me down on the bed and tore a watch he had given me right off my arm. (As usual, the check that paid for the watch had been drawn from my account.) Only the show held me together.

For two summers I had been affiliated with C.W. Post on Long Island. A group of my students from Cleveland came for the semester to study with me, living at the college dorms and taking courses at the college when they were not having lessons. I also gave master classes at the college, something I was being asked to do with increasing frequency at a number of conservatories and universities.

On the basis of that experience, in the summer of 1966 I brought a group of students to live and work at Melodie Hill for six weeks. Each was to have two voice lessons and two master classes a week. Some also took languages at Stony Brook University, and I asked my former accompanist, Jimmy Quillian, to come out and coach them in repertoire each Wednesday while I taught in my Manhattan studio. The kids took turns cooking and cleaning up.

I felt a great sense of responsibility for these young people, and I set some firm ground rules, especially for the days I was to be in the city. Gordon knew I was not drinking, and that there was to be no alcohol on the premises. But when I arrived home from New York one night in June, I discovered that he had brought champagne to celebrate a student's birthday. The place was in a total uproar. I broke up the party and had it out with Gordon. As we argued in the kitchen, he picked up a knife and turned toward me. Suddenly all the steam went out of me. I just looked at him and said, "Go ahead."

After that, I could not risk having the young people around so I sent them home. Gordon's behavior was bad enough when it involved adults, but when I realized he was corrupting my students, *that* was more than I could bear. (One secretary had left me because she could not face what she saw; another became involved with him in my own house. And yet another secretary in my New York apartment said to me afterward, "Oh, Miss Steber, you have no idea what went on here when you were away.")

The situation was intolerable, yet Gordon was so cocksure of his hold over me that he was certain I would never divorce him. He wanted to stay married, to enjoy the fringe benefits of my career and Melodie Hill, but he had no intention of changing his cavalier lifestyle.

Until all this happened, he was not living at Melodie Hill, just popping in and out at his pleasure, but I knew he commuted daily to Connecticut by ferry or stayed with another woman in Port Jefferson. Just before my birthday, July 17, I went down to meet him one night, as did the woman he was living with. Ignoring her, I offered Gordon one final chance to come home with me that very moment. If he did, I said, we would forget everything and start over. He did not choose to come, and I went home alone. Why had I endured so much for so long? I loved the man. I don't understand it, but I loved him.

During that awful, lonely night, I thought my life would end. I walked through my empty house, pacing out the hours. Melodie Hill, the home I thought would be my private heaven on earth, was no longer a home. The night passed like a slow-motion dream, and I began to imagine I really was Vanessa, doomed to perish in that empty house. Yet as I thought and wrote and prayed, I knew God would not let it happen; that I did not have to suspend my life, like Vanessa, and bury myself in Melodie Hill.

The next day I called my lawyer and told him to file the divorce papers. When I picked up my Mexican decree the first week in August, I let Gordon read about it in the papers, as his first wife had read it when he had divorced her eight years before.

Gordon had so depleted my financial resources that about all I retained was my house and my car. I was out of town when he finally moved his things from Melodie Hill, taking many of my possessions as well, including all the expensive recording equipment. That was bad enough, but when I returned from New York and found he had even taken my dog, I threw caution to the winds, drove to where he was living, and reclaimed my dog.

By the time I took back control of my life, it was too late to undo the damage to my career. I began to discover, little by little, how many friends and colleagues in the music business had been alienated by Gordon's high-handed arrogance and by my silent acquiescence. It was not until I sat down to work on this book that I could comprehend how much his influence had to do with the destruction of my Metropolitan career.

For many years I could not admit this; it was easier to cast Rudolf Bing in the role of sole villain. Now I can see that Gordon's behavior drove away all the people who had so successfully guided me during the first 15 years of my career. Add this to my unpredictable private and public reputation, and I must admit, in retrospect, that from Mr. Bing's point of view, he showed extraordinary patience with me.

I look back over the first 25 years of my career and I can see that much of what happened to me I brought on myself, because in my strong-willed, dramatic way, I wanted to have it all, and I didn't want to wait for anything. Perhaps if I had taken time to think a bit, I might not have charged in so quickly where "angels fear to tread"—but if it had been any other way, I might not have been the kind of artist I am.

And I must consider, as I look back, whether it is possible for someone like me to have a normal marriage in the face of the demands of a career like mine. I have serious doubts. I was a divided person through all those years and, except for my music, I have no clear idea of where my head was. I seemed to have been buffeted about by every emotional breeze that blew my way. Not so with my singing!

For me, singing is life! When I am singing, then I am a unified spirit. Singing is something set apart, mysterious and exalting, an unconscious thing, neither male nor female. It encompasses everything that is my "self." God has given me this gift and somehow or other, no matter what I've done with my life—the bad as well as the good—the gift has never been taken from me.

In my personal life, I seem to have been inept at bringing any real happiness to those I love. The realization that I may have brought unhappiness to anyone is a hurt to my soul hardly to be borne. I have had to accept the fact that I was incapable of expressing myself fully except through my voice. The warmth and love that is "me" show through consistently in my art; it is the only way I can fully share what I am.

Survival

I couldn't believe what had happened to me in those last 12 months: my father, my marriage, and the Met gone within a few weeks. But I survived it, and after a time that very survival seemed quite marvelous to me. It gave me a sense of my own inner strength I hadn't known before.

I remained bitter about my forced absence from the Metropolitan. I longed to sing in the big new house at Lincoln Center. I was one of the first American opera stars of my time to work throughout the entire span of her career. Grace Moore had died tragically before her time, as had Leonard Warren. Gladys Swarthout and Helen Jepson retired early because of health problems, and many others had cut short their careers because of family considerations, or other reasons. I really had no precedent to guide me.

Today, of course, more and more Americans are staffing the vocal departments of conservatories and universities all over the country, training singers for tomorrow. But such a philosophic acceptance was impossible for me in 1966. I was still full of drive and always searching for new dimensions in my interpretive powers.

I did love my teaching. Teaching was never a come-down for me. It was the natural and desirable culmination of my entire life, but it was not enough! So long as I had breath and an instrument which would do what I asked of it, I had to sing. Then, as today, it was hard to conceive of living without singing. I *had* to find a means of continuing my career on my own.

In January of 1967 I appeared once more in one of Newell Jenkins's Clarion Concerts, a benefit for Italian Flood Relief. Sharing the program were other guest artists such as Martina Arroyo, Justino Diaz, Giorgio

Tozzi, Gabrielle Tucci, and Blanche Thebom, my old friend of those happy "Così fan Tutte" days.

When Blanche and I sang the two sisters in "Così," we enjoyed a real affinity singing together, and we often spoke about doing some concerts. It took the enthusiasm of Lois Brennan of Organized Audiences to convince us we should try.

Being a couple of divas who were clearly the dark and the light of it, we chose to wear white lace gowns, figuring the contrasts of our coloring and personalities were about all the decor the audiences needed.

We were a smash, and for the next three years we traveled around the country exciting audiences with popular programs of opera solos and duets, including those from "Così," "Butterfly," "Norma" and "Gioconda." We invariably tore up the place with our final encore of "Bosom Buddies" from the Broadway show "Mame."

During the next five years, while I continued to teach at Cleveland, I revived my concert career in a big way, singing a great many orchestra concerts and other programs ranging from Lieder to opera to modern American and British composers. I took a turn as artistic director and narrator for a production of "The Magic Flute" in St. Paul, Minnesota, and became artist-in-residence at the Temple University Music Festival in Ambler, Pa. for five years. I returned to the City Center in the spring of 1967 to sing the Mother Abbess in "The Sound of Music." I sang Mrs. Grose in "The Turn of the Screw" in Washington and, finally, in Schonberg's "Ewartung" in St. Louis. I would add one last role to my repertoire, that of Miss Wingrave in "Owen Wingrave" at Santa Fe, New Mexico a few years later.

In the summer of 1971, I decided to take my first real vacation in years. I'd been so busy teaching and recouping my financial losses, as well as my concert career, I'd had no chance until then. (I still owned Melodie Hill, but for both financial and emotional reasons, had rented it out for some time.) I planned to visit Rome, Salzburg and Bayreuth on my way to judge an international music competition.

The night before I was to leave, I had dinner with Jimmy Quillian. We had gotten very gemütlich and were reminiscing about Grace Moore as we left the restaurant. We decided to return to Jimmy's apartment to listen to her "Manon" record. I was so involved in our conversation that I didn't watch where I was going and stepped into one of New York City's famous potholes. The result was a compound fracture just above my ankle.

Europe was out, of course, but after surgery, I spent some happy weeks at home in Wheeling, making one of my really good early tries at starting this book with the help of my darling Ellen Martin. However, I was in a wheelchair for six months. I missed my first semester in Cleveland while I learned to manage by myself in my New York apartment, maneuvering my wheelchair about quite efficiently.

I was determined to teach the second semester, which I did also from the wheelchair. That meant commuting to Cleveland by air with the assistance of students and friends who got me to and from my planes at either end of the trip. This, like so many things in my life, would have been impossible, no matter how determined I was, were it not for the help of those who have been so eager and happy to be able to help me when I needed it.

Nor did my disability stop me from singing my concerts. I still retained my youthful memory of Jeannette Vreeland singing her Wheeling concert with a cast on her leg. So, undaunted, I kept every concert date, half-sitting on a high stool by the piano, my cast hidden under my gown.

Nine years of commuting to Cleveland were finally enough, and I lost the heart for it after the death of Victor Babin. So in 1971, after the trip to Europe, cancelled when I broke my leg, I joined the faculty of the Juilliard School of Music. I reclaimed Melodie Hill for myself, and began to teach privately, both in Port Jefferson and in New York.

I returned to the Temple Music Festival once more in 1972, and as part of my schedule of performances presented a "Lieder Abend," a perfect little program which included Schumann's "Frauenliebe und Leben," my Strauss "Lebenslieder" group and some Schubert songs. As on so many occasions in years past, I used this concert to warm up a program for my big return to a New York concert which I had planned for the winter of 1973.

As far as musical New York was concerned, I had been just about invisible since 1966. My entire field of activity, except for "Where's Charley?" and "Sound of Music" had ranged from New Jersey westward; and in my business, if you do not sing east of the Hudson River, you are considered "missing."

Never one to undertake things in a small way, I announced a series of three concerts at Alice Tully Hall. That set a few people talking, I can tell you; and John Gruen, an old friend and composer whose song I was singing in my third concert, wrote a terrific piece on me for the *New York Times*. It was a pretty vivid picture which painted some portions of my life in more graphic detail than anything ever printed before; so much so that I felt I had to warn my family. Far from being shocked, my mother responded, "Well, it's true, isn't it?"

Tully Hall was packed with old friends, fans and former colleagues such as Irra Petina, Licia Albanese and Bidù Sayao, and every critic in town. Friends out of my past showed up, and even my first husband, Ed Bilby with his daughter, was there to cheer me on. I am sure not a few people came to hear if I could still sing at all.

I stood off stage, eager and nervous. I took a big breath and swept out on the stage and the crowd stood and roared! It was "Welcome back, Minnie" all over again. I was home. It was a reunion of old lovers, this meeting with friends who had been with me so long.

The reviews for that first concert were all I could have hoped for. They hailed my return at the age of 56 (would they have been more impressed had they known I was really 58?). I hoped that maybe the whole experience of my three concerts, one Lieder, one opera and one of American composers, might have made people realize that I knew what I was talking about when I said, "When you really know how to sing, you can sing forever."

I expect to pass from this world into my next incarnation without ever giving a farewell concert; there are still so many songs to sing! As long as someone wants to hear me, I will sing. But the emphasis of my life today is on the young people I teach and on the Foundation to aid young near-professionals which bears my name.

We inaugurated the Eleanor Steber Music Foundation in 1973, funding it through gifts from lifelong fans, friends and colleagues. I made and sold special records to benefit the Foundation and used most of my concert fees to swell the coffers.

The Foundation has been guided by a board of great philanthropists, musicologists and knowledgeable friends. Since the highly publicized presentation of winners at Town Hall in 1980, additional support from private foundations has increased so that I have great hopes that it will continue to tip the balance for fine young artists for years to come.

It has been a tremendous amount of work, with much of the burden borne by my secretary and loyal friend, Martha Moore Smith, but we have been rewarded by meeting and hearing hundreds of talented young singers. I am concerned for every one of these young people, both winners and losers, for I remember so clearly those desperately uncertain days of my own between leaving the Conservatory and winning the Met

Auditions. That's why there are no strings on how the winners may use their prize money.

My own career evolved its own unique style, almost in spite of myself. Now I am compelled to establish some continuity by doing what I can to help sustain exceptional young American singers as they pursue their own destinies. Who knows, but that some day one of them will pick up the torch and carry it on for a new generation of American artists.

Coda

I have loved singing with every ounce of passion I possess. I have relished my work and enjoyed my travels and the people I have met. With very few exceptions, I have greeted my world with the same *joie de vivre* I felt as a little girl skipping her way to school, filled with wonder at the beauty of the sunlight dancing through the leaves.

I am sure I would have done a great many things differently if I'd known I had the choice. A great deal of my life went miraculously well. What didn't? What did I do wrong? Well, it's pretty hard to pinpoint all your mistakes. I could be flippant and say that my first mistake was in getting married, and that my second was in doing it again. But that's not right either, because I did what I wanted and hold no malice toward either of my husbands, who are both gone, God rest them.

Whatever my strengths and weaknesses have been, I believe my strengths have ultimately prevailed. With my music, there was never a question. Music was and is my life and my profession—not the mechanics of making a career—but the making of music. Music is my strength and my power.

My weakness lay mainly in the fact that I allowed myself to get emotionally confused. I lost control of my life, although I never stopped fighting for it. I have been greedy for life and I have savored it fully. Unfortunately, my considerable appetites for food and drink and, yes, for love, eventually turned on me, clouding my judgment, and sometimes endangering my well-being.

I wanted everything! It's got to be said! And I can accept the blame for my excesses. In many ways, I became a victim of my hunger for happiness, and of my own conscience; but I always kept trying to do the best I could with what I had. Given my heredity and my upbringing, I don't see what else I could have done.

I have had to face the fact that I have often been undisciplined in my private life, and I have deeply resented it when anyone has tried to force discipline upon me—even when I did it myself. Time and again I made real efforts to control my wayward ways, only to find myself entranced or distracted by someone or something, and, once more, my good intentions were lost along the way.

I have always tried to create a happy atmosphere around me, although sometimes it took a tremendous toll of me. I always wanted people to be happy, but, at the same time, to be happy myself. I have been warmly content when I succeeded, and miserable when I did not; but that's the way it goes sometimes.

On the other hand, there is a part of me that is fiercely self-protective—"standoffish," if you will. People have so often misinterpreted my friendliness and presumed an intimacy which did not exist. I've had to withdraw from people I might otherwise have wanted to know better, might have liked as friends, had they given me sufficient time and space, but there is a core of me which I don't want anybody to touch, or even to see.

I do not like to be possessed, to feel coerced into friendship; nor do I like to think my affections are being solicited with gifts or unasked services, something which happens frequently to people of celebrity.

Real affection, lasting friendships, develop slowly. I seldom call people by their first names until I am asked. It's a holdover, I guess, from my parents who were very strict about certain things: salty language, for instance. My father hated to hear me say "damn" or "hell" and my Aunt Ruth was at me all the time for occasionally exclaiming, "Oh, God." So, although in later years I developed a reputation as a somewhat spicy party raconteur, bad language for its own sake is distasteful to me.

Mother always claimed I was a very "innocent" person. If she meant that I seldom saw wrong in anyone, she was right. I believed blindly in many people until I found they'd let me down. Then I would grow suspicious and cynical, feelings I hate in myself.

There finally came a time in later years when I looked around and asked myself, "Where has all the wonder gone? Is this how it ends?" Had I really lost it? I couldn't believe it. And it wasn't quite true. My sense of wonder was simply packed away in my emotional attic while I struggled through the bitter depression which finally overwhelmed me in the late

1960s and held on so tenaciously. I'm still struggling—and winning, I think. At least I've got my sense of humor back.

In preparing this book, I tried to look honestly at my life—to understand the difference between what I may have appeared to be and what I really am. At times this introspection was so painful I turned my back on the book for months, tempted to forget the whole thing. Yet I always returned to it and I have tried to be as strictly honest as my father was.

What is my philosophy? If it hasn't clearly shown through these pages, I am not at all sure I can put it any other way. I am propelled more by senses than by mind—by my senses of hearing, touch, sight, smell, and taste. I'd almost like to add "singing" as one of the senses. Sense and instinct! Intuition! I cannot analyze either my work or my feelings. My "feelings" again. I simply cannot explain myself in intellectual terms. I just feel!

Often I have sat out on my terrace at Melodie Hill, acutely aware of the soft breezes talking to me. I have almost a tactile response to nature's realities even now, just as I did when I was a child lying on the grass in my copse on the hill above Wheeling.

There were moments in the late sixties and seventies when I felt bereft of something very precious. I was empty inside and I couldn't figure out whether it was just a matter of growing older, or that the world itself was becoming more and more joyless. Even the comforting spiritual presence which I had always felt close beside me seemed to have vanished. I wanted my God back.

Now that all the tumult and shouting have died down, I still feel myself drifting sometimes; but, more and more often today, out of the despondency that my own singing career, as I loved it, is past—out of this comes the joy of hearing one of my students give new life to a piece of music.

I have no idea what I've given to the world and I don't know what my students see in me today; but *I* see wonder in their faces. *I* see joy and love for whatever it is I am able to give them. So whatever I am, something is still emanating from me.

Nowadays I try not to think about what I used to sing, except when I'm discussing a piece of music with a student and explain how I used to do it. I'm still making music, only now I'm doing most of it through my students.

During my career, everyone who dealt with me thought he or she knew exactly the right way for me to go. Quite often they were in conflict with each other, and stirred up a great deal of uncertainty and vacillation in me. In the end, my best guide was always my own gut instinct, when I remembered to use it, and to trust it.

Bill Judd used to urge me not to spread myself too thin. He'd say, "Eleanor, you'd better make up your mind what you are going to be. You can be *anything* you want, but you have to choose. You *cannot* do everything!" Why not? I really believed I could do anything that came along. So I tried anyway. Edgar Vincent thought I cheated myself by stretching my abilities too far. I can't believe that. I think I did what I was capable of doing. I don't think I took on too much, although I can understand that people might have thought so. Too much? My God, my work was my delight! It's the love of singing, that's what made me: this subconscious, almost supernatural creative impulse which grows and grows in an artist so that all of a sudden you discover *something within* which enables you to sing so well as almost to supersede it—to go beyond yourself.

It is essential for any artist not only to be able to get on top of the music, but to find more in it than appears to be there. Pianist Artur Rubinstein explained it so beautifully when he described music as purely metaphysical. "You cannot touch it," he said, "it is not visible and it is audible only through its interpreter."

This means that even composers, creative as they are, are bound to staves and notes and bars and written dynamic indications; so that it takes a performer with a concept, faithfulness to its creator, plus that special spirit which is one's "self," to breathe life into a composer's music, no matter how great it is. I have that gift. I was born with it. Nor does success entirely depend upon whether one has the most beautiful voice. Those who have intelligence, the capacity to assimilate style and a feeling for the stage can easily go beyond those who think a big, beautiful voice is all they need. A great big voice, alone, is not enough! There are people who come along who seem to have been born with all the ingredients put together just waiting to burst out. Maybe I was a little like that.

If I was blessed with the essential instinct to know what's right, musically, I can't explain why. It is part of me. It is this instinct that enables a singer to feel a phrase and make it sing; to know how to find the music in music. Take Rubinstein again, for instance, sometimes wrong notes all over the place, but Jimminy Crickets, he made music like nobody you ever heard in your life! "To make music"—this is what it's all about. And each of us gives to the other. Rubinstein learned from Emmy Destinn that piano playing should breathe, and I have learned from artists like him to use my voice as an instrument.

The ear of the listening public has changed since my day, and keeps changing. Audiences may not be interested in the same things which attracted them when I was starting out, and my students will find different rewards from those I found. The only way I can help them is to give them the best I have from my own training and experience. Some things perhaps cannot be taught: how to feel the breadth of a musical line, to sense the inner momentum of a song, how to gentle over the top of a phrase like a violin, how to carry a musical thought beyond the end of its sound.

No matter. I give the only thing I have to give—the sum of what I am. Let them create from it whatever they can. Singing is an intensely personal process and should be as exciting to young people today as it was to me. The joy should be in the journey!

So today, when someone says to me, "Steber, there never was anyone like you," I feel wonderful, and I smile, because I know it's true. I'm the best "Eleanor Steber" there is!

In Gottes Namen!

FAREWELL TO STEBER

Eleanor Steber had the great good fortune and the bad luck to be an American soprano. Good fortune because her Americanness provided a verve and hardiness that made conscientious striving for proficiency second nature. Her optimism and easy belief in herself, manifest in her "can-do" approach to the dimensions of her art, came across as strictly made in the U.S.A. Being an American singer meant, too, that she was not locked by birth into any one repertory, and a rare ability to feel at ease in almost every vocal literature she tackled was allowed its full scope. In fact, it was the central mechanism of her distinguished career. She was the native singer par excellence who made use of this country's mixed-heritage key to music's many parochialisms.

But what worked so wonderfully for this soprano, who died last month at the age of seventy-six, carried its own nagging problem, and this was that Steber never got the kind of acclaim that was her due. As far back as her first decade at the Met, when she scored success after success, most notably in Mozart, her gifts were recognized yet generally taken for granted by audiences and critics alike. Her very versatility acted as a subliminal cue that here was not the ultimate authority—that the last word, the truly revealing interpretation or most exciting sound would come from the Italian and German specialists who were gaining glittering post-war reputations. When these haloed names did arrive on the scene, they invariably snatched the spotlight. How warmly New York applauded Steber—and how eagerly it awaited Seefried, Della Casa, Jurinac, Gueden, and Schwarzkopf. If any of these ladies disappointed or simply failed to materialize, Eleanor would be there to save the day.

This attitude was unfair to Steber, of course, but it also diminished the rest of us, because it interfered with a full appreciation of a rare, beautiful instrument and an artistry that was sovereign in almost everything it attempted. For one thing, the Steber timbre was gloriously individual. Her silvery, bright sound was tinged with a special vibrato that wrought luminous changes throughout the range. Although her highest notes in the best years—before 1960—were always secure, it was the low and middle registers that gave off an expressive warmth unusual in such a lyric voice. Steber used chest tones sparingly; when she did, it was not out of necessity to compensate for unevenly knitted registers but because style and the moment required it. Anyone who recalls the declamatory fire of her Cassandre in a 1959 Carnegie Hall *Les Troyens* can testify to that. One always felt in the presence of a rock-solid technique, a superb facility superbly supported by an intelligence as to how it should be deployed.

Listening to and looking at random personal retrospective in the wake of Steber's death (her "Voice of Firestone" videotape is a lovely souvenir), one notes first of all the breath control that lent her Mozart phrasing its admirable steadiness, fluidity and suppleness. Yes, this was matchless Mozart singing; but when "Pace, pace" was heard, it was not the fine work of a Mozart singer turning to Verdi. The stylistic gestures were equally authentic, the dynamic and tonal shadings neatly calculated yet entirely spontaneous *and* Italianate. This voice—the same voice, but transformed by the subtlest calibrations—next encompassed the ecstasy and hysteria of Elsa, and suddenly Steber became a magisterial *jugendliche Sopran*, one who a few moments later was under the skin of *Les Nuits d'Été* and then convincingly ensconced on Sam Barber's Knoxville porch. What emerged was a conviction: this was a musician so in touch with music's essence and so aware of its varied expressions that to bring them alive was only a matter of opening the mouth and giving utterance. What good fortune for her, and what better fortune for the rest of us, if our appreciation of such uniqueness had been with us all along.

HARVEY E. PHILLIPS
Reprinted through the courtesy of OPERA NEWS

Eleanor Steber's Roles

(Alphabetical, without Articles)

Amelia Goes to the Ball – Amelia
Andrea Chenier – Madeleine
Arabella – Arabella
Arcifanfano – Gloriosa
Ariadne Auf Naxos – Prima Donna
Bobème – Mimi
Carmen – Micaela
Così fan Tutte – Fiordiligi
Damnation of Faust – Marguerite
Don Giovanni – Donna Anna
Don Carlo – Elisabetta
Don Giovanni – Donna Elvira
Ewartung – Woman
Falstaff – Alice Ford
Faust – Marguerite
Fidelio – Marcellina
Fledermaus – Rosalinda
Flying Dutchman – Senta
Frau Ohne Schatten – Empress
Girl of the Golden West – Minnie
Götterdämmerung – Woglinde
Idomeneo – Ilia
Idomeneo – Elektra
Impresario – Prima Donna
Jack and the Beanstalk – Jack's Mother
Lohengrin – Elsa
Madama Butterfly – Cio-Cio-San
Magic Flute – Pamina

Magic Flute – The First Lady
Manon Lescaut (Puccini) – Manon
Manon (Massenet) – Manon
Marriage of Figaro – Countess
Masked Ball – Amelia
Meistersinger – Eva
Otello – Desdemona
Owen Wingrave – Miss Wingrave
Parsifal – First Flower Maiden
Rheingold – Woglinde
Rosenkavalier – Marschallin
Rosenkavalier – Sophie
Siegfried – Forest Bird
Sound of Music – Mother Abbess
Tales of Hoffman – Antonia
Tales of Hoffman – Giulietta
Tales of Hoffman – Muse
*The Abduction from the
  Seraglio* – Constanza
Tosca – Tosca
Traviata – Violetta
Trovatore – Leonora
Troyens – Cassandra
Turn of the Screw – Mrs. Grose
Vanessa – Vanessa
Where's Charley? – Charley's
  Aunt
Wozzeck – Marie

Eleanor Steber Discography

Eleanor Steber is presented on more than 100 recordings from the early 1940s to date. Space precludes reprinting the detailed discography and many of the recordings are no longer available but may be in the process of reissue. Listed below are all initial recordings (excluding reissues) when both old and not-previously recorded performances were issued on cassette, CDs and video.

Contents, Label, Issue and R.P.M.

1942   BACHELET: Cherè Nuit. DUPARC: Chanson Triste. (James Quillian, piano), RCA Victor 18088 (78 rpm)

1943   ORATORIO ARIAS. From *The Creation* and *Messiah*. (Victor Symphony Orch. Charles Connell, cond.) RCA DM-927 (78 rpm)

1944   GRIFFES: By A Lonely Forest Pathway. CRAPSEY-SACCO: Rapunzel. RCA 10-1071 (78 rpm)

1944   SCHUBERT: Auflösung. CIMARA: Canto di Primavera. RCA 10-1099 (78 rpm).

1945   RODGERS & HAMMERSTEIN: *Oklahoma* (Highlights), With Melton, Thomas, orch. RCA M-988 (78 rpm)

1945   MOZART: Arias from *Figaro*. Porgi amor, Dove sono. (Victor orch. Erich Leinsdorf) RCA 11-8850 (78 rpm)

1946   MOZART: Arias from *Don Giovanni* & *Magic Flute*. (Victor orch.) RCA 11-9114 (78 rpm)

1946   GERSHWIN: "Summertime." CARMICHAEL: "Stardust." (With orch.) RCA 11-9186 (78 rpm)

1947   KREISLER: Stars in My Eyes. KERN: The Touch of Your Hand. RCA 10-1248 (78 rpm)

1947   BIZET: Aria from *Carmen*; CHARPENTIER: Aria from *Louise*. RCA 11-0690 (78 rpm)

1947 MOZART OPERATIC ARIAS. From *Figaro* and *Seraglio*. (RCA Victor Orch.) RCA DM-1157 (78 rpm); and WDM-1157 (45 rpm)

1947 BRAHMS: *Ein Deutsches Requiem*. (With James Pease, RCA Victor Chorale, Symph.) RCA DM-1236 (78 rpm); WDM-1236 (45 rpm); LM-6004 (33-1/3 rpm)

1948 FAVORITES FROM THE FIRESTONE HOUR. (With Russ Case, cond.) RCA MO-1234 (78 rpm)

1948 GOUNOD: Two arias from *Faust*. (RCA Victor Orch. RCA 11-9838 (78 rpm); 49-0289 (45 rpm)

1948 GOUNOD: Arias from *Roméo et Juliette* and *Figaro*. (RCA Victor orch.) RCA 12-0526 (78 rpm)

1948 TEMPLETON: Roses in Wintertime; Vienna in the Springtime. (Alec Templeton, piano). RCA 10-1473 (78 rpm); and 49-0421 (45 rpm)

1948 BENNARD: The Old Rugged Cross; FEARIS: Beautiful Isle of Somewhere (With Margaret Harshaw. (Case, cond.) RCA 10-1449 (78 rpm); 49-0569 (45 rpm) (78 rpm)

1949 MONK: Abide with Me; HAWTHORNE: Whispering Hope. (With Margaret Harshaw). RCA 10-1463 (78 rpm)

1949 MADAMA BUTTERFLY. Complete, with Tucker, Valdengo, Madeira, et al. (Met. Opera, Max Rudolf) Columbia SL-104 (33-1/3 rpm)

1950 SONGS AT EVENTIDE. Popular favorites. (Firestone Orch., Howard Barlow) Columbia ML-2105 (33-1/3 rpm)

1950 DRAMATIC SCENES FROM VERDI OPERAS. (Met. Opera, Fausto Cleva) Columbia ML-2157 (33-1/3 rpm)

1950 ROMBERG & HAMMERSTEIN: Excerpts from *The New Moon* (with Nelson Eddy). Columbia ML-2164 (33-1/3 rpm); A-975 (45 rpm)

1951 BARBER: *Knoxville: Summer of 1915* (Dumbarton Oaks Chamber Orch.) Columbia ML-2174 (33-1/3 rpm)

1951 SONGS OF VICTOR HERBERT. (Orch. Percy Faith, cond.) Columbia ML-2191 (33-1/3 rpm); A-1011 (45 rpm)

1951 FAUST. Complete. With Conley, Siepi, et al. (Met. Opera, Cleva) Columbia SL-112 (33-1/3 rpm)

1952 FIFTY YEARS OF GREAT OPERATIC SINGING, Vol. V: 1940–1950. Steber sings *Summertime*. (Made in England for RCA) RCA CSLP 504 (33-1/3 rpm)

1952 GREAT SCENES FROM VERDI'S OTELLO. (With Vinay, Guarrera; Met. Opera, Cleva) Columbia ML-4499 (33-1/3 rpm)

1952 SACRED ARIAS BY THE GREAT MASTERS. (Columbia Symph. Orch., Rudolf) Columbia ML 4521 (33-1/3 rpm)

1952　COSÌ FAN TUTTE. Complete. (With Thebom, Peters, Tucker, Guarrera, et al. (Met Opera, Fritz Stiedry), Columbia SL-122 (33-1/3 rpm)

1953　MOZART ARIAS. (Columbia Symphony Orchestra, Bruno Walter, cond.) Columbia ML-4694 (33-1/3 rpm)

1953　LOHENGRIN. Complete recording, live performance at Bayreuth with Varnay, Windgassen, Uhde, Greindl, Braun. (Festival Orch., Joseph Keilberth) London A-4502 (33-1/3 rpm)

1954　FIDELIO. Complete recording of 1944 broadcast with Bampton, Peerce, et al. (NBC Symphony Orch., Arturo Toscanini) RCA LM-6025 (33-1/3 rpm)

1954　BERLIOZ: *Les Nuits Été*, and other songs. (Columbia Symph. Dimitri Mitropoulos & Jean Paul Morel, conds.) Columbia ML-4940 (33-1/3 rpm)

1955　HEART OF THE OPERA. Six records reissued from 1941 "anonymous" 78 rpm collection: Steber sings on FAUST (CAL-221); LA BOHÉME and MADAMA BUTTERFLY (CAL-222), PAGLIACCI (CAL-226), and LA TRAVIATA (CAL-227). Camden CFL-101 (33-1/3 rpm)

1958　VANESSA, Barber: Complete. With Elias, Resnik, Gedda, Tozzi et al. (Met Opera, Mitropoulos). RCA LM-6138 (33-1/3 rpm); LSC-6138 (stereo)

1959　ELEANOR STEBER AT CARNEGIE HALL. (Live performance, 10/10/58) (With Edwin Biltcliffe, piano) ST/AND SLP-101 (ltd. ed.) & SLP-401 (33-1/3 rpm)

1960　HYMNS OF MARY BAKER EDDY (With Edwin McDonnell, organ) Available from Church of Christ, Scientist, local reading rooms, or Boston Center. ST/AND SLP-402 (33-1/3 rpm); SLP-403 (in German); SLP- 409 (in French)

1961　HYMNS FROM THE CHRISTIAN SCIENCE HYMNAL. (McDonnell, organ) ST/AND SLP-410 (33-1/3 rpm)

1961　ELEANOR STEBER SINGS SACRED SOLOS. (Edwin Biltcliffe, organ) ST/AND SLP-404 (33-1/3 rpm)

1961　ELEANOR STEBER SINGS MOZART. (Symph. of the Air, Robert Lawrence, cond.) ST/AND SLP 406 and SLS 7406 (33-1/3 rpm)

1962　SONGS BY AMERICAN COMPOSERS. (With Mildred Miller, John McCollum, Donald Gramm; E. Biltcliffe, Robert Cumming, piano) ST/AND SLP-411-412 (33-1/3 rpm)

1962　LOVE'S OLD SWEET SONGS. (E. Biltcliffe & Barron Smith, organ; Al Vann, piano) ST/AND SLP-413 and SLS-7413 (stereo) (33-1/3 rpm)

1962　AT HOME WITH ELEANOR STEBER. The World is Waiting for the Sunrise, Danny Boy. (Smith, organ) ST/AND 45-413 (45 rpm)

1962　SYRACUSE MUSIC FESTIVAL SERIES. Bach & Rameau. (Kipnis Baroque Ensemble) ST/AND SLP-416 and SLS-7416 (stereo) (33-1/3 rpm)

1962   SYRACUSE MUSIC FESTIVAL SERIES. Berg: *Seven Early Songs*; Beethoven: "An die ferne Geliebte" and 3 other songs (E. Biltcliffe, piano) ST/AND SLP-417 and SLS-7417 (stereo) (33-1/3 rpm)

1962   BARBER: *Knoxville: Summer of 1915.* LA MONTAINE: *Songs of the Rose of Sharon.* Live performance. (Greater Trenton Symph. Orch., Nicholas Harsanyi, cond.) ST/AND SLP-420 and SLS-7420 (stereo) (33-1/3 rpm)

1963   BACH: *Mass in B Minor.* (With Elias, Verreau, Cross; Phila. Orch., Eugene Ormandy, cond.) Columbia M3L-280 and M3S-680 (stereo) (33-1/3 rpm)

1964 – 1974 multiple reissues except for the following:

1966   GALA FAREWELL (Metropolitan Opera, 4/16/66 . . . complete program) Steber sings in the Quintet from VANESSA. MRF-7 No. 71/72/73 (33-1/3 rpm)

1968   HEAR THEM AGAIN! (10-record album of all-time re-recorded favorites, 89 singers, 122 songs. Steber sings "Summertime." Reader's Digest RDA-49A (stereo) (33-1/3 rpm)

1969   UNFORGETTABLE VOICES IN UNFORGETTABLE PERFORMANCES FROM THE GERMAN REPERTOIRE. Steber sings "Martern aller Arten" (Seraglio). RCA VIC-1455 (33-1/3 rpm)

1974   LE NOZZE DI FIGARO. Metropolitan Opera Broadcast 1/29/44. (With Brownlee, Sayao, Pinza, Novotna, Petina, Baccaloni, DePaolis, et al., Walter. cond.) (ca 10 min. missing at end of Act II) Bruno Walter Society. Opus Records MLG-75/76/77 (33-1/3 rpm)

1974   LE NOZZE DI FIGARO (Same as above; last side contains excerpts from 3/7/42 broadcast of *Don Giovanni*, with Pinza, et al.) Operatic Archives OPA-1033/1034/1035 (33-1/3 rpm)

1974   OPERA GOES BROADWAY. Steber, Melton, Farrell, Peerce, Swarthout, et al. Steber sings "If I Loved You." Star-Tone—ST-223 (Ltd. ed. for Collectors) (33-1/3 rpm)

1974   ELEANOR STEBER LIVE AT THE CONTINENTAL BATHS. Live performance recorded 10/4/73. Arias and songs, with E. Biltcliffe, piano; J. Rabb, violin) RCA ARL 1-0436 (stereo) (33-1/3 rpm)

1975   OPERA'S GREATEST HITS. Steber, Farrell, Tucker, Pinza, Williams, Della Casa (Released in England). CBS Cassette 40-30053

1976   STEBER IN RECITAL Live performance with E. Biltcliffe and A. Rogers, piano. Arias & songs by Handel, Von Weber, Puccini, Verdi, Britten, Bachelet, Fauré, Debussy, Duparc, Berlioz, Wolf. Eleanor Steber Music Foundation, ESMF 1/2/3 (stereo) (33-1/3 rpm)

1976   A COLLECTOR'S "PORGY AND BESS." Steber, Merrill, Stevens, Tibbett, et al. Steber sings "Summertime." (Robert Shaw Chorale) RCA ARL2-2094 (33-1/3 rpm)

1976   THE RECORDED ANTHOLOGY OF AMERICAN MUSIC –
        WHEN I HAVE SUNG MY SONGS – The American Art Song,
        1890–1940. A series of 100 records epitomizing the social and cultural
        history of the U.S. through its music. Steber sings "By a Lonely Forest
        Pathway" by Griffes. New World Records NW-247 (33-1/3 rpm)

1977   CHRISTMAS SONGFEST WITH ELEANOR STEBER, FRIENDS
        AND FAMILY. Live performance 12/17/76. (With Donald Gramm,
        Geraldine MacMillian, Christine Walevska, Stony Baroque Chamber
        Players, Edwin Biltcliffe, organ, Ray Urwin, harpsichord, David Stein,
        piano, et al.) Eleanor Steber Music Foundation. ESMF 4/5 (stereo)
        (33-1/3 rpm)

1978   I'VE HEARD THAT SONG BEFORE. 10 records. Steber sings
        "People Will Say We're in Love" with James Melton. RCA DPL-90100
        (33-1/3 rpm), Cassette DPS-300100

1979   GREAT MOMENTS FROM THE GREAT OPERETTAS. Steber sings
        "Ah! Sweet Mystery of Life" (Naughty Marietta), "One Kiss" (New Moon),
        and "Sweethearts" (Sweethearts) Columbia P6 15093 (33-1/3 rpm)

198?   ELEANOR STEBER – LIVE PERFORMANCES – 1940–1953.
        Legendary Recordings LR 141 (33-1/3 rpm)

198?   AN OPERATIC CHRISTMAS. Steber sings "Silent Night."
        (12/22/47) Legendary Recordings LR-136 (33-1/3 rpm)

1981   MET STARS IN HOLLYWOOD. Steber sings "Out of My Dreams"
        (Oklahoma) Opera Guild. MET 205 (33-1/3 rpm), Cassette MET
        105C

1982   STEBER SINGS "STRICTLY MOZART" – Lieder und Arien Abend,
        Graz, Austria (8/4/79). Eleanor Steber Music Foundation ESMF 6/7
        (33-1/3 rpm)

1983   AN ALL-STAR SALUTE TO THE GOLDEN AGE OF OPERETTA
        (COLLECTOR'S EDITION). Steber sings "Stars in My Eyes" (The King
        Steps Out), 1947. Reader's Digest Cassette KRD 052 A1, A2, A3

1983   OPERA MEETS BROADWAY. Steber sings "The Touch of Your
        Hand" (Roberta). Ariel OMB 15 (33-1/3 rpm)

1985   50 YEARS OF GUILD PERFORMANCES AT THE MET.
        Celebrating the Golden Anniversary of the Metropolitan Opera Guild.
        Steber sings "Porgi amor" (Le Nozze di Figaro), 3-13-43. Met Opera
        Guild, album of 3 cassettes MET 50

1985   THE GREAT OPERA SERIES. The Heart of the Opera, Vol. 2,
        from 1940s recordings of "anonymous" singers. (La Boheme, Madama
        Butterfly). Steber sings both. RCA Special Products, Camden Cassette
        CAK-222

1989   LA FANCIULLA DEL WEST. Steber, Del Monaco, Guelfi, Tozzi:
        Mitropoulos cond. (Live, 6/15/54), Maggio Musicale, Firenze, Italy.
        Cetra. LO 64 (33-1/3 rpm)

1989   A MET MESSIAH. Steber sings "I Know That My Redeemer
        Liveth" (1951). Opera Guild. Cassette MET 208; CD MET 208CD

1990   A NIGHT AT THE OPERA – A MOZART GALA. (Columbia
        Symphony Orch., Walter cond.) Steber sings "Dove sono" (Figaro).
        CBS CD MDK 46579CD

1990   Legendary Conductors. DIMITRI MITROPOULOS-ELEANOR
        STEBER-HECTOR BERLIOZ, "Les Nuits d'Été," N.Y. Phil. Orch.
        (5/4/53) AS CD 619

1990   THE RECORD OF SINGING – 1939 to the end of the 78 rpm era.
        Various singers. Steber sings "Depuis le jour" (Louise). EMI-
        CDHG69741 1840-55 (91)-7 CDs

1991   LA FANCIULLA DEL WEST. Steber, Del Monaco, et al.
        Mitropoulos, cond. 1954, Firenze, Italy. Hunt CD 595

1991   MISSA SOLEMNIS, Beethoven: Live performance, 4/18/48.
        Steber, Merriman, Hayes, Alvary, N.Y. Phil., Walter, cond.
        AS CD AS30

1991   VANESSA, Barber: (Steber, Gedda, Elias, Tozzi, Resnik) Met.
        Opera Orch. & Chorus. Recorded 1958. RCA Victor Opera
        Series, Cassette 7899-2-RG. RCA Victor Gold Seal, CD RCA
        7899-2-RG

1991   BIOGRAPHIES IN MUSIC – ELEANOR STEBER . . . IN
        MEMORIAM. Live performances, 1940–1958. Legato Classics
        CD BIM 712-1

1991   PORTRAITS IN MEMORY: ELEANOR STEBER. Operatic
        selections, "Knoxville, Summer of 1915," Barber; "Zaide,"
        Berlioz; "When I Grow too Old to Dream," Romberg;
        "Summertime," Gershwin. Met Opera Guild Cassette 211C.
        CD MET 211CD

1991   MET STARS SING MOZART. A treasure-trove of great Mozart
        singing. Opera Guild CD MET 211CD (also on cassette)

1991   GREAT OPERAS AT THE MET. Each volume features
        highlights from the opera compiled by the Metropolitan Opera
        Guild on Cassette and CD. Steber sings on the following: LE
        NOZZE DI FIGARO – Cassette MET 504C-2. LA TRAVIATA –
        CD MET 505CD, Cassette MET 505C-2. LOHENGRIN – CD
        MET 510CD, Cassette MET 510C-2. DON GIOVANNI – CD
        MET 511CD, Cassette MET 511C-2. FAUST – CD MET 513,
        Cassette MET 513C-2. OTELLO – CD MET 514CD, Cassette
        MET 514C-1. CARMEN – CD MET 502CD, Cassette MET
        502C-1

1991   SONGS OUR MOTHERS TAUGHT US. Met Artists lovingly
        perform the music of their youth. Metropolitan Opera Guild – CD
        MET 210 (also on cassette)

1991   MET STARS ON BROADWAY/MET STARS IN HOLLYWOOD.
Metropolitan Opera Guild compilation. (CD features 13 songs not on
the cassettes) CD MET 104CD. (also on cassette)

1991   ONE HUNDRED YEARS OF GREAT ARTISTS AT THE MET.
Definitive vocal history of the Met by great artists. "The Johnson Years:
1935–1950" Cassette MET 404C; "The Bing Years II: 1961–1972."
Metropolitan Opera Guild CD and Cassettes

1991   100 SINGERS, 100 YEARS, RCA (8LPM) CRM8-5177; (8CSM)
CRR8-5177

1991   KNOXVILLE: SUMMER OF 1915. (Reissue of 1951 recording).
Sony Classics Master Works CD MPR 46727 (APP) 1991

1991   WOLFGANG AMADEUS MOZART (1756–1791): Legendary
Interpretations. Steber, Pons, Pinza, Tourel, Seefried, Simoneau,
Warfield, Westminister Choir; N.Y. Phil., Williamson, Dir. Sony
Classical CD SMK 47211 (APP) Mono CD

1992   FIDELIO. (The Toscanini Collection). Reissue of broadcast performance
Dec. 10 & 17, 1944. Rose CD 60273-2-RG

1992   ELEANOR STEBER – Mozart/Gounod Arias. Also arias of Bizet,
Verdi, Charpentier, and songs by Schubert etc. RCA CD 60521-2RG.
Cassette 60521-4RG

1992   ELEANOR STEBER IN CONCERT – 1956 & 1958. Live performance
of 1958 Carnegie Hall Recital. Video Artists International Audio CD
VAIA-1005-2

1992   LES TROYENS, Berlioz: (Live 1960 performance). Steber,
Resnik, Cassilly, Singher; Lawrence, cond. Steber sings Cassandra
& Cassandra's ghost Video Artists International Audio CD
VAIA-1006-3

1992   ARCIFANFANO, Dittersdorf: Comic opera with Eleanor Steber and
Anna Russell, Brooks, McCollum; Clarion Music Society, Newell
Jenkins, cond. (1965 live performance). Video Artists International
Audio CD VAI1010-2

1992   ELEANOR STEBER SINGS RICHARD STRAUSS. Four Last Songs,
James Levine, cond., (1970) and excerpts from Die Frau Ohne Schatten,
Karl Böhm, cond. (1953) Video Artists International Audio CD
VAI1012

VIDEO CASSETTES

1990   ELEANOR STEBER IN OPERA AND SONG. Voice of Firestone
Classic Performances. Video Artists International VHS 69102

1990   ELEANOR STEBER IN OPERA AND SONG, VOL. 2. Voice of
Firestone Classic Performances. Video Artists International VHS 69112

1990   CHRISTMAS WITH ELEANOR STEBER. Voice of Firestone Classic Performances. Video Artists International VHS 69113

1990   LEONARD WARREN IN OPERA AND SONG, VOL. 2. (with special guest artist Eleanor Steber). Voice of Firestone Classic Performances. Video Artists International VHS 69110

1991   ELEANOR STEBER IN OPERA AND ORATORIO. Voice of Firestone Classic Performances. Video Artists International VHS 69122

1992   ELEANOR STEBER SINGS LOVE SONGS. Voice of Firestone Classic Performances. Video Artists International VHS 69134

Note: A full-description discography was originally compiled by Wilson Snodgrass, Dallas, Tx. and Margaret Ulmer, Greenville, SC. up to 1964. Donald McCormack, Elmhurst, NY, updated it in 1978. Mr. McCormack and Ellen Martin, Philadelphia, PA have updated it to the present. Recordings issued prior to the mid-1960s are no longer available, for the most part; much of the material has been reissued on other labels, cassettes, and compact discs.